The World of Survival

Colin Willock

THE WORLD
OF SURVIVAL

The inside story of the famous
TV wildlife series

 ANDRE DEUTSCH

First published 1978 by
André Deutsch Limited
105 Great Russell Street London WC1

Printed in Great Britain by
Ebenezer Baylis & Son Limited
The Trinity Press, Worcester, and London

British Library Cataloguing in Publication Data

Willock, Colin
    The world of survival.
    1. Survival (Television program)
    I. Title
    791.45'7   PN1992.77.S/

    ISBN 0-233-97029-0

Contents

List of Plates   *page* vi

1 Opening Titles   9
2 SOS Rhino   15
3 Words and Music   27
4 Karamoja   35
5 The Pioneers   56
6 The Enchanted Isles   63
7 Errors and Omissions   77
8 Portrait of a Wildlife Cameraman   89
9 The Ethiopian Adventure   95
10 Meanwhile in Park Lane   115
11 Beaver Special   122
12 Flight of the Snowgeese   126
13 Safari by Balloon   150
14 Apes and Elephants   160
15 The Ladies   184
16 End Titles   194

Appendix: International Awards Won by
   SURVIVAL   199

Index   201

List of Plates

IN COLOUR

Between pages 24 and 25
A witch from Karamoja (Alan Root)
Snow geese in formation (Des and Jen Bartlett)
Balloon over Kilimanjaro (Alistair Graham)
Fish eagle (Dieter Plage)

Between pages 72 and 73
The extraordinary shoebill stork (Cindy Buxton)
Buffalo in Amboseli National Park (Bob Campbell)
Boadicea's charge (Lee Lyon)

Between pages 120 and 121
A cameraman swims with a humpback whale (Sylvia Earl)
An Afar tribesman of the Danakil (Lee Lyon)
Kasimir, the dominant male gorilla (Dieter Plage)
Orangutans (Dieter Plage)

Between pages 168 and 169
Californian sea otter (Jeff Foott)
The woodpecker finch of Galapagos (Alan Root)
Face to face with a tiger (Mike Price)
Alaskan grizzy bears (Jeff Foott)

IN BLACK AND WHITE

Between pages 32 and 33
Peter Scott with Ted Eales; Bewick's swans
  (Anglia Television; Maurice Tibbles)
A narrow escape for Dieter Plage (Okapia)

Between pages 48 and 49
The flamingos of 'Deathtrap Lake' (Alan Root)
Filming beavers in the Wyoming Rockies (Des and Jen Bartlett)

List of Plates (continued)

Between pages 80 and 81
Cindy Buxton and an ornithological 'first'
    (Cindy Buxton; Jenny Slater)
Two species of giants, the right whale and the humpback
    (Des and Jen Bartlett; Al Giddings)

Between pages 96 and 97
Dieter Plage with the author; an orangutan turns photographer
    (Mike Price)
Early adventures in Africa: lassooing rhino and the
    Karamojong (John Blower; Alan Root)

Between pages 128 and 129
Adrien Deschryver and his gorillas (Dieter Plage and Lee Lyon)
Filming pelicans in Ethiopia (Survival/Anglia; Colin Willock)

Between pages 144 and 145
Housekeeping in Africa and in the Galapagos (Alan Root)
'The Flight of the Snow Geese': preparations, the geese at
the frontier, Fred the crane (Des and Jen Bartlett)

Between pages 176 and 177
The Sultan of Aussa and two of his warriors
    (Joan Willock; Lee Lyon)
Aubrey Buxton on safari and at the 'Emmy' awards
John Forsythe (Survival/Anglia; Anglia Television)

Between 192 and 193
Lee Lyon and a shot from her last film
    (Adrien Deschryver; Lee Lyon)
Two examples of the work of Oxford Scientific Films (OSF)

Chapter 1

Opening Titles

FOR the first forty years of my life, I successfully resisted becoming a team man. A British public school education had inoculated me for ever, I thought, against the team spirit. Six wartime years in the Royal Corps of Marines further suggested to me that, if I had any *esprit* at all, it was not *de corps*. Despite everything the enemy, and, more particularly, my own side could do to me, I remained essentially a lone hand. When I took up a career again, nothing much had changed. There are few working men more alone than a writer. It was to my complete astonishment, therefore, that I later found I had become a member, not to say a leader, of a team. The virus hit me in 1960, though the full symptoms were not to appear until some years later. By then it was too late. It had become a matter of *Survival*. *Survival* is what this book is all about.

Team is perhaps far too tidy and respectable a word to describe the group of people we have gathered around us. On the rare occasions on which several of them come together I look at them and wonder what they would have done with their lives at other times or in other ages.

In the fifteenth century, you might have found their names on the crew roster of the *Golden Hind*. In the late nineteenth, Burton, Baker, Speke, Baumann and Fischer might have found themselves faced with formidable rivals in the exploration of Africa.

In the 1940s, Alan Root would have been flying a Spitfire, Dieter Plage a Messerschmitt. The Australian Des Bartlett? With his tireless kangaroo pace and deep knowledge of jungles from Borneo to the Amazon, he'd have made a fine Chindit. Aubrey Buxton, the entrepreneur who made it possible for us all to come together? I happen to know what he was doing at that time. He *was* in the jungle.

There are so many others. Jeff Foott, a world-class mountaineer and former Teton guide; Bob Campbell from Kenya who spent four years living with mountain gorillas; John Buxton, the imperturbable latter-day Victorian traveller who took his dinner jacket to Uganda when he went to catch rhino. And then the women who share their adventures. Jen Bartlett, Joan Root, Cindy Buxton, Liz Bomford and poor Lee Lyon who was killed. I have been wanting to tell all their stories for so long.

In the beginning there was Aubrey Buxton.

The date was November 1960. In the beginning there was also me. The difference between us was that, as far as the world of television went, Aubrey had what I have come to know through American associates as 'clout'. As a mere programme-maker I was most assuredly cloutless. I did have another equally valuable asset, though: a talent for communications in several media. What we mainly had in common was a burning interest in the natural world.

Aubrey succeeded in direct line from those Georgian Norfolk squires who pioneered new systems of agriculture and composed sonnets in Greek when not otherwise engaged. After a successful career in an international pharmaceutical concern, Aubrey turned to television. He knew and loved his East Anglian countryside as fully and well as any owner of five thousand Norfolk acres. True, Greek wasn't his forte. But he completed the artistic side of the squirearchical equation by being an accomplished painter in watercolours. Most important for what was to come of our association and friendship, he was a dedicated and expert ornithologist.

We had other things in common. Neither of us had a scientific training. We therefore thought of our subject as natural history rather than as zoology, biology, ecology or any other combination of ologies. As writer and producer of countless *Survival* programmes, I have always considered this lack of scientific upbringing to be an advantage. When stuck, you can always ask scientists. There are enough of them around. The trick is to know what to ask them and then how to interpret what they tell you accurately and entertainingly for an audience of millions. You can't learn that sort of trick from books. You learn it, first, by being born with the right sort of curiosity and the desire to tell people what you find out as the result of your inquisitiveness. Secondly, you get it by having had your gumboots repeatedly stuck in real mud.

Aubrey and I had both had our gumboots stuck in mud of much the same consistency since boyhood. I have repeatedly noticed that when he is preoccupied at a business or programme meeting he almost invariably draws wading birds. Either waders or an incredibly intricate maze. I fully understand the symbolism of the maze. The wading birds represent another kind of frustration, though. They stand for the sort of place he would rather be in than in the centre of the current maze. Enough knot, dunlin, redshank have decorated the margins of agenda to populate the tideline of the Wash on a November's day. His love of water birds stems from his boyhood spent on the marshes of Cley, Salthouse and Blakeney on the north Norfolk coast and at Hickling, Horsey and Holkham just inland. A wildfowler since he could hold a four-ten, he learned the ways of ducks and geese as other boys learn to recognize cars and, in his youth and mine, locomotives.

By the time we met I had come to much the same destination by a parallel route. Butterflies provided the bright wings on which I made my first flights into the world of nature. From the age of eight I was a rabid and undiscriminating collector. Though born in North London, all my interests grew outwards towards the countryside. I was lucky to be sentenced to boarding schools first at Liphook in Hampshire – lovely butterfly country – and then at Tonbridge in Kent where my tastes expanded through the school natural history society to include birds and mammals. I kept crows and jackdaws, little owls and an orphaned kestrel. Comparing notes thirty years later, Aubrey Buxton and I found that we had shared similar experiences at school. We had both been keen natural historians. We had both suffered minor martyrdoms for our tastes, our activities being condemned by the mob as 'wet' and ourselves dismissed as 'weedy'. Ah well, things have changed. My own sons, with similar interests at school, were envied for them. Television, no doubt, has played its part in changing the climate.

I had come to television by a now familiar route. I had walked up Fleet Street, stopping at newspaper and magazine offices on the way. When I eventually left via Temple Bar I turned right into Kingsway to the old Air Ministry building where Associated Rediffusion then lived. Over a period of thirteen years I had regularly written for several popular dailies and one august Sunday, the *Observer*, but I had spent most of my journalistic life on magazines. I was editor of *Lilliput* and assistant editor of *Picture Post*.

By the mid-fifties, all magazine journalists were aware that the water was rising fast in the bilges and that it wouldn't be long before we got our feet wet. The general magazines such as *Picture Post, Illustrated, Everybody's* were either sinking or being laid up. They hadn't got enough cargo to carry. The cargo, for which read advertising, was being transferred to the holds of commercial television. It was time for the rats to leave a whole fleet of sinking ships. Practically all the *Picture Post* contingent headed for the BBC where they founded, and made justly famous, *Tonight*. I took the other turning and discovered myself frightened, inexperienced and fascinated on *This Week*. In a moment of aberration, Peter Hunt of Associated Rediffusion, who had been responsible for persuading me to leave Fleet Street, declared me to be deputy editor of this famous current affairs programme. I lived in perpetual dread that the editor would be absent on programme night. There is nothing like a live television programme for making the sweat glands work overtime. It was rather like being asked to fly a Jumbo jet when all you have is ten hours on Cessnas. I was entirely unsuited to current affairs.

Because of my leisure interests, but equally no doubt because I sensed my own inadequacies when it came to politics, economics and the serious stuff of life, I led *This Week*, whenever I could, into rural by-ways. Thus, sandwiched between Randolph Churchill and Dr Hastings Banda, we featured Frank Murgett's Colnebrook maggot factory, the excuse being the opening of the coarse fishing season. I succeeded in relieving the crashing dullness, as I saw it, of prosey politicos and pompous pundits with features on point-to-points and bird-watching. It began to be noticed. This was not what the prestigious *This Week* should be about. In retrospect I entirely agree.

Things were now rushing to a conclusion which, if you believe in fate, was probably foregone. I don't believe in fate. I do believe, however, that if you lean hard and long enough on the metaphorical wall which separates where you are from where you want to be, a brick is likely eventually to give way. The mortar was even at that moment coming loose, strangely enough not in metropolitan London but in deepest East Anglia.

Anglia Television had lately set up there as the regional contractor with headquarters in – with a delightful sense of the appropriate – Norwich's old agricultural hall. One of the founders of that company and its Chief Executive was Aubrey Buxton.

Aubrey saw the outdoors as natural television material, just as I did. The difference was that he had the muscle. The bump on his biceps was a television company and its production facilities. While I was continually grafting and griping away at my metropolitan masters, Aubrey up in Norwich was actually presenting a series of natural history programmes called *Countryman*. One subject was the coypu, the alien Argentinian rodent that was even then ravishing Broadland with its orange teeth. It was this programme that he put forward as a pilot for a network wildlife series.

Rediffusion and Anglia had fraternal ties. And so Aubrey naturally brought his newborn baby to be admired and, with luck, adopted by Rediffusion John MacMillan, Rediffusion's hard-minded and experienced controller of programmes, recoiled sharply at the sight of the coypu but conceded that there was an idea there somewhere. As if setting Hercules his thirteenth and most impossible labour, he said: 'Make me a programme about the wildlife of central London and I'll give you a slot. We'll lend you staff to make it.'

Aubrey, who never looks as if it even occurs to him that anything he means to do may be impossible, replied: 'I hoped you'd say that, John.'

A day or so later when both Aubrey and Rediffusion got down to considering who should make the show, several people simultaneously, and with relief, thought of me. To second me to the task would at least get the maggots out of *This Week*. I was told I was to work with a director called Bill Morton. Bill, who was Sydney Bernstein's son-in-law, got all the difficult or nearly impossible development jobs. Later he went on to help create the BBC's *Man Alive*.

The wall had fallen down. Without knowing it, I was where I had wanted to be all my life.

To get where you want and, more important, to stay there, you need at least three things. (1) the stamina to lean against walls until they get tired, (2) the talent and/or energy to consolidate once you pick yourself up on the other side, (3) luck. The third element is possibly the most vital.

I had two strokes of luck. The first was meeting up with Aubrey with whom I had a great deal in common. The second was that I was at that moment researching a book, which I never subsequently wrote, on wildlife in metropolitan London.

About once every five years I make myself look at that first London programme again. I do so for two reasons: first, to see how far we've come since then; second, to remind myself what it felt like when it was all bright and new. Each time I watch it, I am amazed how brash it was but also how entertaining.

Bill Morton was about as urban as it is possible to be without actually being built of brick. He had excellent taste, programme judgement and was, above all, an innovator. He had no thought for natural history beyond making this first programme. I remember being scandalized when he told me that if the London programme was a success, and more particularly if it was a failure, that was *it* as far as he was concerned. He'd be off, even before it was transmitted, working on a pilot for some other kind of show. What kind of show? It really didn't matter so long as it had nothing to do with the birds and the bees. Meantime he threw his considerable energies into our show.

The wildlife content of the programme seems, in retrospect, a bit of a laugh. Apart from a few feral pigeons, some ducks in St James's Park and a fox let out of a laundry basket on a wild night in a quiet street, just off Hampstead Heath, the wildlife scenes had been shot anywhere but in London. To be fair we never suggested that our puffin *was* standing outside the Thames Embankment entrance to the Savoy Hotel. We merely said one had been found there and then proceeded to show the bird it its wild state – in Pembrokeshire!

If we wanted herons for the well-known breeding colony on an island in one of the Walthamstow reservoirs, we transported them on film from Scotland. The fish we naturally filmed – unnaturally – in tanks. It was a bit of a cheat as the critics, including Maurice Wiggin, were pleased to point out. Bill Morton gave even the fish, and most other sequences besides, a polish and presence, by commissioning John Dankworth to write the score. John, who was then a considerable name in jazz circles but did not enjoy the general fame he does today, wrote some highly original music. This appalled the purists but told the general viewing public that, as far as this show was concerned, natural history had shaken off the greenery-gallery dust and was in there competing for the ratings with the best of them.

Despite the fact that hardly a true wild thing, apart from some bomb-site plants, was shown in its London setting, the programme gained authenticity by taking its cameras into all the appropriate London locations. We also took Aubrey Buxton on location to 'do the links'. Aubrey performed gallantly, popping up amid the mallard in St James's Park, the pigeons on a City bomb site and at the seat of his Rolls-Bentley on the night we nearly lost the fox off the Spaniards Road, Hampstead. I think he confused a few people by looking a little, mainly around the domed forehead, like Peter Scott. He made one deathless fluff which is to this day embalmed on the sound-track of that first film. 'Meet me,' he invited, through a curtain of rain and the lowered window of the Bentley, 'tomorrow in *daylate*.' God knows why we never reshot the scene. Possibly the combination of losing the fox and filming at night in a downpour and gale of monsoon intensity discouraged even Bill Morton.

All we now had to do was to find a suitable title. 'Tooth and Claw' remained a front-runner for some time. Both Aubrey and I objected to it on the grounds that nature was not really like that. In the end we came up with *Survival*. It was adopted for the reason that most titles are eventually adopted. No one can think of anything better. As it turned out, it was a good and lucky choice.

That first programme, subtitled, with enormous breadth of imagination, 'The London Scene', went out from Rediffusion in January 1961. It gained a considerable audience and fair critical success. I can remember someone at Rediffusion saying next day: 'I can see that there may be another two subjects, but what do you do after that?'

At the moment of writing the answer is 280 half-hours and 30 one-hour Specials. What follows is the story of the people who made those shows.

Chapter 2

SOS Rhino

A MONTH after 'The London Scene' was transmitted, I was working at home on the second *Survival* programme.

After the excitement of the London show, it was a decided anti-climax but it was the best we could do as a follow-up. We'd been caught out by our own success. There wasn't a similarly lively rabbit hidden in our hat. Instead we had produced a bird, a beautiful bird it is true. The second *Survival*, 'The One that Came Back', told the story of how the avocet, a rare wading bird, was brought back to nest in East Anglia. I was half-way through the film treatment when the phone rang. It was Aubrey. 'Would you,' he asked, 'be willing to go to Uganda next Thursday to film the capture of some white rhinos?' There's only one answer to that. When I'd put the phone down I realized that I'd committed myself without knowing (a) precisely where Uganda is in Africa (b) what qualifies a rhino to be called white (c) whether I was expected personally to catch the brutes and, if so, how. All I knew was that it sounded a lot more exciting than the return of the avocet.

After the success of 'The London Scene' I had been loaned to Anglia Television, which shows how much *This Week* missed me, to develop *Survival*. Bill Morton had left on schedule, as he had predicted, to plough a new furrow in the ether.

The day after the Uganda summons I reported to the Hospital for Tropical Diseases for my jabs and to Brook House, Park Lane, Anglia's London headquarters, for my orders.

What had happened was this. Through his old friend and fellow naturalist Peter Scott, Aubrey Buxton had learned that the Uganda National Parks intended to catch the one remaining pocket of twenty to thirty white rhino left in Uganda. They were in the Madi District of West Nile. Once caught, the rhinos were to be moved two hundred miles to Murchison Falls (now renamed Kabarega) National Park where they would be safe from poachers. Rhinos the world over have the misfortune to grow up with a horn (in African species *two* horns) on the end of their noses. Alas, tired old gentlemen all over the Far East regard powdered rhino horn as a remarkable restorative for their waning powers. Rhino horn has no more aphrodisiac quality than chopped-up hair. In fact, that's exactly what rhino horn is – compacted hair. I tried to remember this later whenever I saw a three-foot horn coming fast in my direction. Its aphrodisiac inefficacy has no bearing on the price paid. Those who risk their lives for it earn only a few pounds per pound. Middlemen and Far Eastern merchants make a fortune from the trade. And so poaching flourishes.

The Uganda Parks were ready to sell the exclusive film rights in the white rhino operation to pay some of its costs. It was typical of Aubrey that, without knowing how we were going to film the catching, he decided that Anglia would put up the ante – £1,500. This doesn't sound a lot of money today. In 1961 it was a bold gesture for a regional television company to make. Why Africa? anyone on the Anglia board might have asked, and for all I know, did ask. Acle, Aylesham or Attleborough: these places fell within the proper East Anglian field of operations. But Africa? Aubrey's answer was that he intended to follow a sound evolutionary practice, namely, that where there is a vacant niche in the eco-system occupy it. There was certainly a vacant niche in Independent Television. Since Granada was winding down its excellent zoo unit under Desmond Morris (remember Congo, the painting chimpanzee?), there was no wildlife programme department in ITV comparable with the BBC Natural History Unit, Bristol. The remarkable tool-using woodpecker finch of the Galapagos got its start in life by noticing there were no woodpeckers on those islands. Anglia spotted the holes in the network of ITV branches. *Survival* was the tool it used – along with its drama productions – to make the most of the situation.

That £1,500 stake was important in other ways. It was the start of Anglia's relationship with national parks, conservation organizations and scientists all over the world that was to become *Survival*'s passport. More often the tie was not a financial one but one of trust. This sounds smug but it happens to be true. To people like park wardens and zoologists working in the field, television is a dirty word. To them most TV crews are a pest who first interrupt their work and then misinterpret it. From the start we had one great advantage. Aubrey Buxton had all the high level wildlife contacts necessary. But these would have been useless had we often put a foot wrong with the men who were doing the real hard and often dangerous work in the field. From the start *Survival* had to make sure it would always be asked back, and not simply because it had paid to come in in the first place. It was for this –

rather than for family reasons – that when looking for a cameraman who would be willing to risk his neck catching rhinos in some unspecified but probably highly dangerous fashion, Aubrey thought of his cousin John Buxton.

John Buxton had had – that important qualification – his gumboots in the mud since an early age, and Norfolk mud at that. His father Anthony Buxton, a famous ornithologist, lived at Horsey Hall, on Horsey Mere, Norfolk, mainly because marsh harriers and bitterns nested in the reed beds. John had been brought up to shoot, fish, and to watch and film birds. He had an ancient 35mm Mitchell camera encased in a kind of wooden box which he had inherited from his father (I wouldn't have been surprised to have learned that he had got it from D. W. Griffiths). This he insisted on taking to Uganda along with his more practical 16mm equipment. He also, as I said earlier, packed his dinner jacket 'just in case we meet any Buxtons out there'. Over the years I was to discover this was no idle boast. Buxtons or their relatives lurk in the least likely places in every corner of the globe.

So John and I set out together without truly knowing what we were going to do or how we were going to do it. All we knew was that we were to rendezvous with the rhino-catchers at Entebbe. We had no transport and we had a nasty feeling that if we were going to do a proper job, we'd need a second cameraman.

Ralph Dreschfield, constitutional adviser in Uganda and Chairman of the National Parks, was the key figure in setting up the operation for us. As far as Africa went we were as green as the papyrus in Lake Victoria. John Blower, who was then head of the Uganda Game Department and is now an old friend and an FAO wildlife adviser in Indonesia, met us at the old airport building. This was later to be shelled by Idi Amin's tanks when ousting the régime of Milton Obote and later still to become the objective of the famous Israeli raid. These events were a long way in the future. Uganda was still under British rule and hadn't yet tasted the joys of *Uhuru* – freedom. At that moment all seemed sweetness and light. If anyone had been asked to put money on which of the three East African countries would pass most successfully into self-government the betting is that in 1961 he would have staked his all on Uganda.

Lord knows what John Blower was expecting to meet – a couple of TV freaks, possibly. John, tall, thin, bush-jacketed and silk-scarfed, was more or less what I had been expecting. He didn't make any concessions to us, just threw our stuff in the back of his Land Rover and drove off to the Lake Victoria hotel. On our side we didn't try to impress him, probably because we knew it would be useless. However, when he waved an arm towards a swamp close to the airport and said 'Supposed to be sitatunga in there,' he obviously wasn't entirely

2

disgusted when John Buxton asked: 'Aren't they the antelope with very long hoofs adapted for living in swamps?'

John Blower has a laconic narrative style. What to us was then utterly abnormal he described in a manner that could have been little more dead-pan had he been reading the instructions on a packet of fish fingers. The rhino-catchers' trucks 'looked as though they had been worked over by multiple pom-poms'. Blower didn't amplify this but it was quite clear that what they had been worked over by was elephants and rhinos. They were late at Entebbe because they had had an accident with one of their jeeps. Blower added that, as a result of this accident, the jeep was 'flat enough to play on a gramophone'. It only emerged several sentences later that what it had had an accident with was one and a half tons of angry hippo. The catchers were apparently still in the south on the Chambura River where they were attempting to lasso baby hippo at night as their *quid pro quo* for catching the white rhino. Baby hippo commanded a good price at the time in zoos. The Uganda Parks were delighted to make the exchange since they had something like ten thousand hippo too many in the Kazinga Channel and lakes Edward and George which the Kazinga connects. Looking back on that first conversation with John Blower at the Lake Victoria Hotel, I don't believe he was deliberately trying to make us apprehensive. After all this time, I'd just like him to know that he succeeded.

Next day, helped by Blower, we started to shop around for the essentials of life. In Kampala we managed to hire a clapped-out diesel Land Rover. Blower had warned us that it was unlikely the catchers would let us ride on their rhino-riddled truck. We'd need a vehicle to follow the chase on our own. It would have to be able to keep up across country at speeds of thirty and even forty mph. Diesel Land Rovers will pull an elephant out of a mud wallow if necessary, but they are not best known for rapid acceleration. This one, as we soon discovered, was less fast through the gears than most. In certain conditions of over-heating, the only thing that could persuade its clutch to take a grip on itself was to pour Fanta lemon – it liked that better than orange – into the clutch housing.

We also shopped for a second cameraman. Bombo Trimmer, the last European Director of the Uganda Parks, had a suggestion to make. A trustee of the Parks Board called Chiels Margach, who had a plantation at Kinyala near Masindi, on our route to Murchison Falls Park, had shot some 16mm nature film for the Parks which was 'pretty good'. Bombo's idea of pretty good might not coincide with ours. Chiels! It was obviously an African name. There was no reason why an African naturalist cameraman shouldn't be brilliant, but mightn't there at least be problems of communication?

I was to find over the next few years that when Bombo said something was pretty good it was as if it had a hallmark on it. The first sighting of Bombo was guaranteed to deceive anyone. He looked the typical ex-King's African Rifles colonel, which he was, and gave the impression of being a small round bomb, primed with blood pressure and fused with gin and about to explode at any moment. Bombo, in fact, was the opposite of most of this. He drank gin, yes, but not until after sundown, then he drank it fast and in large quantities for a stipulated period. Then he stopped. But he was very much not the chuffer type ex-colonial colonel. For example, Bombo wrote plays about issues of the day, and, having written them, stuck them away in drawers, never to be heard of again. He was highly imaginative and sensitive and a first-class administrator. He's gone now, alas, died, probably of blood pressure, in Fiji, on the way to visit his wife Kay's son in New Zealand. On our initiation in Africa he struck both John Buxton and me as larger than life. Everyone in Africa struck us as larger than life, including Chiels Margach, whom we met two days later. Bombo had been right about Chiels. It was I who was wrong – on two counts. First, Chiels, as it turned out, *could* shoot decent film. Second, when John Buxton and I coaxed our lemon drop of a Land Rover in among his rubber trees at Kinyala, we were greeted not by an African but by a little man in a panama hat three feet wide who spoke in a soft Scottish accent. Margach! I should have guessed. Chiels? An abbreviation from his Scottish childhood, a dialect diminutive meaning 'child'.

Chiels lived in a glowering replica of a Scottish manse, built among the bougainvillaea and jacaranda trees. His father had been one of Uganda's few white settlers after the First World War. Chiels carried on the tradition in a despairingly resigned sort of way, confident that he was being robbed by his African staff, as well as the Uganda Government, certain that disaster lay ahead with the coming of *Uhuru* (he may well have been right there). Despite his air of gloom, he was probably at that moment in 1961 a very rich man.

Over dinner I told Chiels what was in our minds. Dinner *chez* Margach was always a colourful meal as I found a year or two later when dining at Kinyala with my wife. On that occasion one of the kitchen boys murdered the cook with a carving knife between the paw-paws and the eland steaks. On this first occasion nothing more serious happened than a violent argument in Swahili and ripe Scottish abuse between Chiels's demonic-looking house servant and his African grey parrot. The parrot, Kousouku, lived off wild red peppers and had a temper to match. He couldn't stand the house boy near his cage and told him so in language of which the Gorbals would have been proud.

Chiels needed no persuading to join us. He gave the impression that the plantation would carry on just as inefficiently without him. In fact I am certain that it ran well and profitably. If ever a Scot was canny it was Chiels. But the lure of joining an expedition like ours was too much for him. He would have passed up a favourable deal in paw-paws, pineapples, ginger, rubber or cotton, all of which he grew, for a chance to jump on the rhino-catchers' truck. Looking sadly at the succulent pineapple we were eating, he said: 'Do you know, the Margachs have been farming here for forty years and this is the first pineapple I've ever succeeded in getting into the house. I know it's one of mine but even then I had to buy it from some bastard by the side of the road for ten cents.' It was Chiels's way of saying that the farm could go to hell and might just as well do so while he took off with us to film the rhino catch.

Next day John Buxton and I drove on to Murchison Falls National Park where we were to meet the rhino-catchers. They were still three or four days behind schedule. In the meantime we were handed over to John Savidge, head warden, for some basic training in bushcraft. For openers he took us stalking black rhino on foot. For newcomers it was an impressive initiation. The sharp end of a black rhino at thirty paces when you have nowhere to go if it turns nasty except up a tree is a memorable way to start. It was a long way from Anglia's London base in Brook House, Park Lane. In *Survival* programme files I came across a letter I wrote to Aubrey:

> We've had our moments these first few days. We walked into a hippo in the dark while laying cable to record hyenas on an elephant carcase. A few minutes later I found myself alone and looking at four pink soup plates. These turned out to be the eyes of two more hippo. I sorted out a good tree just as the warden had told me. Fortunately the hippo moved on inland. I haven't been so scared since those first nights after the landing in Sicily. The dead elephant gave the authentic flavour to the occasion . . .

If John Buxton was alarmed by any of these adventures, he never showed it. John was unflappable to a point which often irritated me. Why should he be able to stay so calm when we walked into a lioness and cubs and came within inches of being charged? I certainly wasn't calm. Perhaps John wasn't either but somehow he managed to give the impression that, after he had been delivered from annihilation by John Savidge's bushcraft, he was simply thanking Savidge for putting a second lump of sugar in his tea. John is almost a caricature of the intrepid Englishman. Yet there is nothing put on about it all. 'Thanks *awfully*,' he would say, after someone had pointed out that a second rhino was about to charge the truck from behind. And when he had got the shot, there sometimes came a rare and excessive gush of emotion: '*Smashing!*' We only fell out once. While waiting for the rhino-catchers, Savidge invited us to take part in an anti-poaching operation. In the mêlée that took place, a raider was shot with a Greener gun and killed. They'd crossed Lake Albert (sorry, Lake Idi Amin) from the Congo (now Zaire) side by dug-out canoe and were netting antelope in the park. I wanted John to film the incident and he refused. Subsequently I believe him to have been right but I was considerably exercised by his lack of news-sense at the time.

The rhino-catchers turned up three days later. No one had exaggerated about them or their transport. They might have walked straight out of one of those magnificent Frederic Remington paintings of the old West. I could imagine them all in America of the mid-1800s as buffalo hunters or Indian fighters and I found myself casting them in Wild West roles. Ken Randall, the boss, would have been the boss in any outfit you cared to name. Tough as rhino hide, never speaking a superfluous word, with features almost as battered as his trucks, Ken was nevertheless a thoughtful, even sensitive man. Richard Boone would have played him to perfection. His partner Pat O'Connell was the gunfighter in his prime, aggressive, sure of himself, never willing to be put down. Then there was Louie Wedd, Ken's son-in-law, the youngster, courageous but certain eventually to choose the wrong man to call out. Lastly, Ken Stewart, small, intelligent, self-sufficient. I saw him as the gambler with the Derringer in his sleeve.

Pat O'Connell sorted us out straight away. 'If you've come to Africa with any left-wing *Daily Mirror* views about the equality of man, forget 'em. And if you get in our way when we're catching and fall off the truck, don't expect us to stop for you because the rhino won't stop for anyone. Apart from that, welcome.'

Ken Randall confined himself to comments about rhino, with whom, it was easy to see, he was deeply in love. 'Some people,' he said, 'think rhinos are stupid bastards but I'll tell you this. They can't see a goddam thing but if you put a ginger biscuit on the side of the truck and they decide to charge it, short-sighted or not, they'll hit it right on the button.'

On the subject of white rhinos he was properly cagey. 'They're supposed to be fairly docile but that's because no one's ever tried lassoing a full-grown one. My guess is that they're not going to like it all that much.'

Four days later in Madi District of West Nile we found out he was right. Our first catch was a quarter-grown calf. We chased the three and a half ton mother and her one ton calf for two miles flat out across the bush, crashing trees to splinters and touching the ground at rare intervals. We ran the mother off and roped the calf without any real difficulty. As we started back to catch mum, O'Connell said with relish: 'Boys, this is going to be different. This is the big one.'

The set-up for catching was as follows. The truck was an open ex-WD Chevy 15 cwt. Bolted to it, on either side front and rear, were two stout tree trunks to act as mooring bollards. The lasso artists, Wedd and Stewart, were stationed behind the cab, each holding a long bamboo pole to which was attached, with soft wire, the noose in the end of a one inch sisal rope. The other end of this rope was coiled on the floor of the truck and, of course, attached to a tree trunk. The technique was for Randall to drive the truck alongside the galloping rhino and for the catcher on the appropriate side to slide the noose over its nose. Randall then slowed down slightly, the noose broke away from the catching pole and the rhino was hooked. During the chase, one of the catchers gave hand signals to Randall through the open hatch in the cab roof. Such was the noise that it was impossible for the driver to hear shouted directions such as 'hard aport' or 'slow down'. The rest of the crew, those who were to tie up the rhino when caught, just hung on where they could. For the first catches I sat next to the driver, right beneath the open hatch in the cab roof.

So we set off after 'the big one'! The noise and the jolting in the front of the cab made you feel like a dice being shaken in a tin box. Randall smoked imperturbably while he drove. Once a hand flicked down through the open hatch above my head indicating a change of direction, and we reared round to port. A few seconds later, there was the rhino's jinking backside ahead of us again. The creature had apparently taken advantage of a thick patch of tall grass to change direction almost at right angles. Trees came up and smashed against the windscreen. I had not yet schooled myself not to duck each time this happened. By now the chase seemed to have been going on for a good ten minutes. I suspect that the real duration was a tenth of this time, but we still weren't up with our quarry. However, there was now a long stretch of plain ahead of us, fairly level, though broken with rocks, termite heaps and trees. The howl of the truck became almost more than I could stand and there was a strong smell of burning. Slowly the rhino's hindquarters crept nearer to us. Even more slowly, we overhauled her. She crept back past the bonnet of the truck rather like the rear coach of a train being overtaken by a second train travelling at a slightly greater speed. The size of her at close quarters was appalling. At last her head was coming within range of the ropers. As that huge front horn became level with the bonnet, she gave a couple of savage sideways hooks at us, but without slackening her pace. Randall was now shouting for O'Connell to rope and indeed O'Connell was desperately trying to do so, but a situation, new even to the catchers, had developed: the front horn was longer than anything they had ever met before and the lasso noose was just not wide enough to go over the tip and round and under the rhino's lower jaw. There were some desperate seconds of juggling. Randall was swearing at the top of his voice. I'll never forget the sensation of tearing along beside that beast even though it was separated from me by the width of the cab. Randall, however, was practically eye to eye with her with only about a foot separating the pair of them. After what seemed twenty minutes, a second lasso pole dipped into view. Wedd had crossed the cab to reinforce O'Connell and this time his noose, which was a little wider, went home. I heard a shout from up top that the rope was on, and now we were slowing and the distance between us and the rhino lengthening again. This time the creature was attached to us by twenty yards of rope.

The battle started. The rhino's first move was to try and shake herself free. She did this by backing away and heaving her huge head up and down. The rope jerked and strained and the tree trunk to which the end was lashed creaked and groaned, but it held.

Now the rhino tried to break for it and run. Randall drove after her cautiously, keeping her on a tight line and trying to lessen the sudden stresses on rope and rhino. The rhino checked and backed off again. This time Randall drove the truck round her in a slow circle, keeping the line taut while the animal fought it out. The whole process was exactly like that of a skilful angler playing, and tiring, a very large fish.

Without warning, the rhino changed tactics. She galloped left-handed across our front so that the rope whipped over our screen and strained out at a forty-five degree angle on the nearside of the truck. Now the rhino was looking at me and I began to feel very acutely the absence of a door on my side of the cab. The fact that Randall had assured me a door was no protection if a rhino really decided to come aboard did little to reassure me. Just as you feel a little better with some cover, even if it is only a bush, between you and the enemy, so now I felt that door might have done a lot for my morale. The rhino seemed to guess how I was feeling. She came straight in and charged. At first her trajectory seemed to be taking her right into the cab. I wriggled off my seat and shared the centre of the floor with the gear lever. But at the last second she swerved and the uppercut she gave with her horn hit the body low down just forward of the cab. The tip of her horn appeared through the metal. There was something utterly primeval about this furious animal seen at close quarters and I do not mind admitting I have never been more frightened. She did not back away but stayed where she was, plunging and lunging with her horn and rocking the truck at every slash. I had had enough. Ken Stewart had told me the night before that if a rhino really *did* stick its head into the cab there was always the escape hatch in the roof. I used it now, and emerged on top of the cab just as the animal made a run round the front. It seemed I could hardly have done a worse thing. I felt the rope moving under me and jumped just in time to save myself being swept to the ground by it. The rhino had by no means finished with us yet. She was giving the treatment to the front of the bonnet now, alternating uppercuts with trip-hammer blows which she delivered to the top of the radiator by letting her head crash down on it. You had the feeling of being on a very small tin island battered by a monstrous sea. What O'Connell did at this moment fills me with admiration even to this day. He went over the side with a short length of rope in his hands and, while the rhino was busy savaging the front of the truck, nipped practically under her belly and got a rope round one of her rear legs. The others followed him down, dodging when the rhino hooked and turned, scuffling in the dust with her, distracting her attention so that O'Connell could come in again and take the rope round her other back leg. This, it seemed, was the moment of truth in rhino-catching. Once the back legs were haltered a good deal of steam went out of the creature. Wedd was still in the truck shortening rope. The rest of the Lilliputians swarmed over her. O'Connell, Stewart, Randall and the African ropers slipped and tightened a second rope round her front legs and then all heaved together so that she went down on her side. It was only then that I saw with relief that Chiels Margach had been in close to cover all this from the side while John Buxton had filmed the whole battle, more or less continuously, from the top of the catching truck. As O'Connell had said: it had been the big one.

All told twelve rhinos were caught. Two died after capture. Ten

The wearer of the black ostrich feather headdress is a witch from the Karamoja region in north-east Uganda. Alan Root was violently attacked by her when filming a woman's ceremony for the documentary on this vanishing people called 'Karamoja'. The warriors of the five tribes that make up the Karamojong peoples are extremely warlike, continually raiding and killing each other. Alan Root experienced fewer problems with the warriors than with this lady and her companions.

Overleaf: A skein of snow and blue geese fly in formation with the camera. These flying shots were the ones that amazed all those who saw the Emmy-winning Special, 'The Flight of the Snow Geese'. Some viewers even asked if they were done with models. One of the dilemmas when making the film was to decide whether to use the sequence that gave away how these scenes were taken. In the end it was decided to include it.

were released to breed in the wild and successfully secure the species a foothold in northern Uganda. Several years later, when drugs had been developed that enabled rhinos to be caught by darting without the shock and stress of the lasso technique – the only 'safe' method in 1961 – another batch was caught and released in Murchison Falls Park. That time the darting was carried out by helicopter. We made a *Survival* about that operation, too, called 'Bolt from the Blue'. It was a goodish programme but it never measured up to that original film shot by John Buxton and Chiels Margach.

When John and I returned to England there were endless technical inquests about the quality of the film, the sharpness of some scenes, the colour variations and so on. But then the technicians had never tried using as a camera platform a bucking catching truck with a three and a half ton rhino attached to it by a one inch sisal rope. Finally, when the experts had had their say, we went ahead and the editor cut the film. It was the real thing, all right. Not a bit like that Hollywood capture epic *Hatari*, with Elsa Martinelli frolicking around with John Wayne. Ours had the roar, dust and danger of the chase in every frame. I remember no more exciting scene in a wildlife film than the one in which that first big cow 'played' the truck on the end of her rope. John Dankworth's score exactly complemented the rawhide quality of the action. The film was called 'SOS Rhino'.

More than any other show, perhaps, it put *Survival* on the map. As far as I was concerned there could now be no question of returning to Rediffusion. Aubrey invited me to join Anglia.

'What do you want to be called?'

'How about Head of Natural History Unit?'

Previous page: 'Lengai', Alan and Joan Root's hot-air balloon passes slap over the crater of Africa's highest mountain, Kilimanjaro, at the first attempt. Note how little snow lies around the crater itself. Though dormant, Kilimanjaro still retains some warmth. The snows at the top, of which Ernest Hemingway wrote in his famous short story, are in reality large ice-fields. A small pack of wild dogs was recently seen to cross one of these. The story of the Roots' adventures was told in 'Safari by Balloon'.

Dieter Plage's classic shot of a fish eagle about to take its prey. The target was a large fish, a tilapia which was careless enough to surface with its dorsal fin showing above the surface of Botswana's Okavango Swamp. The African fish eagle, a close relative of America's national bird, the bald eagle, throws its talons forward at the last moment, hooks them into the fish and uses its forward momentum to lift the catch clear of the water.

From that moment on Anglia Television had a Natural History Unit. It consisted almost entirely of chiefs and very few Indians. One of the chiefs, who had also been posted from Associated Rediffusion, was a programme director, Stanley Joseph.

Chapter 3

Words and Music

LIKE Bill Morton before him, Stanley Joseph wasn't truly interested in wildlife, even less did he understand it. To his last days with *Survival*, which came some ten or more years later, he referred to antelope as 'deer'. Even when he knew better, he still, out of sheer egregiousness, called them deer. Deer had horns and, as far as Stanley was concerned, that was it. Stanley was out of his element in the great outdoors. Nevertheless he had ideas and style and these he gave to those early *Survivals* in generous measure. His instincts, being those of an urban sophisticate, at least as far as films were concerned, always led him towards production techniques and away from the finer detail of wildlife behaviour. This, so long as someone was there to put the brake on his wilder exuberances, was not a bad thing. *Survival* had deliberately set out to capture the widest possible audience, leaving the specialized wood-notes-wild viewers to the BBC. Aubrey Buxton had declared from the outset that we intended to present wildlife as entertainment. The London programme had set the key. Who can blame Stanley if, as resident director, he played theme and variations in that key.

The three of us soon found that we were operating in a branch of the film business for which there were no rules. We had to make them up as we went along. We had started out with the premise that we could buy in film from talented amateur naturalist cameramen and build *Survival* by sticking this together with links and location shooting done by full television film crews. This is what we did first with 'The London Scene' and next with 'The One that Came Back'. In the first instance the film came from a number of sources, including Hungary. In the second, the main footage belonged to the Royal Society for the Protection of Birds, the rest was from Holland. The weaknesses of this system were immediately apparent. The first years of *Survival* were exclusively black and white years. But even in this modest medium, the differences in quality that arose from the use of different cameramen, of differing ability, often using different film stock, gave an overall result that was very far from perfect. Though the idea that we might one day sell the show worldwide had not yet occurred, there was the nagging thought that we didn't own the material and therefore the rights in it. I called it postage stamp film-making. It was like sticking a whole lot of interesting individual exhibits down in an album. Without any of us realizing it at the time, 'SOS Rhino' changed all that. We had commissioned two wildlife cameramen, supplied their film stock and therefore owned the result to the last fogged frame.

Those programme-makers who had been in the field before us had solved these problems in different ways. Peter Scott's *Look* for the BBC had been highly successful for years. It was essentially a nature chat show with film clips, the naturalist film-maker concerned being there in the studio to talk to the anchorman about his work and the wildlife featured in it. *Look* was good, old-fashioned television and, in its day, none the worse for that.

Granada's *Zoo Time* relied on a special film unit based on the London Zoo. Desmond Morris supplied the expert knowledge and on-screen personality. Inevitably, though, it dealt with captive animals in a captive situation.

Armand and Michaela Dennis were true pioneers. They had as cameraman, and later as partner, a brilliant Australian, Des Bartlett, of whom much more later. Armand Dennis Productions was based in Langata, a suburb of Nairobi. Wildlife material of the very first quality was shot in the bush by Des, and his wife, Jen. Armand and Michaela turned up, occasionally *On Safari*, but increasingly on what Hollywood would call 'back lots' to shoot the links in which they spoke to camera and to each other. The audience, of course, believed implicitly that they were always in, or at least close to, the lion's mouth and even that they had shot the film personally. TV audiences are like that and who's to blame them except the poor writers, cameramen, directors, who actually do the job? All that matters in the end about a programme is that it works. *On Safari* worked. Moreover both it and *Look* created a TV climate and an atmosphere that made it possible for *Survival* to thrive when it arrived on the scene.

At first we accepted the convention that in-vision links with an introducer speaking to camera were necessary. Aubrey did the job. He even spoke the commentaries of our earlier programmes. He popped up not only in London but also in Norwich Museum among stuffed rhinos, on Norfolk river banks, beaches and inevitably at his beloved Blakeney Point. Loyal to the last drop of his East Anglian blood, Aubrey believed,

I think, that Norfolk, if not the sand dunes and marshes of Blakeney
Point itself, could produce any setting needed to match any location in
the world. Fortunately, at that time *Survival* had not begun to range as
far afield as the Andes or the Himalayas. When we eventually did so,
in-vision links by the Chief Executive of Anglia Television, or by
anyone else for that matter, with the occasional royal exception, had
long become a thing of the past. *Survival* favoured 'pure' film. How to
get the raw material for such films? Well, that basically is what this book
is about. What we all three began to see at quite an early stage was that
we had somehow to build up a permanent team of naturalist cameramen
who worked exclusively for us.

For the moment, though, we were absorbed with problems of
presentation and in achieving a style. Much of that style was to come
from the use of music. This was basically Stanley's province. He had a
good sound knowledge and appreciation of music. He was, however, not
a musician any more than I am. At that stage we were both naïvely under
the impression that we could influence and steer composers. Stanley's
directives to our resident maestro, John Dankworth, and his arranger
and fellow composer, David Lindup, were minor masterpieces in
themselves.

Music was a centre of controversy from the beginning, not only among
ourselves but also with the viewing public. Aubrey, who during the
early years of *Survival* liked to be involved at the main stages of every
half-hour we made, is a leading exponent of the I-know-what-I-like
school of musical appreciation. What he likes is, in fact, percussion. He
has an excellent sense of rhythm. For the rest, Shostakovich is probably
a Russian general and Bix Beiderbecke a German fighter ace of the
First World War. Hence a continual plea for some 'real African music'.
What he means by this is *drums*. Real African music in any Western
sense just does not exist despite Dankworth's 'African Waltz' or 'A
Swinging Safari'. Try those on the Maasai or the Matabele!

Numbers of viewers held decided and forceful views on our use of
music. For them it was intrusive, distracting and superfluous in a
natural history film. What the complainants wanted to hear was the
wind on the heath and, oh brother, not in the brass section. For them,
the birds and the bees sang sweetly enough. 'Disgusted of Saffron
Walden' switched back to *Look* never to defect to the Independent
channel again. It didn't do to take too much notice of such complaints.
It never does. In the end you must always please yourself and, in so
doing, hope to please the majority of others. Those who bother to write
in about a television programme are very distinctly a minority. People
rarely write to tell you how wonderful you are. The letters come from
axe-grinders and those who want you to know why they switched off.

For every viewer who complains there are thousands, maybe millions, sitting at home who don't know, don't care or thoroughly enjoyed the show. In this situation all you have to go on are the mystic 'ratings', audience viewing percentages derived from a balanced sample of monitored sets. In those days the oracle was the great god TAM. TAM suggested that we were very much on the right lines.

So Stanley continued his splendidly detailed briefings to our composers. The following examples, addressed to John Dankworth, are intended as musical guidance for sequences in the first African compilation show we made called 'Tomorrow May Be Too Late'.

> M.4. Rescue deer from water at Kariba.
> Smooth, soft 'deer-like' music, broken harshly at the tenth second. Then becomes more of a rough and tumble up to twenty-fifth second. More opportunity for jazz in those fifteen seconds, between the tenth and twenty-fifth.
> M.5. Baboon rescue
> It may be just the similarity of the words, but the baboon makes me think of 'bassoon' and even 'buffoon'. The animal can't help raising a laugh in this sequence in his buffoon-like struggles and his refusal to be rescued. The musical clout he gets on the head at the tenth-plus second should contain all the exasperation of the men who are irritated by the 'ingratitude' of these animals. Yes! surely bassoon music: (what about the old-style Ragtime?)

It goes without saying that when Stanley wrote 'deer' he meant antelope.

What I have painfully come to realize over the years is that no matter what you say to a composer as you sit viewing the fine-cut of the film frame by frame, he then goes away and writes something that bears no resemblance to what you had become convinced was a joint conception.

The next stage in total disillusionment comes when you ask him timidly: 'Can't you play the theme (you, of course, mean tune) to me on a piano before we go into the recording studio?' We once even bought a broken-down piano for this purpose and installed it in our viewing theatre. It was never used except by the pub pianists among the editing staff. The reason should have been foreseen. A non-musician, any composer will tell you, is quite incapable of visualizing or, more accurately, hearing, what the completed sound will be like once the 'tune' has been arranged and orchestrated. People like myself are just not capable of speaking or understanding the language. Bitter experience over the years has convinced me that this is truly the case, so much so that I long ago ceased going to music recording sessions.

What happens at such a session is baffling in every respect, not least in the expertise shown by the musicians. Up to thirty top instrumentalists arrive with seconds to spare and uncase their instruments. All know each other by Christian names although some may only perform together a few times a year. The arrangements are produced, often with the copyist's ink still wet on them. The composer and possibly his musical director arrive. The musicians, some of whom may have been playing the previous day with Jack Parnell, others perhaps performing that night at Covent Garden or Sadler's Wells, briefly regard the sheet of music they have never seen until that moment. The first clip of film to which the composer has been writing starts to run up on the monitor. 'M One. Take One', announces the recording engineer. The orchestra or rather 'line-up' responds to the composer's or MD's baton. Often they get it right first time. Sometimes there are several takes. Miraculously music fits action. If it doesn't, the composer snips a bar or two out as if cutting film. As producer you are powerless to do anything but admire such professionalism. Sometimes you love the result, often you hate it. Either way you know that until you get the music back home and start marrying it with commentary and sound effects you won't know what works and what doesn't. More than anything else in film-making it is hit and miss.

The subject of the use of music in wildlife films is a fascinating one to which I shall be returning later. For the moment I must confine myself to music in our early days. We were most successful when the film gave the *Survival* team scope for fun and didn't concentrate too heavily on natural history. The best examples came from the show in which we used Rolf Harris as narrator, singer, lyricist and often composer as well. Stanley himself was no mean librettist. Rolf, who is always at his best with young people and wildlife, fairly bubbles with good humour and wit. The result was often irresistible, even if it sometimes shocked the stuffier naturalist viewer.

The first time we used Rolf was in a programme about how Australia was mistreating its wildlife. For this we borrowed the title of his famous song, except that we called this *Survival* 'Mow Me Kangaroo, Down'. Rolf adapted the lyric of the song and gave a bitter twist to the kangaroo's tail. If the lines don't always seem to scan, that is because Rolf is a brilliant and lightning artist at both aside and ad lib. Hence such throwaways as 'Oho! Steer clear of the wombat, mate.'

> Watch that wallaby behind you,
> Hey! Watch that other one go – woohoo!
> They're no sluggards for speed, mate:
> And take a look at the ears and the shape

of the other features and their size and
you can see how they differ from the 'roo.
(Spoken)
Well, the kangaroo is usually very much bigger.
The duck-billed platypus – hey, that was quick,
 where did he go?

Well, we'll talk about it later.
Here's old fat-bottomed wombat: he's bad-tempered,
 of course,
No one ever attacks him because he turns his
 fat padded base to face his attacker
And a kick from his back leg – boing! –
Could flatten a horse:
Oho! Steer clear of the wombat, mate. . . .

No one cuddles the echidna – aoh! – he's all spikes
 from his day of birth
And he's so shy when he meets you that he tilts
 down his snout
And the rest of him follows
And he digs and he digs and he digs
Until he's some feet underneath the earth.

In a later Australian half-hour called 'Roo', Rolf wrote a marvellous
action lyric to a sequence of CSIRO (Commonwealth Scientific and
Industrial Research Organization) scientists catching – and often
missing – kangaroos in a wired-in compound.

. . . They shoved me in a bag
That reminded me of Mum,
So I snuggled there without a care
About things to come.
I'll leave it to me cobbers
Who're out there in the sun – . . .
That's a little too close for comfort mates,
They're starting to hem me in.
But the slightly superior speed I've got
And the highly superior spring
Gives a wonderful sense of freedom
And a bubbling urge to sing.
Ohhh! They got me! . . .

I say, you there,
Release that kangaroo there.

Peter Scott, Scientific Adviser to *Survival*, with Ted Eales, warden of the National Trust Nature Reserve, on Blakeney Point, Norfolk. Ted was one of *Survival's* first wildlife cameramen. Peter's umbrella is painted on its outer surface to resemble reeds and provides an instant hide on the marsh. On this occasion, they were working together to film the story of the wild Bewick's swans which travel each winter from Siberia to the Wildfowl Trust's reserves at Slimbridge, Gloucestershire, and Welney in Norfolk. The swans are individually recognizable by the patterns on face and bill and are logged in daily at the Trust's reserves. Below, 'Zoop' and 'Primrose' greet each other after a quarrel with neighbours. Both starred in the programme 'Never Forget A Face'.

Cameraman Dieter Plage has a very narrow escape. The incident occurred in the fishing village of Vitshumbi in the Virunga National Park, Zaire. This bull elephant normally lives at peace with the villagers, strolling casually amongst them and even rubbing himself against their houses. Outside the village, on the shores of Lake Edward, he occasionally reverts to type. Dieter had been filming him peacefully for some time when he suddenly became irritable and charged. Unfortunately Dieter was attached to his camera and heavy tripod by a battery cable. The tripod collapsed and the bull mercifully stopped in full charge to examine the camera, placing his foot on it. Not even the camera was damaged!

You know, Australia is an impossible place
For a self-respecting kangaroo to live in.
It's a bloody disgrace.
I suppose it's the thrill of the chase.
But then, they're a dreadful race.

Not even the conservationist fuddies could object to this. Such songs put over the message. They were also, without doubt, fine entertainment.

There were other issues that taxed us during those early days. One of these was how far we should go in showing nature in the raw. If the lion pounced on a zebra that was OK. But if it was shown with the rest of the pride finishing it off in the frequently messy way to which lions are prone, could the viewing public stand it? Should they be asked to stand it? Here I usually found myself in a minority of one. Where big animals are concerned, life in the wild is, ninety-nine per cent of the time, peaceful. But when action erupts between predator and prey it is violent, brutal, necessary and without any of the overtones that accompany human violence. Such adjectives as 'vicious' just do not apply to a predator though they are often used just the same.

Aubrey and I had laid it down as one of the tenets of *Survival* that we would always avoid sentimentality and that we would never allow our-selves to be accused of anthropomorphism. Starting from this base, I argued rather priggishly that we had what practically amounted to a duty to show nature in the raw when the situation called for it and the footage allowed. I should add that I am not at all squeamish. Stanley took the opposite view, but then he was not only squeamish – I couldn't imagine him paunching a rabbit or gutting a trout, occupations in which both Aubrey and I were well versed – he was also intel-lectually opposed to violence. He recognized its role in nature but was averse to emphasizing it. Aubrey was opposed to prolonging scenes in which creatures killed and ate each other for quite a different and far more practical reason. He argued that anything that caused the viewer to switch off from a sense of shock or horror was defeating the whole object of the exercise. I did not agree with him at the time. I'm forced to admit that I have largely come to share this view since.

Aubrey wrote memos to us both on this subject, one of which I particularly treasure for the handwritten footnote. I imagine that he read the memo when his secretary presented it to him, thought it was a bit much and sought to soften the blow. Across the bottom he had scrawled, 'It was a wonderful *Survival*.'

Up to that point when reading the memo, you might never have guessed it. Nevertheless, the points he made which bear on the

3

permissible stress on 'cruelty' in wildlife films were all goodish ones. He wrote:

> There is no doubt that 'Elephants Have Right of Way' was an outstanding programme. Nevertheless it is agreed that we only bother to *criticize* programmes.
>
> I think we have a knack, perhaps an unnecessary one, of making people feel sorry for animals. This was the case with the hippo and the young buffalo.
>
> There is no question here of inhibition or squeamishness. We are trying to sell peak time entertainment, with a strong message.
>
> Therefore anything that detracts from the peak time entertainment objective need not be included unless it is vital. The hippo culling sequence was all right on film when I saw it, and it was very carefully cut, but the commentary made it slightly gruesome.
>
> Catching the baby buffalo. I remember positively stating that the branding should not be included. This may have been overlooked but I do not want to get to the stage where we have to have minutes recorded of all our discussions.
>
> What also made people sorry for the buffalo, instead of glad that it was being looked after, was the bogus squeaking. The result was unnecessarily pathetic.
>
> You may feel that these points stem from inhibitions, but do not forget we are trying to sell programmes at home and abroad, especially in the States. The hippo sequence may well prove a formidable obstacle.

And then that handwritten footnote.

> It was a wonderful *Survival*. A.B.

Aubrey, as I have said, took a deep personal interest in our slender output of five or six programmes a year. At first this was all we produced. Like many of us he was perhaps never at his best when committing his reactions to paper. If either Stanley or I had taken some of them to heart, we would have gone mad or resigned. Still, *Survival* was his baby. It was natural at first that he should be apprehensive about how we would bring it up.

Chapter 4

Karamoja

AUBREY had been to Africa before and during the war. His first post-war visits were with his wife, Maria, as a guest at the Uganda and later Tanzania *Uhuru* celebrations. It was as a result of these two trips that we were to find two of the finest wildlife cameramen in the world. Aubrey made one of these contacts in the Queen Elizabeth National Park in southern Uganda. A young Kenyan called Alan Root and his wife, Joan, were staying with the head warden, Frank Poppleton, while filming in the park. Alan wanted to take a short cut home through what was then the Congo, at that time in the grips of a bloody civil war. The Roots had no visas in their passports. It was highly unlikely they could have got them, even if they'd tried before leaving Nairobi. Without appearing to give it a thought, Alan and Joan, plus a parrot, set off to drive three hundred miles through Congolese territory full of disaffected military and, for all they knew, Simba guerrillas. Aubrey was deeply impressed by this. It was, in fact, the disaffected military who caused the trouble. When the Roots were inevitably stopped by drunken soldiery at a road-block, a Congolese NCO tried to take away Alan's passport. Alan hit him hard in the stomach, retrieved his passport and drove off to the frenzied and disorganized clicking of submachine-gun bolts. The Roots were round the bend before anyone could open fire.

Aubrey's second contact was with Des Bartlett in Nairobi. He asked me to follow this up in 1962. My wife and I found Des, Jen and their small daughter, Julie, camping in the bush close to a forestry research station outside Kampala. I had sought Des out with the sole purpose of asking him whether he would come and film for us. His answer was that he had heard what we were doing and would like nothing better. Armand Dennis had been very good to him, though, and as long as Armand Dennis Productions were making television programmes he'd stick with them. Ask him any time after that and he wouldn't find it hard to be persuaded. That moment didn't come until nearly four years later.

I formed the impression at that first meeting that Des was perhaps the most personally dependable man I was likely to meet in a lifetime. For once, first impressions were correct. My wife was equally captivated by the Bartlett entourage. It was her first time in Africa. She suffered from that feeling, hard to suppress at first, that when you walk bare-legged in the bush, snakes are waiting to strike in every clump of grass. Before long she wanted to spend a penny. The forest and scrub just beyond the Land Rover and tent were thick and seemed to be just the sort of places favoured by puff-adders and spitting cobras. She admitted to Jen Bartlett that she was not quite used to the sort of out-door conveniences provided by Africa. So Julie Bartlett, aged six, acted as her guide and then insisted on taking her for a long walk in the bush to show her that snakes were very good at minding their own business. During the course of this conversation, Julie mentioned casually that she'd once been carried off by a lion. She had, too, one of those semi-tame beasts that hunters and wardens sometimes raise from cubs and keep about their camps. The lioness, a fully grown one, had leapt at Julie as Jen Bartlett was lifting the little girl on her shoulders and had run two hundred yards into the bush with the child in her mouth. Fortunately she was not mauled.

Much of Julie's composure undoubtedly comes from her mother. Jen is, if anything, even less likely to be stampeded than is Des. She'd been an up-and-coming Australian tennis star before she'd married Des and had even played at Wimbledon. From the moment that Armand Dennis discovered young Bartlett in Australia and asked him if he'd like to film in Africa for him for six weeks – in fact Des stayed over ten years – the Bartletts were literally 'on safari'. From that moment on, their home was never likely to be much more permanent than a Land Rover and a couple of tents. When Julie came along, Jen took on the appalling job of educating the child herself. She knew all about the excellent Australian educational correspondence courses designed so that mothers can teach their own children on outback sheep stations. She had begun this exacting task when we first met her. Over six years later when my wife and I made our first field trip with the Bartletts in the deserts of Arizona, Utah and New Mexico, she and Julie were still hard at it. 'Hard' is the only possible word.

No one but a wildlife cameraman, or his wife, would choose the life they lead, though they themselves consider no other life possible. There are no hours except all hours. Very rarely do they take holidays because the next project always seems to depend on a season or event which, once missed, will then be a further twelve months away. The weather is by no means always fair. Travelling is often long and exhausting. For the wife, the moment the caravan stops she faces organization, catering, cooking, secretarial work, logging and dispatch of film, shot-listing, indexing of still photographs. And on top of all this, in Jen's case, there was Julie's education. I have seen Jen Bartlett, at the end of a five hundred mile drive, get out the arithmetic books and supervise the little girl's study in the back of a station wagon. I've seen her climb out of a light aircraft and take a class in French immediately the family reached a motel bedroom.

For Julie Bartlett the strain can hardly have been less with the distractions and the temptations of the wilderness her daily and often only playmates. Nevertheless, when Des and Jen at last decided to send their daughter home, aged fourteen, to a boarding school in Australia, she was ahead of her classmates in almost every grade. Today she is on the way towards being a promising marine biologist and is an extremely poised and attractive young lady. We will meet the Bartletts later in this book. They are one of the mainstays of *Survival*.

In this account of our first moves towards building a film team, I must not overlook the name of Bill Cowen. Bill ran a successful optician's and chemist's in Kampala. His wife had died on a photographic trip to Africa several years before. I believe it was Bill's dearest ambition to do the same. His passion was wildlife photography and in pursuing this passion he certainly came close to dying several times. Once he was even horned in the backside by, of all things, a wildebeest. In the course of filming 'SOS Rhino', Cowen met Chiels Margach. They got on so well together that I suggested that they team up. The Cowen-Margach combination shot two of our earliest African *Survivals*, 'Explorer's Nile', which contrasted the explorations of Samuel Baker on the Victoria Nile with the scene there today; and 'Elephants Have Right of Way', which was about the day-to-day running of the Queen Elizabeth National Park by head warden Frank Poppleton. I worked on these films on that same trip in 1962 on which I sought out Des Bartlett. My wife and I lived part of the time with the team on the Nile in the twenty-three foot ketch Chiels had designed and built himself from logs personally selected from the Budongo Forest.

Bill Cowen, the blunt Northumbrian from Keswick, must have been pushing sixty even in those days. Alas, he never achieved his ambition of living out his days in Africa. Typically he 'illegally' escaped from Idi Amin's oppression with enough of his worldly goods to have got himself clapped in gaol. He got out by the simple ruse of walking through the normal passenger channels of Entebbe airport.

Inevitably, as the business of wildlife filming became more and more technically demanding, the Cowens and Margachs dropped out of our life but I, for one, will never underestimate the part they played in the early days.

Des Bartlett and Alan Root were Nairobi contemporaries. They are old friends and in some respects rivals, as all naturalist cameramen are. Aubrey Buxton had more luck with Alan than I did with Des at our first meeting. Alan was pleased at the prospect of filming for *Survival* and said so. Like Des he had a loyalty to an older man and mentor, though, in Alan's case, the loyalty, fortunately, was capable of being adapted. That mentor plays a very large part in *Survival*'s story. This, then, is the moment to weave his thread into the pattern.

Professor Bernhard Grzimek (pronounced Jimmek) is at this moment one of the most respected figures in world conservation, certainly as far as Africa is concerned. In the late 'fifties he and his son, Michael, made a remarkable film together which became a world box office hit. It was called *Serengeti Shall Not Die*. To do this they learned to fly, bought a German light aircraft, a Fieseler Storch, very similar to the communications and artillery spotting plane used by the German army in the Second World War. They painted it in zebra stripes and flew it by easy stages to Tanzania, or Tanganyika as it then was. One day Michael took off on a routine flight from the floor of the Ngorongoro Crater in Tanzania. Some time after he'd climbed away beyond the crater walls, he hit a vulture which jammed his controls. He crashed and was killed. Bernhard Grzimek had already met the same young couple Aubrey was later to encounter in the Queen Elizabeth National Park. He was equally impressed. Alan had done some filming on *Serengeti Shall Not Die*. There is little doubt that Alan came partly to fill the role of Michael in Bernhard's life. Possibly, even, the relationship worked in reverse. A strong bond was formed. Alan was soon doing a great deal of wildlife work on both stills and cine for Bernhard Grzimek. Yet Bernhard's need for Alan's services was limited. He showed the material on his own highly popular TV wildlife show in Germany but could not possibly use Alan full-time. Thus Alan, with Bernhard Grzimek's approval, was able to film for *Survival*. The partnership continued for many years. For a long time we shared Alan's unique talents. This was by no means all that we derived from a long friendship with Professor Bernhard Grzimek. Grzimek is a great fund-raiser for conservation. He uses his German TV programme for this purpose. He has possibly more influence with rulers of emergent nations, especially in Africa, than anyone else alive. He is constantly travelling and initiating exciting new wildlife projects for which he somehow manages to raise funds. Over the years, Bernhard Grzimek was to let *Survival* in on the ground floor of many exceptional wildlife stories. He also much later brought us the third of our great wildlife cameramen, Dieter Plage from Darmstadt.

The forging of our bond with Alan was done by Aubrey Buxton on his second visit to Africa. He persuaded Alan and Joan to take him on a safari into the remote, wild north-eastern part of Uganda called Karamoja. Karamoja is, or at least pre-Amin was, occupied by five magnificent warlike tribes, called collectively the Karamojong, whose national sport is bloodily raiding each other for cattle and for women. Aubrey wrote an account of his safari with the Roots. In the great British stiff-upper-lipped tradition, Aubrey is inclined to underplay things. Nevertheless in this account written at the time, I detect the authentic sound of the explosive charge that is wild Africa hitting a newcomer right between the eyes.

The Roots headed first for the Kidepo on Uganda's northern border with the Sudan. The Kidepo was then gazetted as Uganda's third national park, which it has since become. It has always had its problems with raiders both tribal and military from its northern neighbour. At one time Bren-gunning of game from armoured cars manned by Sudanese troops was fairly common. At the moment of writing, since the régime of Amin stopped tourism dead, no one can say precisely what the state of the game is there. But when Aubrey wrote these impressions in 1962 both the Kidepo and the country of Karamoja to the east were unspoiled wildernesses.

Towards evening, the western sky aflame beyond the mountain ranges of the Sudan, we reached Opotipot, a police post on the frontier. This will also be the headquarters of a new wildlife national park now being laid out at the far tip of Uganda. At present there is only a cluster of round huts on top of a small hill. After delivering some mail and some vegetables we continued north for another ten miles through the bush to the Roots' tents under a great thorn tree near the Kidepo river.

It was now dark and as we ploughed through tall elephant grass the eyes of birds and game were everywhere glinting ahead of us. Nightjars with bright red eyes crouched in our path until the last moment, herds of kangoni, oribi, reed buck, and zebra gazed intently for a moment before dashing off into the night. For the first time (and the last) I suddenly asked myself what on earth I thought I was doing, a family man with an establishment to support, with a sheltered life and various responsibilities, settling down under a tree in the ancient unchanged heart of Africa without a single weapon of any sort. At Opotipot they were all in high spirits because they had captured three poachers that day, Dodinga people from over the border. There were a hundred poachers in the party they said, all armed with spears; the engagement was 'just by your camp'. This apparently was a huge joke.

'Are there elephants? I enquired as we ground onwards into the blackness. 'Yes, they say they're nasty up here,' replied Alan Root. 'The other morning we found droppings in the camp.' Would an elephant sit on my tent in the night, or worse still throw it into a tree? 'Any rhino?' I asked, trying to sound like a wildlife expert, and not a nervous tourist.

In the vast open spaces with so much room for everybody and everything, and particularly in the reassuring company of the Roots, you at once settle down, though when during the first night I heard a tree being pushed over, or the deep guttural rumbling of elephants close at hand, my heart would insist on pounding in a way it hadn't since the war in Burma, and I felt irritated with myself as the Roots slumbered peacefully next door. Then a huge branch was torn off and came crashing down not a hundred yards away, and elephants rumbled again. I sat up with a start, and then someone shouted loudly three times. 'Good for the cookboy,' I thought, 'he's driving them off,' and sank back and slept uneasily. Next morning I asked Alan to enquire about the incident, and there was hilarious laughter when he interrogated the boys. 'The other boy says the cookboy was shouting in his sleep.' So now I knew the Roots did not even wake up when the elephants came or people shouted, and that proved to be the best way to get a good night's rest in the bush . . .

From the Kidepo we moved out into vast stretches of grassland, yellow and brown in the dryness, where the heat haze made it difficult to watch animals at more than a mile. Further on in the centre of a magnificent landscape, with towering blue mountains as a backcloth, we saw first one elephant, then a dozen, and then three hundred. The biggest herd I had ever seen was packed solid across its own primeval untouched setting. This was just as things looked hundreds of years ago, or thousands. And this is how they looked to that fabulous if misguided character Karamoja Bell, the great elephant hunter, at the turn of the century.

The herd was moving steadily from the open country towards a valley of trees, browsing as they went. Occasionally there was a sharp crack and a rending crash in the distance as a tree went over; there were intermittent disputes on the fringe as one animal would lumber out of the throng being chased by another, with much trumpeting and snorting. There was a full complement of young, some tiny babies smaller than Shetland ponies.

In our detour we crossed some of the bush they had passed through. The grass, normally six foot tall, was flattened like a parade ground, the bushes torn to pieces and uprooted, full-sized acacias knocked flat or split through the middle as if struck by lightning. Only a brigade of tanks preceded by a bombardment could have matched the havoc.

Alan decided to take his camera on foot and get into position ahead, and with transparent bravado I felt unable to stay behind and watch him go. Joan Root was to sit in the Land Rover, poised ready to hurtle forward if the situation demanded it.

When the elephants came within a hundred yards of our position, about three hundred yards from the Land Rover, they halted. I do not know whether they could see or smell us; the hot dry wind kept changing. Alan shot some film, but the elephants were all in the trees and it was not what we wanted. So I walked back to ease them out of the trees with the Land Rover, Alan having promised to leave his camera and sprint like an oribi if necessary. When I reached the Land Rover the battery was flat as a pancake and Joan could not have started it in hours whatever the emergency.

I lost pounds cranking up with the sun straight overhead, and after some gentle and careful work to and fro in bottom gear we finally eased all the elephants out into the sunlight. We had kept Alan in sight all the while and now we re-joined him. We had been with the elephants for three hours and they seemed to be getting used to us. We went up within a hundred yards and got some fine film of a majestic subject.

Hollywood seems to dream only in terms of charges, blood and thunder, when featuring Africa and big game; and they like to fake and stage these activities. Nature as it really exists is our line of business, so when Alan had shot all the footage desired we decided to call it a day and take a few stills from the Land Rover. I particularly wanted a shot of the periscopes, and to 'up' these all you had to do was to drive a little nearer. We were now about sixty yards away, and there was a restless old cow without a tail butting and buffeting her neighbours on the perimeter. Alan was standing on the top, I was standing on the seat clicking my camera through the sunshine roof, and Joan was at the wheel with the engine ticking over. We wanted no cranking at this point. We all at the same moment became aware of a wild rustling of grass, and then an earsplitting sound like a dozen saxophones burst upon us and compelled our attention in a direction where none of us had been looking. Thundering towards us like a Sherman tank not twenty yards away was the tailless elephant.

Alan fell flat on the roof clutching on to what he could, I grabbed him under the armpit, and we both expected the Land Rover to bound forward and accelerate. But Mrs Root is made of other stuff. She thought her husband would fall off if she shot forward, and was not prepared to move until she knew he was secure. When two shouts of 'Go' reassured her, the elephant was only five yards away (I could only see its upper half over the back by then), and could have bowled the Land Rover over long before we got clear. And then for some reason she stopped, trumpeted and flayed her trunk about in the air, and wheeled back angrily towards the herd.

That first encounter with a herd of three hundred elephants must have been almost too impressive. It certainly looked very impressive as it appeared in a one-hour *Survival* completed two years later and called 'Karamoja'. That film was, of course, shot by Joan and Alan Root.

Alan Root was born in Enfield, north of London. He was nine years old when he first met Africa. His father had returned from the Second World War looking for an opportunity and place to develop a career in the meat business. He picked on Kenya and went out ahead of the family to weigh up the chances. They seemed good, so he bought a house on the outskirts of Nairobi. With pardonable exaggeration he wrote a letter to his young son still in England. 'On a clear day you can see out of our windows the snows of Mount Kenya on one side and the snows of Kilimanjaro on the other.' So, when Alan packed his precious belongings to make the journey to Africa, he insisted on taking his toboggan with him. Since then Alan has climbed Mount Kenya and made the first flight by hot-air balloon over Africa's highest mountain, Kilimanjaro. If someone bet him he couldn't, I daresay he'd slide down its famous snows on his toboggan. In Alan exists a compulsion to put one foot over the rim of every available precipice. Some people think that this compulsion will one day cause him to put both feet over the edge. He has certainly been close to it on a number of occasions. I devoutly hope that he will draw back from some chasms in time and not even approach many of the others towards which he seems irresistibly drawn. Alan is too much of a character – albeit an infuriating one at times – and too clever a film-maker ever to be allowed to disappear wantonly from the scene.

Alan Root was a born naturalist from early youth. Even during his days in Enfield, Middlesex, he spent hours in woods and by streams. Africa, with its teeming wildlife and bright birds to meet him even in his Nairobi garden, was what he had been waiting for. He learned his craft as all naturalist cameramen must in the first instance – by buying a camera and just filming animals. Technique and technical knowledge could come later. For Alan, a camera is a thing you use, not a precision-made god to be worshipped. Likewise an aircraft is a thing you fly to get quickly from A to B, or, in Alan's case, from A to Z and further. You don't have to understand its finer points of aeronautical design, any more than a good rider has to know the exact anatomical construction of a horse. Such knowledge may help some airmen and some horsemen. On the other hand, many horsemen are born to the saddle. Riding technique is what they learn. The rest is the seat of their pants. Thus with some pilots. Alan flies by the seat of his pants. He is a brilliant and natural pilot. Alan brings the same sort of natural intensity to film-making. He claims to be innocent of technology but the results deny this. Nevertheless he puts technology second to a born film-maker's sense and flair. Technique has, however, built up over the years. It was beginning to accrete when he first started filming for *Survival* in 1962.

Alan started his filming career at a time when Des Bartlett was setting up shop with Armand Dennis in Nairobi. There were other good naturalist cameramen in the making in that city at the same moment. They, too, were teaching themselves the trade. Two of these were Bob Campbell and John Pearson. There was thus a stimulating if competitive atmosphere for these followers of a lonely and highly specialized craft.

One of Alan's first stories for *Survival* concerned the Ngorongoro Crater where Michael Grzimek had crashed a few years before. The story was one Aubrey had found on his first visit in late 1961. It concerned the supposed contest for grazing between the cattle of the nomadic Maasai and the resident wild animal population of the Ngorongoro Crater. It also typified the conflict of views about what is being done and what should be done that is common to most conservation problems.

The crater, or rather caldera, since its walls have long since collapsed into a mere two thousand foot high rim, is about the size of Paris. On the savannah formed by its floor live thousands of wildebeest, zebra and gazelle. There are also a number of eland, black rhino, giraffe and lions. This virtually self-contained community – there is little animal traffic in and out to the surrounding Crater Highlands and the plains of Serengeti beyond – living in its unique and majestic setting, justifies the title we gave to the programme: 'The Eighth Wonder of the World'. One school, represented by John Owen, who was then the forceful and most successful Director of the Tanzania National Parks, held that the limited grazing in the crater, and therefore the wild animals who lived on it, were in danger of being obliterated by Maasai cattle. Far too many Maasai, this argument went, were allowed down into Ngorongoro in the dry season to water their cattle at its lakes and streams and to feed on its grass. Since Ngorongoro had been excised from the Serengeti National Park some years before and made into a separate ecological unit, a conservation area, there was not much the Parks could do about this except moan. The Conservator, a cultured and gentle agricultural expert called Henry Fosbrooke, was known to be in thrall to the Maasai. Indeed it is very easy to become fascinated by this handsome and proud tribe of warrior pastoralists. Henry was said to be a 'Maasai lover'. He maintained that the crater was in no danger from the nomads and their herds. In a dry season contest for grazing, the game would always win. The permanent Maasai villages inside the Ngorongoro supported only a few hundred people and a thousand or so head of cattle and therefore constituted no threat. The real threat, he maintained, came from the agricultural tribes in the hills around the crater's rim. By clearing and burning the forests, they could seriously affect Ngorongoro's water supply and that could drastically upset the balance for everyone.

I followed Aubrey's trail to Ngorongoro in 1962. I listened to all the arguments but started, I fear, biased by the report I had received. Alan Root moved in after I left and shot some beautiful footage which excellently illustrated the problem. Stanley Joseph and I made the film and invited Henry Fosbrooke to view it, complete with pilot commentary, during an unexpected visit to England. It was heavily slanted towards the Maasai-must-go viewpoint. Henry and his wife courteously pointed out that I had perhaps bent over a little too far in that direction. I accepted some of their points and amended the commentary but the result was, I feel, not entirely fair. I believe that subsequent events have shown the Fosbrooke argument to be the right one. Ngorongoro is still there. So are the animals. So are the Maasai. The gravest threat came when the Tanzanian Government proposed to open a tourist hotel on the crater floor close to its one small forest, the Lerai. Fortunately they pulled back just in time and built their new lodges where they should be, on the crater rim. I had a letter from Henry Fosbrooke while I was writing this book. He is again advising on agriculture and ecology in Tanzania and asked for a copy of 'The Eighth Wonder', made fifteen years before, for lecture purposes. So it can't have been all bad. What is certain is that the filming was first-class and it was one of the films that began our partnership with Alan and Joan Root.

Even in his first films it was clear that Alan had story sense, a very rare thing to find in a wildlife cameraman, many of whom can only see the scene they're shooting at the moment. Not a few otherwise excellent operators – and there are possibly just a dozen real top-liners in the field today – only see a series of sequences or a general way in which these sequences might be connected. Very, very few have the whole thing in their mind *before* they start shooting. That is why they need the teamwork that a producer, writer, a back-up such as *Survival* or the BBC Natural History Unit can give them. Alan Root has developed that overall sense. He is therefore genuinely a film-maker in his own right. I like to think he feels he gained some of this from his early connection with *Survival* but I doubt very much if he would agree. Like the leopard which he temperamentally somewhat resembles, he is very much a cat that likes to walk alone.

In his first year of working for *Survival*, Alan tackled a one-hour project which we would today call a 'Special'. Alan and Joan took off in their Land Rover to Karamoja to make the tribal documentary which had occupied Aubrey's mind since he had been on safari there with the Roots a year before. Aubrey felt that the last chance to make a documentary record of these fine warrior tribes was upon us. He was right. Milton Obote, the first Premier of Uganda, had sworn that he would put all these naked savages into long trousers, if necessary at gunpoint, within a few years, for is not nakedness a sign of barbarism? The appalling Amin went further and practised wholesale slaughter against these and other northern tribes after he deposed Obote. So we were in there at the last possible moment in history.

In May 1962 I wrote to Alan what now seems an extremely patronizing letter.

> The Karamoja project is definitely on. Now, just one general remark about *Survival*. I think we are trying to do a different job from the Dennises or anyone else, in that we are endeavouring to produce complete documentaries with the standard of editing you would find in a feature film. . . . I saw the notes about the disturbances and I certainly hope it doesn't prevent you getting there or endanger you when you do.

I obviously didn't know my Alan Root. 'Disturbances' is a mild word for what had just been going on among the Karamojong. One of the southern tribes, the Pian, had set about their non-Karamojong neighbours, the Suk, and killed about a hundred of them in a cattle raid.

Alan and Joan Root headed north to country temporarily at peace and made contact with the Jie (pronounced Jee-ay). It was the first time we had worked together on a major story. Alan's reports from the field are models of their kind. In our kind of film-making, a two-way flow of information between writer-producer back at base and cameraman in the field is of crucial importance. I shall expand on this later. What we are doing ninety per cent of the time is making highly specialized films by remote control. The cameraman never sees his 'rushes'. The producer has therefore to act as the cameraman's eyes, interpreting what he sees on the newly processed film, steering the story, making suggestions as to how it can best be developed, giving technical advice on how scenes might be improved as well as a purely technical report on what, if anything, went wrong. At *Survival*, producer or writer, as well as a technical expert, view the original the day after it reaches us from the laboratories. Reports go off to the cameraman within twenty-four hours, by telex or cable if he is within reach of civilization. He very seldom is, and so hideous opportunities for delay occur. It goes without saying that the writer or producer has to know his subject and it helps enormously if he has visited the scene of the action first. This is by no means always possible. Just the same, we have all now spent a great deal of time in the field in most of the countries in which we operate. I most certainly had not been to Karamoja at the time Alan and Joan Root were shooting the picture. So a steady flow of information from field to base was all the more important. The writer of a *Survival* programme relies heavily on the background the team in the front line can give him. Alan's Karamoja notes, extracts from which I now quote, are still hard to beat. The collected reports give possibly the most complete day-to-day picture of life among the Karamojong ever compiled.

17 June 1962

The main filming problem has been, not getting them to allow us to film, but getting enough light. They start everything at crack of dawn, the latest hour we have filmed has been about 9.30 am when we got a couple of girls doing another's hair. The afternoons are out, as at about 11 am it starts to cloud up and, with clockwork regularity, it starts to rain at 2 o'clock and drizzles and thunders for the rest of the day. Still, this too has provided footage, and by racing far enough downstream we were lucky enough to get a wide dry sand river starting to flow after months of dryness . . .

All the Karamojong have been disarmed, which is a great shame because these big men look pathetic walking around with just a stick. Fortunately we have been able to persuade the Administration to give us ten spears and, though guarding them in an unlockable tent is a constant worry, it means that we are going to be able to make the men look genuine. Out in the cattle camps, apart from the way of life and the collecting and preparing of blood, we hope to film them making the stools which every man carries, both as a seat and a headrest. Also the men fixing up their hair in their varied and elaborate hair-dos.

The Karamoja cattle scheme is quite a thing, because after an inter-tribal raid the police often confiscate a lot of stock – the Karamojong, knowing this, will sell as many cows as they can to the scheme and then a week or two later, when things have quietened down, go and pinch some of them back before they have been slaughtered. Everyone here is waiting for a big raid which they know is due soon against the Suk – after the slaughter of about 106 Suk last month, the police confiscated many hundreds of Pian and Bokara cattle and gave them to the Suk as compensation. Apparently many warriors have been overheard saying 'That's good, the Suk have got nice fertile country so we will let them have our cows, fatten them up for a couple of months, and then we will go and swipe them back again . . .'

The marriage customs are roughly as follows:

A man can have as many wives as he can afford, and the senior son has priority over the others when it comes to paying for wives with family cattle. The bride price is high and involves about fifty cattle and large numbers of sheep and goats. The groom provides between twenty and thirty cattle and the remainder will be begged by him from his friends and relations. It is the groom's job to collect all this stock from all the various people who have an interest in the marriage.

If a man wants to marry and does not have enough cattle, he can still visit the girl. After she has had a child she builds a hut with its own courtyard within her mother's courtyard, where her lover can visit her. If the families consider the couple to be suitable they may become engaged on the payment of about five cattle. This gives the man complete sexual rights to the girl and he is expected to pay up the remainder of the cattle as soon as possible. He cannot do it on the h.p. but must wait until he has the full price. If he is a long time in collecting the cattle, someone else can come along and marry the girl if he has ready payment, even though she has several children by her fiancé . . .

Thank you for your comments on the migration filmlet* – you know, that is something that we ought to do a full programme on sometime. There is so much of interest that comes into it that I am sure it could be a winner.

---

* This was some footage Alan had shot for the Director of the Tanzania National Parks on the Serengeti wildebeest migration. Alan's comment is interesting because some twelve years later he was to make the classic *Survival* Special 'The Year of the Wildebeest'.

29 June 1962

Towards the end of Rolls 1424 to 1429 shows Jie women removing winged termites from their trap over an anthill. The anthills round the settlements are individually owned by the women, who keep an eye on them, and after heavy rain when they see that the winged termites are going to emerge for their nuptial flight, they set their traps. The termites emerge from many small holes all over the hill, and the idea of the trap is simply to place a cow hide, supported by sticks, over part of the hill where there are most holes. Earth is packed all around the hide except for one small exit, and at this point a circular pit, six or eight inches deep, is dug, the sides of which are made smooth with mud. The exit is then walled up with mud to leave a small hole just above this miniature pit. When the ants emerge they are channelled from their several holes to the one small chink of light at the exit, and just as they get to it they fall into the small pit. They can of course climb out of it in time, but it serves to accumulate them so they can be lifted out in handfuls. They are then taken back to the homestead, fried in their own fat, and then spread out to dry in the sun. Later that day they are winnowed to get rid of the wings and they are then eaten . . .

Rolls 1460 to 1462 and part of 1463 still in camera, show an initiation ceremony with the sacrifice of an ox. I was bitterly disappointed and frustrated about this sequence. We have been trying to get on to one for the whole time we have been up here, finding one already three-quarters finished and hearing of others that we were unable to get to. Finally, when we got on to this one, we had to have the worst bit of luck possible. First, the initiate, who has to spear his own ox, did not make a very neat job of it, and after the third spear thrust the ox rampaged around the boma and I, who was hampered by the tripod, could not get out of the way quickly enough and was charged. The brute went and trod straight on my light meter and completely wrote it off. I suppose I was fortunate really for it could have damaged the camera. The loss of the light meter would not have been serious, except for the fact that one of the standard afternoon storms started to come up and after darting in and out, the sun was finally hidden behind very dense clouds. Finally it started to rain so we had to give up anyway. I hope that what I did get will be usable, but under the foul conditions we had, I am afraid I doubt that my estimated exposures will be very good.

Roll 1460 shows the initiate spearing the ox and the next shot is of it down and dead. I did not get it going down because, after

'Deathtrap Lake' was the name *Survival* gave to Magadi, the soda lake in the Rift Valley of Kenya where over a million flamingoes made the disastrous decision to nest in 1962. So super-saturated is the lake with soda that the legs of the newly hatched chicks soon became encrusted with anklets of solid soda. The calamity was discovered by Alan and Joan Root, when filming at Magadi. The Roots quickly organized help from the East African Wildlife Society and from the army in Kenya, with the result that at least 10,000 flamingo chicks were saved. Joan Root frees a days-old flamingo from its soda leg-irons.

Much of the 'World of the Beaver' was filmed at a beaver pond high in the Wyoming Rockies with the Teton peaks as background. Des Bartlett prepares for a swim beneath the ice watched by his daughter, Julie. Massage and liberal doses of sherry were needed to restore circulation after prolonged bouts of filming beneath the ice. The beaver's lodge can be seen in the background. During the winter, the beavers store their food under water and dig deep, ice-free channels to reach it. Bartlett obtained remarkable material of their life beneath the surface and inside the warm, secure lodge, including a pair rearing and feeding a family of kits. The film followed the growth of the young to maturity.

chasing me, it smashed its way through the stockade and finally died in one of the women's courtyards and had to be dragged back . . .

On Roll 1414 you say that the plough is a modern steel one and that you can see the trade name. Yes, this is meant to be so. The advent of these inexpensive ploughs has had more effect than almost any other contact with civilization, for it enables them to make the best use of what agricultural land they have. Before they had these ploughs they used a primitive sort of hoe, which I will be showing when I get shots of the women weeding the growing crops.

There is an amusing little story about these ploughs – in order to get more people to buy and use them, the Government offered to pay a third of the cost on any that were bought. They were delighted when the people over in the west near Labwor seemed to be really taking agriculture to heart and were buying large numbers of them. A little later, however, they found that the reason for their enthusiasm was that it was an extremely cheap way of getting hold of enough metal to melt down and make half a dozen or so spears . . .

25 July 1962

The end of 1474 and 1475 show bits of a great gathering of women. We at first understood this to be a rain dance, but later found out that apparently in Lango, over in the west, a woman gave birth to what was obviously just a deformed child. The women swore that it was actually twins, a snake and a guinea fowl. The evil spirit that caused this lives on Mt Moroto, but as he must have been in Lango for this to happen, they held a series of ceremonies all across the country to escort him back to the mountain.

I got on to fairly good terms with the head witch at the ceremony and she said that she would allow me to film the whole thing in exchange for an ox – which I was going to get cheap from my friend in the cattle scheme. However, when I brought out the camera and started filming, the women turned nasty and after I had got a few shots inside the dancing mob, and tried to get into the middle where the witches were placating the spirit, they just threw me out. As anyone out here will tell you, the women are far more dangerous than the men at times like this, and I just did not have a hope. I was pinched and prodded with the sticks which you will see them waving, and finally just forcibly chucked out. I was able to get some shots of the outside of the great circle of women, and more shots when they marched off to escort the spirit towards Mt Moroto, but although these are impressive because of the large

4

numbers of the highly decorated women, they just do not make a complete sequence . . .

On my 1962 trip to Africa I had met, at Aubrey's suggestion, an East African Airways captain called John Pearson. John was then flying DC3s on East African's internal routes. Apart from flying, his passion was wildlife filming. He had briefly been in partnership with Alan in their early experimental days but two such different temperaments were unlikely to complement each other for long. Where Alan is mercurial, quick to move in any venture, John was inclined to be cautious, to plan and move slowly. John was, from a technically photographic as well as a naturalist standpoint, extremely knowledgeable. He had already made two excellent promotion films for East African Airways, one on marsh harriers, the other on Lake Naivasha. Sitting on the verandah of the Norfolk Hotel, where Lord Delamere once tied his horse and propped his dusty boots, John and I had spent several hours discussing Lake Magadi. Everything John Pearson told me about this weird soda lake (that's what the word 'magadi' means) convinced me it was a wonderful subject for a wildlife film.

Magadi, seventy-five miles south down the Rift Valley from Nairobi, is an extreme, almost hellish, environment. At just over a thousand feet above sea level, it is appallingly hot. The lake itself manufactures soda faster than the Magadi Soda Company with modern barges, grabs, dredgers and suction pipes can extract it. Like much of the Rift, it is a thermal area with hot springs at the southern end into which a little fresh water flows. The surface is blinding white and only exceeded in inhospitality by the pink and even more hellish soda lake, Natron, to its south. Despite this, game lives around its shores. Wading birds and the larger water birds patronize the brackish southern end. Even in the hot springs a little fish, *Tilapia grahami*, is able to thrive on algae, though a browse-line in the bottom of the pools shows where it gets too hot for even *grahami* to venture. All in all, it was obviously a marvellous *Survival* subject. So John Pearson and I planned how the story of life's adaptation to extremes should go and, when I returned to London, we commissioned John to shoot it.

John did his homework as thoroughly as I subsequently discovered he invariably did. He got co-operation from the Soda Company, set up Dexion hides out on the hell's broth of the lake's surface and, in between flying for East African, began to build up his story. Both he and I knew it was bound to be a long-player if only because flying duties allowed him only limited time on location. And then events overtook us all. The first hint of what was happening came in a letter from Alan Root, written just after he returned from Karamoja.

8 August 1962

Just an hour or two before I received your letter, I had sent off a cable asking if you were interested in film of flamingoes breeding. Then in your letter you mention that one of the programmes you have in mind is about Lake Magadi, and by the strangest of chances that is where the flamingoes are breeding. We got back to Nairobi just as the August Bank Holiday started, so as we could not get anything done in town, we did a recce down to Magadi after one of my little birds told me of the flamingoes. It was such a fantastic sight that I straight away went about getting permission to film and camp there, and the next day set up camp and left my boys there.

I am now in Nairobi preparing hides and so on and will be going back down there in a day or two, with the blessings of the Game Dept and the Magadi Soda Company. I think I am right in saying that this is the first time for forty-seven years that they have bred on Lake Magadi, and, as you probably know, flamingo breeding colonies in Africa have not yet been filmed professionally. Leslie Brown, the flamingo expert, got some shots of them nesting a few years ago, but it has never been covered properly.

If you are doing a Lake Magadi programme there is no doubt about it that now is the time to get at least the flamingo shots. Otherwise, of course, this would be fantastic material for colour TV.

I am going down to get stuck into it immediately for they have been there about two weeks so the eggs will be hatching soon. I will just be shooting on spec, for I know that someone will want this material, so if you would like it, please let me know.

We let Alan know. There was no telling whether John Pearson would be sufficiently free of flying duties to cover the flamingo invasion or even whether the birds, over a million of them as it turned out, would stay to face the rigours of Magadi. The possibility of a cameraman's confrontation amid the caustic wastes of Magadi seemed high. But then none of us owned Lake Magadi. Anyone, with the Soda Company's blessing, was free to film there.

A second letter dated 19 September gave the first indications of a far larger story. Alan wrote:

19 September 1962

Thousands of the young flamingoes have been getting great balls of soda building up around their legs as they walk around in the saturated solution near the breeding area. I have not been filming this because it is so gruesome and just ends up with them slowly dying. What we have been doing though is catching them by the hundred and washing the anklets off with fresh water. When John Williams, the ornithologist at the Coryndon Museum, saw this he went back to Nairobi and stirred up a great campaign in the Press to collect money for us to set up a couple of teams so that we can rescue a lot more of them.

The story of the great flamingo disaster reached *The Times* the same week:

SODA LAKE THREAT TO FLAMINGO
Fledglings Dying in Thousands   NAIROBI

Fears for the future of the world's flamingo population were expressed here today when it was reported that 300,000 fledging flamingo face death at the soda lake of Magadi, 60 miles away. The flamingo went to Magadi after being forced to leave their ancient breeding ground of Lake Natron in Tanganyika when it dried up in last year's drought.

They flew to Lake Nakuru, another favourite haunt, but arrived as the drought broke, filling the lake with flood waters which destroyed the soda conditions in which flamingo thrive.

As a result of these twin disasters and migrations more than two million flamingo are believed to have died, halving the world population. The survivors made their way to Magadi. Wildlife experts believe that 90 per cent of the world's flamingo population – about a million breeding pairs – now live there.

But the soda content of the lake is proving too much for the fledglings, which are dying in thousands because of solid soda anklets which build up round their legs until they prevent all movement.

The problem can be dealt with by bathing in fresh water, which removes the soda. A Nairobi game photographer, Mr Alan Root, and his wife report that they have saved hundreds in the past fortnight by this method. 'If we had £500 we could employ a washing team and save most of the birds in the next three months.'

In the meantime vultures are reported to be gorging themselves on dying birds. If the young birds are not saved it is feared that flamingo could be virtually extinct in six or seven years.

The reports of the flamingoes' imminent extinction were, of course, greatly exaggerated. You just can't wipe out a bird that exists in such numbers and has adapted so successfully to an environment, a soda–ry one, that is poisonous to practically all other animals. And there was little doubt that a similar crisis had befallen the greater and lesser flamingoes of the Great Rift Valley several times before. A fossilized soda anklet, very similar to those forming round the legs of the young chicks at Magadi, has already been found elsewhere in the Rift.

What was valuable about the rescue operation organized by the Roots, John Williams, the East African Wildlife Society and even the army, was the publicity it brought to the cause of conservation which in Africa was only then getting off the ground. It was only a year since the famous Arusha Conference at which African heads of state and world conservationists like Bernhard Grzimek, Sir Julian Huxley and Peter Scott had met to find common ground in protecting African wildlife. It had been a very practical conference as the statement made by Dr Julius Nyerere, future President of Tanzania, made clear:

> I personally do not greatly care for wild animals. I cannot imagine that I should ever spend my holidays looking at crocodiles. But I know that Europeans and Americans enjoy this. I shall see to it that they are able to see big game in our country. It is my view that wild animals will be Tanganyika's third most important source of revenue after sisal and diamonds.

The flamingo rescue operation at Magadi may have saved the lives of a hundred thousand young birds, both by freeing chicks trapped in leg anklets of soda (the Roots discovered these were best tapped off with a light blow from a hammer, just as if freeing a prisoner's leg-irons), and also by chasing unfettered birds out of the area of water that was super-saturated with soda.

As it turned out, the film shot by John Pearson and Alan Root were superbly complementary. Despite the statement in his letter that he found the sufferings of the soda-shackled chicks too gruesome to film, Alan's sense of story won the day. He had filmed the whole natural tragedy movingly and dramatically. What, I suspect, had largely persuaded him to do so was that the rescue workers had found something positive they could do to free many of the young birds. John Pearson had filmed many other aspects of the flamingo invasion of Magadi, including scenes of Egyptian vultures stealing eggs from the cone-shaped nests made of soda and hyenas stalking and catching young flamingoes at the water's edge. John had not, however, filmed the rescue operations in whose value, I discovered later, he did not believe. He even wrote to Peter Scott to suggest that the rescue of a proportion of the chicks was a sheer waste of time in preserving the flamingoes of the Rift. They were quite used, he argued, to taking that kind of calamity in their stride. Peter, of course, did not agree and nor did I, but then we were both in our separate ways interested in the propaganda value of what had happened at Magadi.

The resulting film was perhaps the best *Survival* had made since

'SOS Rhino'. It had story, drama, a partially happy ending and the overwhelmingly beautiful spectacle of one million pairs of pink flamingoes nesting on a blinding white surface. It was called 'Death Trap Lake'.*

Before I leave the Alan Root of those early days – I'll be returning to his adventures and major achievements later – I must describe briefly one other project.

Alan was then, and is even more so now, strong on the notion that the smaller animals, lesser mammals as well as birds, reptiles and insects, are largely overlooked by the film-maker. And so, when he visited London in 1963, he and I planned the outline of a film with the working title 'Africa's Little Game'. The idea was that the tourist visits the game parks to see lions, rhinos, hippos, elephants and giraffes. Meanwhile all around him is a smaller world of far more fascinating animal life which he doesn't even know exists. The sort of 'game' we were talking about included tree squirrels, dung beetles, termites on their nuptial flight, egg-eating snakes, chameleons. We would start with a scene showing tourists watching elephants at the water-hole in front of Kilaguni Lodge, Tsavo Park, Kenya. The elephants move off. The tourists read magazines or doze off, complaining that 'nothing is going on'. As they do, a mud-building wasp begins to build its nest on the beams directly above their heads.

Alan contrived all his small game dramas so that the wasp led to the dung beetle, the egg-eating snake connected with the termites hatching close to the base of its tree. In the final scenes the elephants return and the tourists sit up and take notice, relieved that at last something is happening once again.

If ever a wildlife film was shot to a script, a rare enough event in itself, 'Nothing Going On' was that film. In my original discussions with Alan I made one serious miscalculation. Alan, who has a highly developed sense of humour, especially when he makes the jokes himself, which are usually good ones, was taking 'Africa's Little Game' seriously. To him each of the little gems he shot was a straight behavioural study. Stanley Joseph and I had a rather different approach. You could say that we sent Alan's master-work up. We asked Rolf Harris to speak the commentary and I wrote the script accordingly. Though putting across most of the essential natural history information, I wrote a decidedly jokey commentary. For instance, the final sequence was of two large male agama lizards enjoying a territorial battle on the

* John Pearson was shot dead in a tragic accident while filming in the Ngorongoro Crater in 1978. His own game guard mistook him for a marauding Maasai tribesman in the early morning light, firing a shot at random. He had just completed filming a Special for 'Survival' called 'Hunters of the Plains'.

wall of Kilaguni Lodge, right by one of the sleeping tourists' feet. Between us Rolf and I constructed an all-in wrestling commentary for this fight with lines like: 'That's Schultz in the lizard-skin shorts.' He spoke it in the tones of breathless awe used by wrestling commentator Kent Walton. Rolf also spoke the lines I wrote for the supposed American tourists on the lodge verandah. In fact, the 'Americans' were friends of Alan's from Kenya. The result was exactly what we had meant by education wrapped in entertainment. It was also highly amusing.

Alan was not amused, at least not at the time. He was now beginning to emerge as a serious film-maker in his own right. He made it clear we had gone too far. He was to shoot one more one-hour Special for us on the Galapagos which became a turning point in *Survival*'s evolution. But after that he wanted to try film-making on his own. What he actually did was to turn to the BBC in search of a more serious image. We said *au revoir* with regret but in the certain knowledge that you should never try to stop real talent seeking to do its own thing. What's more, we were fairly sure that, sooner or later, he'd be back.

As will emerge, he was. But I am firmly convinced that when we turned 'Africa's Little Game' into 'Nothing Going On' we temporarily pushed this remarkable and likeable prima donna out of the door.

Two or three years later, Alan Root admitted to me over drinks on the identical verandah of the Kilaguni Lodge that featured in the film, that 'Nothing Going On' had become his favourite programme! Just the same, though we remain firm friends, I don't think he ever forgave me for it. We've certainly never had the same personal programme relationship since.

Chapter 5

The Pioneers

SEVENTEEN years after it all began, we have been fortunate to enlist the finest team of wildlife cameramen in the world. They are highly versatile people. Several fly their own aircraft. Lord knows how much camera equipment these stars of the wildlife game own. Des Bartlett not uncommonly carries £40,000 worth of cameras and recording equipment around in his location vehicle and he deposits dumps of the stuff in storerooms round the world. In these days of star cameramen and extreme sophistication it is easy to forget the wildlife cameramen who got us started in life. Some of them still film occasional *Survival* stories. Some I have already mentioned. There are others who must find their place early on in this account.

First, almost literally first, was – and, mercifully, is – Ted Eales. Ted is warden of the National Trust Nature Reserve at Blakeney Point in Norfolk, as was his father before him. Ted is as Norfolk as the big church at Blakeney and stands about as four-square to the sky and sea though possibly not quite as hallowed. Nelson picked his crews from this north Norfolk coast because he knew where good seamen were to be found. If he was looking for a ship's company today I've no doubt he would call on Ted Eales. A latter-day Royal Navy did exactly that. In the Second World War, Ted, who was brought up with one foot in a saltmarsh creek and the other in a small boat, became a chief petty officer. Had Admiral Raeder known about this he might have slept less well at nights. Ted Eales today films for Anglia Television in his spare time and appears regularly live on the air in his own wildlife spot.

Even before Aubrey Buxton showed Associated Rediffusion his first pilot wildlife show on the coypu invasion, he had been presenting what amounted to Anglia's version of *Look*, a regional film and wildlife interview programme called *Countryman*. To provide one regular source of local film for *Countryman*, Aubrey had taken an inspirational chance and presented Ted Eales with a 16mm Bolex camera. Ted not only had a highly educated and observant countryman's eye, he was throughout the summer in an ideal place to shoot wildlife film. In the summer months Blakeney Point is home to a large nesting colony of common terns. Ringed plover, oyster catchers, redshank also breed there. So do Sandwich, little and occasional Arctic terns. Skuas turn up on raids. Short-eared owls hunt in the marram grass of the dunes and common seals bask on the sandbanks just off the Point. All summer Ted lives in the old lifeboat house at the tip of the Point. His family run the boat service which brings the visitors across from his home village of Morston for the day. When the visitors return on the last tide, the Point belongs to Ted, his wife Betty, his assistant warden, and the birds. In the long light summer evenings – and when he can fit it in during the day – Ted is free to film what he calls 'little dramas'.

When he gave Ted Eales that movie camera, Aubrey had no idea whether the warden of Blakeney Point could use it adequately. But then in those days Aubrey was new to the whole conception of film-making. To him, shooting was still something you did with a twelve bore. There is a story that when Dawn Addams was rehearsing in a play at Anglia's Norwich studios she declined a lunch date because she was shooting at Elstree next day. Aubrey is alleged to have said: 'Oh really. Who's got the shooting there?'

In Ted Eales's case the two meanings of the word could justifiably be confused. Ted had been brought up with a gun in his hands. He had crouched in the salt creeks of Morston and Blakeney since wigeon grew wings. He had a shooter's reflexes and instant recognition of flight attitudes that told him what a bird was going to do next. Thus he turned out to be one of the best followers of bird flight that *Survival* has ever known. Just as a pheasant or a mallard would be placed dead centre in the shot pattern had Ted been wielding a gun, then so was the jinking skua or diving tern centred in the frame when he was holding a camera. He knew the birds and mammals of the Point as his familiars. He captured many remarkable scenes which were the highlights of such early *Survivals* as 'Continuous Performance', the round-the-year story of the Point, and the appropriately titled 'Shotgun Wedding', which showed how wildfowlers and conservationists were co-operating to preserve ducks and geese.

Those were good times. We were a lot more relaxed in every way in those early days. There was time to potter round the Point with Ted, a remarkable wind-burnished figure with tousled hair, red face, and wearing gym shoes so decrepit that it was said he could feel flounders buried in the sand through the soles. Those are some of the best memories I have. I think it is fair to say that Ted came off best on his own patch which was the north Norfolk coast. His cameras seemed to be able to set their own apertures to suit the deceptive light reflected from the sands of the Point. The cameras often shared the back of a battered Land Rover with a kedge anchor and a sack of mussels. The vehicle itself stood out winter and summer on the Blakeney Point. Nevertheless cameras and vehicle always responded when asked in this salty environment. Ted was strictly a wet-the-finger-and-hold-it-up-to-the-wind man. He distrusted all technicians and experts, as well as most Londoners. He referred to the Norwich studios as the madhouse and to the *Survival* Unit in Brook House, Park Lane, as a loony bin.

I have one particular memory of Ted that sums up his wonderfully independent and robust character. We were on the way to Holland together, I to research a *Survival* about the draining of the Issylmeer, Ted to film avocets, spoonbills, godwits, ruffs and purple herons. The usual customs ordeal faced us on the outward journey, the checking of numbers on cameras and innumerable lenses in order to ensure there was no question of duty having to be paid when we brought them back into the country again. To make things easier, our air agent had drawn up a list of numbers against which each item could be checked. Moreover he had a gentleman from HM Customs and Excise obligingly standing by, since time for boarding the aircraft was getting very close.

Something had kept Ted, probably his terns were hatching out on the Point. When Ted at last arrived on the scene, with a battered suitcase held shut with rope, there was about five minutes to go. The customs man was distinctly frayed and became even more so when Ted un-knotted the rope, allowing the suitcase to fly open. There were no lenses immediately apparent. Admittedly they weren't entwined in old fishing net or lengths of seaweed, but they were wrapped up in socks, pants, vests. One was even inside a sponge-bag. They took a lot of finding. Ted rummaged round like a mad rat, making the job of checking numbers almost impossible. The customs man had adopted the air of hurt ambassadorial hauteur which is the speciality of his species.

'That's all right, Charlie,' Ted told him. 'Keep your gold braid on, mate.'

I had never heard anyone speak to a customs officer like that. Nor had Charlie. He signed the form and turned away in a state of deep shock. We boarded the aircraft just as they were pulling up the gangplank.

The other character cast in this kind of mould was George Edwards. I write in the past tense only because George has retired from active filming. George, as I once told him, looked like a curate from the Missions to Seamen coming aboard a lightship in a force eight gale. He wore the sort of grey flannel trousers whose cloth seems to have been galvanized against rust, these topped off with a turtle-necked sweater straight out of the ship's stores of a 1914 minesweeper. Actually George had no nautical background at all, beyond the fact that some small ship was always taking him to a remote oceanic island and dumping him there on behalf of *Survival*. He had made more migrations to the southern ice than an Arctic tern.

George was a bird man to the tips of his primaries. As a bird photographer he was a contemporary of Eric Hosking though, where Eric had stuck to stills, George had moved on to movie. Like Ted Eales, when not away filming, he was a warden on a bird reserve. As a Yorkshireman he naturally chose a Yorkshire reserve, Spurn Head. He lived in a caravan there, acting as assistant warden, until summoned by us to work on a film. George had been making bird films long before the birth of *Survival* for, among others, the Royal Society for the Protection of Birds.

George first went south for us to Signy Island in the South Orkneys. He was almost as much part of the British Antarctic Survey ships *John Biscoe* and *Kista Dan* as the smoke from their funnels. The BAS cheerfully freighted him, complaining goodnaturedly about the decibel level of a narrative style that could cut through a South Atlantic fog further and louder than the ship's siren. George was good company and, what is more important, 'fitted'. You can't afford an odd man out in a small tossing bucket like the *Kista Dan* and even less when you arrive at your destination, a group of huts set on a chilly, snow-flecked rock.

Sitting on rocks was what George was very good at. Loneliness meant nothing to him. And as Mike Hay, *Survival*'s general manager, once told him: 'The good thing about you George is that you can live on a ship's biscuit a day and a sniff of an oily rag.' For a man used to wrestling with in-field expenses of thousands of dollars a month, with unexpected bills for helicopter hire and, in one case, the construction of a one-man submarine, it was spoken from the heart, if general managers can be said to have hearts.

So we sent George Edwards not only to Antarctica but to the Falklands, Tristan da Cunha, the Seychelles, Aldabra, St Kilda, to name but a few isolated rocky pinnacles far out to sea. There was a grand design behind all this. George was not only the most economical of cameramen: he was also the least mobile. He had passed a driving test way back in the thirties shortly after the test was introduced. But he much preferred the bicycle, perhaps because of the panache that cycle clips gave to those famous trousers. It followed, then, that if you could set him down in a place where filming locations were mainly capable of being reached by bicycle, you had largely solved his transport problem. George's ability to drive a motor car had, once neglected, withered away in much the same fashion, no doubt, that the flightless cormorant of the Galapagos lost its wings. George did occasionally need outside help and when he did so it was usually on a grand scale, a battleship or two, or, anyway, a Fisheries Protection vessel of the Royal Navy. In this way he reached an isolated member of the Falklands Island group called Beauchene, whence he brought back remarkable film of rockhopper penguin rookeries. Other hitched oceanic lifts were more hazardous, as when he accompanied the Tristans in their canvas long-boats on an annual egging and birding expedition to distant Nightingale Island where the great shearwater nests in countless thousands. It was to Nightingale that some of the Tristans withdrew when the volcano erupted right beside their village, known as the Settlement.

As sailors on long lonely voyages once carved ships to put in bottles, George Edwards when not filming filled shorthand notebooks with jottings and sketches. They are lively documents containing shrewd and sometimes unrepeatable comments on local conditions and in-habitants. They are filled with first-hand information on birds and beasts, invaluable to myself when later making the films. Sometimes we got letters, too, though a ship did not pass most of George's locations all that often.

The following extracts give some of the authentic Edwards flavour.

Falklands, 26 December 1965

Firstly, although the navy have taken Ian and me to Beauchene, we have had such ghastly and continuously wet weather over the past two months that I have still not yet exposed three thousand feet of film. Just to put the cap on everything, on *midsummer's day* we had snow – and snow is not regular here even in winter!

I have made several day voyages to Kidney Island which pro-duced material but later we had four days there in the little living hut and scarcely got out for more than the odd half-hour because of frequent and prolonged hailstorms. Later I was given the opportunity of sailing round the Falklands on the tiny mail steamer with the object of disembarking at West Point Island where there is a large black-browed albatross colony and good concentrations of upland and ruddy-headed geese; but we ran into heavy weather and had to anchor in a remote creek for forty-eight hours with only sheep to look at. Just before we got away from the creek a radio message came through to say that HMS *Protector* would be taking us down to Beauchene 'the day after tomorrow'! I was about one hundred miles away from Stanley at the time but on the following day we managed to get round to Jox Bay and I caught the Beaver seaplane back to Stanley without ever reaching West Point Island.

Falklands, 11 February 1966

Since the New Year, I have been over on the small islands in West Falkland where for much of January and early February we had vastly improved weather, although for the last seven days prior to coming back to Stanley I have been unable to get out. During that period I have been working on black-browed albatross colonies intermingled with rockhopper penguins and found some of the islands had large numbers of fantastically tame birds. My only trouble was that I was obliged to work alone and the tussac birds walked over my camera, then over me, neither of which situation was much good for photography. I should have some nice stuff of them standing on the backs of elephant seals, and some good cine material of kelp geese negotiating rough seas.

I had to make one special trip down to New Island in order to get at a fur seal colony but they were very obliging and did a lot of tricks for me in the off-shore waters. They (the owners of the island) made me ride a horse in order to reach the fur seal colony so now I only need a bicycle ride to have run the full range of transport in these islands. So far I have used two Research Ships, a coastal steamer, three private sailing boats, rowing boats, Land Rovers, cars and jeeps, two Beaver seaplanes, two helicopters and a warship. Where none of these was available I walked!

Tristan, 10 March 1967

After the birdlessness of Tristan, Nightingale is certainly one of the ornithological experiences of a lifetime. The air is filled with shearwaters to the same extent as when one looks up into a heavy snowstorm. They are tame enough to walk over my boots and often allow themselves to be stroked. I have filmed them taking off from a rock on which a man was sitting. I have included shots of the islanders taking young albatrosses (mollies) and shearwaters for food and there should be some good sequences of the famous Tristan long-boats in full sail. I have pretty well covered every activity of the islanders' everyday life – crawfishing, thatching roofs, spinning wool, bullock carts, volcanic activity and I hope, stacks of scenics to gladden the heart of any film editor!

We owed a lot to the often brilliant and always courageous camera mercenaries who contributed much to *Survival*'s earliest success.

To Iris and Rupert Darnton who stumped around Ceylon and Africa to bring us back first-class wildlife film. Iris, a lady of outstanding charm and force, was cast in the model of Lady Baker, to whom her husband, Samuel, on recounting their adventures in discovering Lake

Albert in 1861, paid the highest imaginable compliment. 'Lady Baker,' Sam Baker wrote, 'was no screamer.' Nor was Iris Darnton, who was still cavorting among hippos and buffalos in her late sixties, accompanied by her equally indomitable game-legged husband, 'Rupe'.

Many took considerable risks in pursuit of their stories. John Buxton, of 'SOS Rhino' fame, nearly met his end beneath the hoofs of a stampeding bison herd in Wood Buffalo Park, north-west Canada.

His letter to me, dated 27 June 1964, could only have been written by a man with sufficient sangfroid to take his dinner jacket on a rhino-catching expedition.

> Dear Colin.
>
> I have been on a buffalo chase to Fort Smith and am very glad I fitted it in indeed – the material of this should be useful and it has more of the excitement in it than any other sequences so far I have met. Some of the herding was quite thrilling as I persuaded the helicopter pilot and Park Warden to land me in front of the herds so that I could get in the path of their driving manoeuvre. Thank God the tree I was in remained standing. It would have been a great chance for anyone else there to see and film one of your photographers at work!
>
> The trickiest part was changing film in the middle of the operation with one hand and one foot holding on to the tree and the other hand inside a changing bag, the whole apparatus resting precariously on my spare knee. Bloody uncomfortable in fact! And poor prospects if I fell off. Anyway, if there is some unsteadiness in the sequence please forgive pans and zooms in the haste of the moment. I am afraid this was also a completely unavoidable case of no slates. It had dropped out of my pocket as I ascended and I would never have 'hit' it if I had shot it anyway up there.
>
> I had originally planned to crouch on a dead tree stump and shoot between the upturned roots at the charging herd. It is possibly fortunate that I changed my plan and went aloft because on inspection of this particular upturned root system after the on-slaught of panicking bison there was only one root left on the tree – the others had all been broken off by passing buffalo! Anyway, I feel this will make a good sequence.

It did, and was eventually used in a *Survival* called 'How the West Was Lost'.

Chapter 6

The Enchanted Isles

IN 1964 Aubrey Buxton, who occasionally accompanied Prince Philip abroad as an honorary equerry, was aboard the royal yacht *Britannia* when it visited the Galapagos Islands, four hundred miles out in the Pacific from the coast of Ecuador. He returned, like every other member of the party, including Prince Philip, awed by the strangeness, diversity and, above all, tameness of the animals there. He was also aware of the fact that the Galapagos, possessors of a unique oceanic fauna and inspiration of vital observations in Charles Darwin's *The Origin of Species*, were in urgent need of scientific research and preservation. Already human intrusion over the centuries had done its damage by the introduction of rats, cats and goats that thrived at the expense of the indigenous animals. It was an obvious subject for *Survival*. At once, woe-wishers outside our organization pointed out that the Galapagos had already been 'done'. The distinguished German naturalist cameraman, Heinz Sielmann, of black woodpecker fame, had been there previously with 35mm cameras and had filmed the wildlife – in black and white.

In those days there were still very few colour TV sets and, though we shot everything in colour, we still tended to think of black and white films as competition, simply because *Survival* itself was received by most viewers in black and white.

Fortunately, we ignored the woe-mongers. I believe one should always do so. I steadfastly refuse to be put off because the BBC, NBC, CBC or anyone else has, say, just made a film about boa constrictors. All you have to believe is that you will make a better film about boa constrictors. At the very least, yours will be different from theirs. And so, believing just that, we sent Alan and Joan Root to the Galapagos. By agreement, it was the last film the Roots were to shoot for *Survival* for some time.

For a naturalist cameraman of Alan's standard, the Galapagos archipelago was as exciting to the lens as it had been to Charles Darwin's scientific notebook when he visited the islands in HM Survey brig *Beagle* in 1835. Now there was another *Beagle* sailing between Hood Island and Santa Cruz, Albermarle and Isabella. A converted Brixham trawler, this *Beagle* belonged to the Darwin Research Institute, then directed by Roger Perry. She was inadequate, leaky and picturesque and she carried Alan and Joan Root from island to island in their quest for film. They had excellent help and advice. Besides Roger Perry and Carl Angemeyer who lived on the islands, there was an Ecuadorian biologist studying the three hundred pound giant tortoises; Dr Mike Harris working on frigates and other sea birds; Bryan and June Nelson studying red-footed, blue-footed, masked and brown boobies. Bryan, one of the most articulate of scientists and one of the few who can not only understand but sometimes speak the language of communicators like myself, is the world's greatest expert on boobies and gannets. He has travelled the oceans in pursuit of knowledge about these spectacular fish-catchers. Bryan became a firm friend of *Survival* during the Galapagos operation and has remained one ever since.

The actual filming operation was not ideally planned. To be truthful, it wasn't planned at all. To get the Roots to the islands, Aubrey had to move fast. Some high level diplomacy was called for. When the Roots took off, their brief was not much more sharply defined than: 'Film all the wildlife you can; film everything that bears on Charles Darwin's observations, above all, film the woodpecker finch in action.'

The woodpecker finch is one of the few tool-using animals on earth. How Darwin would have reacted had he watched the little bird breaking off cactus spines to winkle grubs out of rotten trees I can only guess. He never actually saw this bird perform although some of his crucial deductions about evolution were based on the diversity of forms into which the Galapagos finches had evolved from what must have been one basic finch. These birds are now often referred to collectively as 'Darwin's finches'.

For those who missed the film, or perhaps never read *The Origin of Species*, it may be helpful to recount what actually happened in the Galapagos Islands in an evolutionary sense and why scientists get so excited about it. Between one and three million years ago, this group of volcanic islands rose from the sea. They were for some time bare of all life. Then seabirds began to visit. Most of these, like the brown pelicans, frigate birds and the boobies were what you might call standard models, free to roam the oceans like sailors, calling in where it suited them for food, water and to breed. In time, almost certainly a great deal of time, other immigrants arrived, including iguanas, smaller lizards, tortoises and obviously that first basic finch. Those little finches must have come on freak winds. To fly westward from the coast of Ecuador cannot have been a chosen migration route for them, unless they wanted to end up in the sea. The land animals travelled on floating rafts of vegetation and perhaps tree trunks. It is hard to imagine this happening but there can have been no other way. Once they were there this basic stock colonized the several different islands of the group. Strong winds and even stronger currents prevented any further interchange. So the tortoises, finches, iguanas, cormorants settled down to adapt to the individual needs of their particular islands. Hence all evolved slightly different characters. To Darwin this was evident from the finches and from the vastly different shapes of the shells of the giant tortoises from several islands. To the scientist, therefore, the Galapagos are a living laboratory of evolution. To the layman, their animal inhabitants are a source of wonder. It was this sense of wonder that Alan's cameras so successfully captured.

In one respect the wildlife of the islands is a cameraman's gift. The animals show no sign of fear. It is a shameful reflection on the human race that this should be so. The same is true of the seal and penguin colonies of the Antarctic. The animals in both cases have not been persecuted within recent history and therefore have not come to look upon man as their deadliest enemy. So, during the months that Alan and Joan camped in this island Eden, mocking birds perched on the edge of their cups as they drank, sea lions rolled and basked like dogs around their tents and, like dogs, allowed their tummies to be scratched. They filmed amazing scenes of sea lions body-surfing; of marine iguanas, the only lizards adapted to living and feeding in and below the surface of the ocean, grazing algae off the rocks ten feet down; of Bryan Nelson's beloved blue-footed boobies diving in formation at the whistle signal of their flight leader; scenes of the waved albatrosses of Hood Island beak-fencing in courtship in a style very reminiscent of human osculation; and, as they say in the commercials, so much more besides . . .

The 'so much more' included the most important of the named wild-life targets, the unique behaviour of the Galapagos woodpecker finch. The filming of this finch raises one of the more controversial aspects of wildlife filming.

To get his remarkable sequences of the finch breaking off both twigs and cactus spines in order to probe grubs and moths out of holes in rotten timber, Alan had first to catch his finch, or rather finches. He did so with the requisite research permits and by use of mist nets. Long before he caught the stars of the performance he built a netting

5

enclosure, a theatrical 'set', except that in this instance the set was a piece of wild Galapagos bush with a suitable rotten tree centre stage. He had to catch several finches because it quickly became clear that not all members of the species knew the trick. Some were experts with cactus spines. Others had learned to prod out insects with a small length of broken twig. Once caught, the birds were released into the enclosure to settle down and to learn to accept the blind that held the cameras. The result of all this preparation was that he obtained sequences of both spine-probers and twig-snappers going through their complete routine, including the rejection of twigs found unsuitable for the job after the bird had broken them off the parent branch.

Now there are those who argue that this is, at best, setting things up; at worst, faking. I have even heard super-purists contend that one scene shot in the wild is worth ten full sequences obtained by what is euphemistically described as 'controlled shooting'. To the super-purist, it doesn't seem to matter if the image is in soft focus, in long or mid-shot or the product of imperfect exposure. All that appears to matter to this school is that 'it is the only shot of a wild panda in existence'. Never mind if it appears as a black and white blur. Happily, competition has largely made this viewpoint untenable. There are still those who believe that if you set a scene up with a captive animal or anyway an animal that has been caught and habituated, you should declare the fact in the film's commentary. On American network television you are required to add a disclaimer in the closing titles of a wildlife film which says: 'All the scenes in this pictorial essay, whether actual or created, represent authenticated facts.' God knows what it actually means and it still doesn't tell you *which* scenes were actual or created. It's there simply because of the outrageous faking, sometimes detrimental to wildlife, that occurred in some early network specials.

Our view is simply this. Provided the 'controlled shooting' exactly represents the behaviour of the creature in the wild and was obtained without harm to the animal or its environment, then the film-maker should not only use it but should use it without explanation, disclaimer or apology. We say this because we are certain that the viewer wants to see a fascinating piece of wildlife action, sharply defined and in close-up, and controlled shooting is sometimes the only way to guarantee this. When you make a wildlife film you are often creating mood and atmosphere as well as giving information. Why shatter that mood, or interrupt the flow of information, just to say: 'This sequence was shot in a tank . . . in a laboratory . . . in a section cut through a pine log . . .'? Critics of these methods sometimes overlook the fact that only an extremely skilful naturalist cameraman can obtain such sequences. He has first to understand the biology of the creature concerned and then to produce conditions that will persuade it to lay or hatch its eggs, catch its prey, slough its skin, dive and catch fish underwater – or whatever.

There are good and bad examples of setting up. Disney, who did so many wonderful things in his early days, produced one of the classic worst in *The Living Desert*, the famous square dance of scorpions. The scorpions were, it is said, placed on a warm surface to make them react as they did and then the action was reversed and the dance created in the cutting rooms. Good fun, no doubt, except possibly for the scorpions, but certainly not natural history film-making. Alan Root's woodpecker finch was an example of justifiable setting up to capture a unique piece of behaviour.

As an example of excellent controlled shooting, I prefer the classic hornbill nesting sequence from Alan's much later 'Secrets of the African Baobab Tree'. The male hornbill walls his mate into a hollow tree with mud and then feeds her and her brood through a vertical slit until female, and later young, are ready to break out. The hornbills steadfastly refused to use the baobabs of Alan's choice. In the end he took an old acacia trunk with a likely hole in it and literally set it up, in Tsavo National Park, Kenya. Behind the nest hole he had already inserted a glass panel through which he hoped eventually to film. For twenty-one months Alan flew regularly from his home on Lake Naivasha to Tsavo to inspect his tree. One day, through binoculars, he saw mud at the entrance to the nesting hole. He was in business. The filming *from* the *inside* of the whole hornbill nesting sequence has become part of wildlife filming history. It also revealed unknown facts about the birds' behaviour. Should Alan Root have paused in the commentary to explain that what people were watching, spellbound, was a 'fake'?

When the last foot of film was in from the Galapagos it seemed that Alan had shot an outrageous amount – 23,000 feet. In those days we had a fairly restricted outlook on shooting ratios. A half-hour (twenty-five minutes allowing for commercials) programme uses just under 950 feet of 16mm film. A normal documentary unit might expect to shoot 5–6,000 feet to obtain this result. Allowing for the uncertainties of wildlife filming, we were, in the early days at least, prepared to double this. But 23,000 feet! For a half-hour. We reassured ourselves with the oft-quoted platitude that film stock and processing is the very least of a film-maker's costs. Nowadays we have long since become resigned to high shooting ratios though even now we would regard 20,000 feet for a half-hour as pushing things a bit.

There were dramas about quality, in some ways similar to the ones we had experienced with 'SOS Rhino'. Some of the footage had a strange blue quality. When analysed by the experts it was found that this was unavoidable, a by-product of the light reflected by the blue-black lava floes of the coast. As we viewed the rushes, it became more and more clear that we had a mass of exceptional and possibly never-to-be repeated footage. The question was inevitable. Will it make an hour? The answer just had to be 'Yes'.

The next question, posed by Aubrey Buxton, was: 'Supposing Prince Philip agreed to appear in it and speak the commentary?'

There's no way you can say 'No' to that. After all, Prince Philip had visited the Galapagos aboard *Britannia* with our producer as one of his guests. As Chairman of the British Appeal of the World Wildlife Fund, Prince Philip felt more keenly than most the need for preservation and research in the Islands. The Darwin Research Station did need a replacement for the leaking and inadequate converted Brixham sloop *Beagle*. If a Galapagos *Survival* could raise funds towards a new vessel, then royal support might become a possibility. Royalty can, of course, only lend its name to an enterprise with a deserving cause at heart and furthermore a cause that does not clash with the equally deserving claims of other royally supported causes. Conservation, obviously, was such a cause and so Prince Philip was sounded out and made encouraging, or at least not discouraging, noises.

The first thing, however, was to produce a worthwhile film and this is where the problems began. There are basically two ways to make a wildlife film. One, the ideal way, is to plan everything in advance, or at least to start with a detailed outline, knowing that nature in one form or another will take a hand and upset the scheme. The other is to take off into the blue, shoot everything you can and rely on someone back at base to bolt the result together with a mixture of foresight, hindsight and a substance which is at best known as commentary and at worst called 'word-glue'.

In the case of the great Galapagos puzzle I had several things working for me. First, some excellent and unique film material; second, a very good co-scriptwriter by name Charles Darwin. It also seemed highly likely that we had a star, though that might conceivably complicate things. It eventually turned out that we had a star-cum-scriptwriter, which made three writers working on the project! At least Darwin, good as he was, couldn't answer back. He'd already written his lines in *The Origin of Species*. Some of these were incapable of improvement, for example his reactions to the strange forms of life that he found on the Galapagos. 'Here, both in time and space, we seem to be brought somewhat near to the great fact, that mystery of mysteries, the first appearance of new beings on this earth.'

Darwin and his voyage in the *Beagle* had obviously to be a main thread in the story. In many cases Alan had shot wildlife sequences that perfectly illustrated his words.

Of the marine iguana Darwin wrote:

> The nature of this lizard's food, as well as the structure of its tail and feet, absolutely prove its aquatic habits . . . This lizard swims with perfect ease, by a serpentine movement of its body and flattened tail, the legs being motionless and closely collapsed on its sides. I do not recollect having observed the seaweed on which it feeds in any quantity on tidal rocks. I have reason to believe it grows at the bottom of the sea at some little distance from the coast.

Darwin, unlike Alan and Joan Root, did not have diving gear to follow the iguanas down through the icy water that lapped the gun-metal-coloured lava. His observations are, therefore, all the more remarkable. Alan, however, was actually able to swim with the iguanas underwater. His film confirmed every detail of the great Victorian naturalist's conclusions. One marine iguana sequence I remember in particular showed a Galapagos sea lion playing cat and mouse with a big iguana in the water, seizing it by the tail and dunking it every time it tried to swim ashore but without harming it in the least.

So I had Darwin. The wildlife had, it seemed, to be played in two ways. The main theme would be built round what Darwin saw and the evolutionary conclusions that he drew. Variations in a minor key would illustrate what had happened since his day and what might yet happen to Galapagos wildlife.

The first task was to edit all the very best wildlife sequences that the material provided. As I recollect, there were about twenty of these. On Aubrey's advice I decided to ignore local geography. The archipelago consists of fourteen islands. We would say on which island the action was taking place only if the facts required it. For instance, Hood Island tortoises demonstrably occur only on Hood Island. For the rest we would let topography go hang. The island pattern was too complicated. Simplification is always a problem where the fleeting images of TV are concerned. Over-simplification is a constant trap.

By this time it was obvious we had a one-hour film. Prince Philip was given a private viewing of the assembled material and agreed to speak the commentary. A location for filming the in-vision to-camera links had to be found. The dinosaur hall of the Natural History Museum was selected as an appropriate location. From a technical point of view it was pretty ghastly. The powerful lights needed for interior filming, known by the delightful colloquialisms of the trade as 'brutes', 'pups', and 'bashers', threatened to 'kick back' off the glass cases that are essential furnishings of any museum display you care to name, even one playing host to fossilized skeletons as large as *Tyrannosaurus rex*. The echoing sound quality of the hall would have done credit to Hammer Films' most haunted castle.

As a precaution, we had a dress rehearsal. An evening dress rehearsal, as it happened. We had to make this dummy run after museum hours. For one night, I was Prince Philip. I remember that I was going to a charity ball. So I did my stand-in bit, speaking Prince Philip's lines to camera, togged up like an old-time BBC announcer in a dinner jacket. When midnight struck it was Prince Charming who was late for the ball. I never did discover whether the Natural History Museum found my glass slipper.

Survival had worked with Prince Philip once before, back in the very early days, when he had introduced a composite black and white hour about the wildlife situation in Africa. The programme, called 'The New Ark' had won our first international award, the Golden Nymph at the Monte Carlo Film Festival. That first filming, done in the private cinema at Buckingham Palace, had been a fairly simple operation. Nevertheless, it had made very clear to all concerned that HRH is a very precise, very professional performer who expects things to work first time and if they don't, doesn't hesitate to suggest how they might be made to work the second time. Practical as most of the suggestions are, they don't necessarily make for a speedier outcome. At various times he has demonstrated that photographers and film crews are not perhaps his favourite species. Couple with this the fact that he is no mean stills photographer himself and you are liable to get a situation where he suggests that the director or cameraman doesn't need to cut to close-up at that point. You can reason sweetly, which usually works, though in the event of an impasse there is no course but to go along with the star's wishes. Well, many stars of the silver screen are like that. Perhaps the tension wasn't eased by the fact that Stan Joseph, who was directing, showed republican tendencies and found it hard to oil the wheels with an occasional 'Sir'.

In the event, the link shooting in the cavernous dinosaur hall went reasonably smoothly, though it would be idle to pretend it was all relaxed fun. But then no such filming is, in my opinion, all relaxed fun, which is why I have never had the ambition to be a film director. I just give a big sigh of relief when it's all in the can. At the end of the afternoon, it was.

Long before we shot these links it had occurred to us that Prince Philip should be asked to speak much of the commentary to the wild-life sequences. They were, after all, pretty much what he had just witnessed in the Galapagos. In addition, he has quite a reputation as a bird-watcher and photographer and, indeed, as an all-round naturalist. So I wrote what I hoped he would say, recorded it myself to picture and took this pilot commentary to Windsor to show him.

This occasion was far more relaxed. I remember that we set up the projector in a viewing room papered wall-to-wall with old Dutch masters. The star entered dead on time in a sloppy Joe blue sweater, looking rather as though he had just been gardening. I had done my homework fairly thoroughly. I had consulted, among other authorities on the Galapagos, Dr Bryan Nelson, booby expert supreme, who had recently returned to England.

The booby material was among the best bird footage in the film. Alan had shot a marvellous sequence of a male blue-footed booby going through his display ritual. Part of his routine involved a low level flying approach to the female in which the male, just before touching down, suddenly raised his webbed blue feet in mid-air as if trying to show his lady love the soles of his boots. Bryan had assured me that this was exactly what he *was* doing. This foot drill was part of the bird's courtship. I wrote the commentary to the scene accordingly. It seemed to me that with the aid of Bryan Nelson, world booby expert, we were conveying a previously unrevealed and fascinating piece of information.

Prince Philip looked at the upturned blue feet, listened to my commentary and asked brusquely: 'How do you know?'

'A world expert on boobies told me so.'

I knew that he knew Bryan and had in fact met him in the Galapagos.

'I'm always suspicious of experts.'

'This was Bryan Nelson,' I said.

'How does *he* know?'

'He's an expert.'

'Exactly. Look, the other day some nice archaeological chap took me round a ruin. There was just the outline of the walls left. He pointed to a small rectangle about ten foot by twenty and said: "That was the kitchen." I asked him how the hell he knew. "Well," he said, "that big room was obviously the living room. The second biggest was where they slept. They had to cook somewhere, so it must have been in the smallest room. Yes, that was the kitchen." ' The star paused. 'See what I mean about experts?'

I did see what he meant. To anyone possessed of such a lively and enquiring mind it must grow irksome to be taken round everything, shown everything, by experts. The only defence in the end must be to question their findings and opinions. I saw all this but I didn't see what bearing it had on our blue-footed booby.

HRH wasn't going to let an expert win the day, even though in this case he knew Bryan well and eventually wrote a foreword to his book

The Galapagos. Being a pilot, he suggested an aerodynamic reason for the raised feet. Couldn't they be air-brakes? It was my turn. I know a bit about aircraft, too. The angle of attack of feet to airflow obviously did not fit this explanation. In the end Prince Philip conceded that the air-brake theory wasn't really tenable. I agreed to go away and modify the passage to accommodate all concerned, including the booby and Bryan Nelson. Meantime HRH would make a few alterations to suit his own colloquial style.

We happily nit-picked through the rest of the script. In contrast to the agonies of filming the links, I enjoyed this commentary session. Boobies aside, Prince Philip's comments were shrewd and usually very much to the point. Nevertheless my heart was filled with the cold dread known to all professional film-makers when an amateur, however with it, starts amending a commentary script. There is one inalienable constant in cut film, namely the film itself. It says what it says by showing you a series of images. Moreover, it only shows you each image for a set time that is defined by the length of the shot concerned. Laymen – scientists are the prime offenders – don't seem to realize this. They write in lines of absorbing interest to themselves, regardless of what is happening on the screen. Words and picture no longer fit and the result, especially on the ephemeral medium of television, is a confusing disaster.

Some scriptwriters, I am told, work with a timed shotlist and stop-watch. I don't know how they do it. I work with the picture on an

Was this the face? No wonder the first people to find the skull of the shoebill or whale-headed stork imagined that they had come upon the fossilized remains of a small dinosaur. The large hook on the beak helps when catching fish. It has been suggested that the vastly flattened shoe-shaped bill acts as a ploughshare when digging up lungfish and other mud-dwelling species, but it is far more likely that it has evolved to deal with large quantities of weed scooped up with fish. The bird now only occurs in remote swampy areas of Africa. Cindy Buxton produced the first film record of the shoebill in 'Almost A Dodo'.

Overleaf: Kilimanjaro, its summit covered by recent snowfall, provides the classic background for African big game. The scene was shot by Bob Campbell when filming the one-hour Special, 'The Dusts of Kilimanjaro', which dealt with the problems of Kenya's Amboseli National Park. The buffalo herd has come to drink at one of the two spring-fed swamps which make Amboseli so attractive to wild animals as well as to Maasai cattle. A big bull lies on the right. The bird in the foreground is a cattle egret feeding on insects disturbed by the buffalo.

editing table, writing to the actual film which I can run backwards and forwards as often as I please. Prince Philip certainly didn't have one of these machines at Buckingham Palace or Windsor and anyway he didn't have the cutting copy of the film. I'm sure he had a stop-watch but he didn't possess a timed shotlist of the sections he was to narrate and hadn't asked for one. I feared the very worst.

I needn't have worried. When his amended script came back I rushed to the nearest editing table to check the alterations with picture. I confess I wasn't looking forward to going back and arguing the toss line by line. There was no need. Words and picture fitted in practically every case.

We recorded the commentary in the air-raid shelter at Windsor Castle among a clutter of superannuated royal toys including some giant model railway engines. The shelter was the only place in the castle immune to the whine of jets which were that day using the western approach to Heathrow. Windsor must be quite a noisy residence to have when the wind's in the wrong direction.

I said that there were several ways of making a wildlife film. Of them all this was certainly the most difficult, if not the worst. Because of the royal commitments it had been necessary to book and record the star before the final shape of the epic had gelled. We now had everything – links, royal commentary, twenty marvellous wildlife sequences, Darwin and a narrator to act as word-glue where necessary. Welding all this into a coherent, cohesive whole that had to look as though the result was exactly what we had planned at the outset, was like trying to make one jigsaw from the pieces of at least four different puzzles. At least Prince Philip's in-vision links had been written to lead into either his own or Darwin's commentary. In the end, though I am not particularly proud of admitting this, I tackled it exactly like a jigsaw. I cut out thirty-six pieces of cardboard. On each, in differently coded colours – blue for Darwin, red for Prince Philip links, yellow for wildlife and so on – I wrote the name of one of the ingredients. I spent the best part of a morning shuffling these around, discarding a few in the process, until by some miracle I seemed to have a homogeneous and yet varied shape

The most imposing elephant the author – and a good many other people – has ever been charged by. Lee Lyon took this picture of Boadicea during the filming of 'The Family That Lives With Elephants' dealing with Iain and Oria Douglas-Hamilton's study of the Lake Manyara elephant herds. Boadicea was the matriarch who dominated one of Iain's main study groups. Her charge, which usually stopped short at six foot range, was extremely impressive. But then it was meant to be. As Iain said: 'Elephants have been perfecting their threat charges for several million years.'

with highlights and climaxes occurring more or less in the right places. Stanley made one or two suggestions and then Denys Coppard, the film editor, bolted it all together. Miraculously – and one hardly deserves to be that lucky – with relatively few adjustments, it worked. Two days later, after the picture had been fine-cut to ten minutes over length, we showed it to Aubrey who now revealed that he felt confident enough to go for a royal première at the National Film Theatre in November.

We weren't out of the cactus yet. Aubrey has today evolved into that most splendid of producers who leaves the film-makers to get on with the job while reserving the right to tell them in no mean fashion that he doesn't like what they've done, if such should be the case, after they've done it. But it was still early days and he could hardly be expected to stand completely aside with a first royal première at stake. The rock we hit just off the Galapagos Islands was a well charted one. Stanley got down to a set of his famous music notes. He instructed John Dankworth:

> I think we have agreed that the music for this film should tend to the rhapsodic. The title will probably be 'The Enchanted Isles' and it is this quality of enchantment that we want to get across. The Galapagos are one of the last havens of animals who have not yet learned to fear man and this feeling of innocence and unspoilt-ness is what we are after. If we could base the music on, say, three themes or so, then it would keep the film musically concentrated and reflect the simplicity of the film itself.

The composers, John Dankworth and David Lindup, this time took Stanley's suggestion of a rhapsodic theme seriously. Possibly the rhapsody was more Cornish than South American but it was certainly melodious and even haunting. To enhance the latter quality they used a group of siren voices in harmony over the romantic opening sequence of the *Beagle* under full sail. Stanley and I both thought it very effective if a trifle schmaltzy. Our producer did not and fired an almost Darwinian broadside in a private note:

> It is most important that when we express our views it is not taken as criticism, otherwise my remarks would be rather wounding. These are my opinions, and I am no connoisseur of music, and everybody else is entitled to their opinions.
>
> My main reaction to the recording so far is that we are starting from the wrong standpoint. If I have to summarize, the music is totally inadequate in my view to the majesty of the subject. The music sections seem to me frivolous, irrelevant, and have no Latin American element at all, as I had previously suggested.

It was a good idea to try the Lorelei voices, but it is my view that they become intensely annoying. The opening sequence may be pleasant enough, but in no sense matches the introduction of a *Survival* epic . . .

Albatrosses: It is difficult to go on describing the same reaction. Here it seems to me that the instrumentation is offensive to the mating ritual.

The end titles: This would be quite all right and appropriate for the end of an average half-hour *Survival*, but seems to me quite inadequate for the big show.

I have no musical vocabulary and therefore I cannot use anything except the above severe words. If it seems insulting, I apologize. It is merely the instant reaction of a rather unmusical viewer.

So we had what, in the trade, is known as an 'all-tracks' run when music, effects, commentary, sync. links are put up on separate channels in the dubbing theatre so that it is possible to combine or eliminate any element you wish. One thing became immediately clear: there was far too much music, something like fifteen different pieces in all. Some of them *were* harsh, irrelevant and discordant, but then some of them always are. Some clashed with commentary but then quite a few always do. Certainly there was no Latin American element but then neither Stanley nor Dankworth had considered the Galapagos particularly cha-cha-cha. But at least we won the day with the siren song which started and ended the film – which was called, as Stanley had forecast, 'The Enchanted Isles'. The title came from *Los Enchantodos*, the name given to the Galapagos by old-time sailors who found the archipelago difficult to come up with because of contrary winds and currents.

There were still minor problems to be overcome. The late James Robertson-Justice seemed ideally cast as Charles Darwin. The gruff bearded persona of 'Doctor in the House' was misleading. Jimmie Justice arrived at the recording studio, gave a virtuoso performance of major eccentricities by demanding to be called 'Dr' Justice (which he was), stripping to the waist in the recording booth and drinking white wine from the bottle between takes. Sadly, the voice so robust when combined with the physical presence was strangely light when used on its own to picture. This unsuitability for commentary is by no means a unique experience where well-known actors are concerned. Come mentary speaking appears to be something that demands a techniqu- and timbre of its own, even when the actor is playing a part such as Darwin. In the end Stephen Murray gave Darwin's voice just the right degree of precise ponderousness. Aubrey himself made almost his last vocal appearance on *Survival* as narrator. We had our royal première.

The Roots flew from Africa to shake hands and chat with the Queen, Prince Philip and Prince Charles. The sirens sang and everyone was as enchanted as the islands of the title.

There is always a certain amount of mopping, not to say sweeping up, to be done after any major victory.

Casualties, apart from the nervous systems of one or two of those most closely concerned, were fortunately light. Poor old Darwin himself nearly became one of those posted as missing in action. While researching this book, I came across a letter I had written to the Executive Secretary of the Linnean Society of London.

> Dear Mr O'Grady,
>
> I was rather aghast to hear that your Darwin bust hasn't yet been returned, as I was under the impression our messenger had taken it back immediately after we had finished filming it.
>
> I now discover that he put the bust, for safety, in a cupboard here and then forgot about it in the general pre-Christmas rush . . . I do hope you have received the cheque we sent as a donation to your Library . . .

The other item of mopping up that followed the royal première and transmission of 'The Enchanted Isles' in the UK and across much of the rest of the world wasn't to come until over a year later. But it was arguably the most important thing ever to happen to *Survival*. 'The Enchanted Isles' became the very first natural history show ever to appear on American network television.

Chapter 7

Errors and Omissions

IN the late 1960s *Survival* was still very much a three-man team. Inevitably the team dropped a few catches. A number of balls went through to the boundary. This is mainly about the ones *I* failed to stop. One of the unfielded 'sixes' had the name Ron Eastman on it.

In those days we used to see any naturalist film-maker, amateur or professional, who wanted to show us some film. I suppose we still do, though nowadays there are at least four writers to view such material and the increasing perfection of the genre has imposed its own filters that ensure that only the likely or encourageable get through. When Ron Eastman from Hampshire wrote to say he'd shot some film of king-fishers I naturally said that I'd be delighted to view it. After all, one never knew . . .

The thousand or so feet he showed me was the result of his first year's experimental filming on the River Test of that most beautiful of British birds. As with all rushes there were a few wonderful shots, some excellent ones, some passable and some scenes that were technically poor. One expects all that. At that moment in time I couldn't see *Survival*, with its get-up-and-go image, making a complete half-hour about one little bird, however spectacular. Just the same, some dim, and that is the exact word, showbiz instinct, told me that Ron Eastman had something. So I suggested that he take his kingfisher material to the BBC as it was more 'their sort of thing'. I think I even phoned up Jeffrey Boswell at the BBC Natural History Unit to make the intro-duction. I didn't want to see all Eastman's hard work and enthusiasm come to nothing. It didn't.

The BBC rightly saw the essential quality of the work and the appeal of its subject and sent Ron and his wife Rosemary back to the Test with a lot of film, a commission and instructions to try again next season.

The Eastmans did exactly that and came up with 'The Private Life of the Kingfisher', a BBC classic that won three awards.

Oh, well, not even *Survival* can win them all . . .

The next dropped catch was less of a fumble, certainly from a prestige point of view though not, perhaps, from a commercial standpoint. About the same time as the 'Kingfisher' episode, I got a phone call from Ian MacPhail, the bearded laird of the clan PR, who was then busily and successfully promoting the World Wildlife Fund. Ian had a nose for a story. He it was who talked the *Daily Mirror* into giving the best part of one complete issue over to the launching of the WWF in 1961. Now he had seen an American TV series about a cross-eyed lion and a vet in Africa which he thought Anglia ought to snap up for British television. He sent round a couple of the shows on film. This time my reaction was negative but for the opposite reason. With a reputation as a natural history unit, we certainly couldn't be connected with anthropomorphic rubbish like that, however entertaining it might be. So I told Aubrey that we should certainly turn 'Daktari' down. Though he's never quite forgotten the 'Kingfisher', he seldom mentions 'Daktari' more than once a year so perhaps he had his doubts, too. One serious naturalist told me several years later that he thought I needed my head reading. Des Bartlett felt strongly that 'Daktari', which was made by that highly successful entrepreneur Ivan Tors, had its heart in the right place. The minor inaccuracies, such as tigers in Africa, were always explained by the script. The important thing about it was that it appealed to children and got them hooked on wildlife and conservation at an early age. I daresay he was right. At the time I plainly hadn't got *Survival*'s image quite in focus. 'Kingfisher' was too straight; 'Daktari' too bent. What, then, was *Survival*? Kinky? My opposite number at the BBC, Jeffrey Boswell, coined a phrase to describe our style. He called it: 'Pop. Nat. Hist.'. It wasn't too far from the truth. The trouble was that where assessing opportunities was concerned, I seemed at this period not to know my Pop. from my Nat. Hist. Incidentally, I thought I detected in the coining of that phrase at least one decibel of admiration. I wouldn't go as far as envy. Certainly, though, the sedate BBC wildlife shows were tending to hoist up old Auntie's skirts and dance to music, just as if they knew what Pop. Nat. Hist. was all about.

Since I am presenting my jugular vein I might as well go through the whole obeisance ritual and admit there were other misjudgements.

In 1962, two Oxford lecturers at the Commonwealth Forestry Institute, called Thompson and Skinner, entered a film they had made about the alder woodwasp for a BBC Natural History film-making competition and quite deservedly won. They were insect experts. Their film miraculously showed how the woodwasp bored a hole with its ovipositor deep into a tree and laid its egg in the living wood. It also showed, even more incredibly, how its parasite detected the grub that had hatched and lived deep inside the tree, bored another hole and laid its egg on the grub. Thompson and Skinner were not men to be overlooked. Having presented its prize, the BBC did not appear to be immediately interested in making use of their talents. *Survival* was soon on its way to Oxford to ask them what they were doing next and who they were doing it for?

Gerald Thompson was, he told me, extremely interested in stickle-backs. He had already shot quite a lot of film of the males fighting, building nests and swimming through them to entice the females to mate. He had also obtained sequences of the male in its red breeding livery being extremely aggressive to a dummy stickle whose throat was painted the appropriate red. I remember thinking that this was pretty academic stuff and too close to the territorial tricks David Lack had made robins perform with dummy red breasts and even with pieces of cloth dyed the correct shade of red. True to form, I turned it down. Several years later, the BBC picked this footage up and producer Mick Rhodes built around it 'The Making of a Natural History Film' which, surprise, surprise, won the Prix d'Italia and many other awards.

On the subject of awards, *Survival* soon became possibly the most decorated programme on the air (see Appendix). We even won quite a few in conjunction with the brilliant and highly specialist outfit, Oxford Scientific Films, into which the original Thompson and Skinner partnership evolved, after Eric Skinner retired. *Survival* has won thirty-four international awards. People in TV pretend awards don't matter to them, but of course they do, if only because the product itself, their brain-child and art-baby, disappears down the cathode plug-hole so devastatingly fast and completely, far faster than, say, films made for the cinema.

In connection with this, I came across, in the files, a series of rather shamefully different letters I wrote on receiving a piece of bronze from behind the Iron Curtain. The award, given at a Hungarian Film Festival, was for a lovely *Survival*, shot by Oxford Scientific Films, about a pair of blue tits raising their brood inside a nest box. Here the letters are:

To the organizers of the Festival:

> Thank you very much for the totally unexpected and very handsome award from Hungary.
> We are absolutely delighted with this and will display it proudly

in our show-case at Anglia House, Norwich. Incidentally, it is quite one of the nicest plaques we have received.

To Gerald Thompson at OSF:

I am sure that you are thoroughly bored with collecting awards, but I thought you would like to know that we have just been given a rather nice bronze plaque by the Scientific Film Association for our entry in a Hungarian film festival. This was for 'Inside Story', otherwise known as 'Blue Tits'.

To Ron Pope, who edited the film:

I am delighted to be able to tell you that 'Inside Story', which you so excellently edited for us, has won an award at the Hungarian Festival of Scientific Films.
If you are ever up in Norwich, at Anglia House, you will see a handsome lump of bronze that testifies to your victory.

To John Gooders who wrote the commentary:

You will be glad to know that we have just won an award for 'Inside Story' at the Scientific Film Festival in Hungary. Another goddam brass paperweight! But, seriously, this is to thank you for your most valuable contribution towards this award-winning film.

To the Stills Department, Anglia Television, Norwich:

We have just won another of those ugly lumps of bronze from a Hungarian Film Festival. It is for an Oxford Scientific Films' epic, called 'Inside Story'.
I would very much like to get a nice 10 × 8 shot of same and ask Graphics to mount it for us so that OSF can display it. Could you chaps very kindly take some shots of it. It's not big enough to use as a doorstop.

One OSF show that did not win an award though it almost certainly should have done I dropped and then caught first bounce.
Oxford Scientific Films consists of seven or eight super-specialists. They are all academics. All have an equal say in their own affairs – which makes negotiation with them rather like a meeting with a supreme soviet in which there are eight heads of state, loosely grouped round the presidency of Big Daddy, Gerald Thompson, who started it all. (Eric Skinner, his original partner, retired from active film-making after 'Alder Woodwasp'.) The group now consists of Sean Morris, all-round zoologist and former Oxford rowing Blue; Peter Parks, specialist in

Cindy Buxton scored an
ornithological 'first' when
she became the first person
to witness, let alone record
on film, the private life of
one of the weirdest looking
birds on earth, the shoebill
or whale-headed stork. To
do so she lived for six
months in the heart of the
immense Benguelu Swamp
in Zambia. The shoebill now
exists in only a few of
Africa's remote marshy
areas. When the first skulls
of this bird were found, it
was suggested by their
non-scientific discoverers
that they were the fossilized
remains of a small dinosaur.
Survival called the
shoebill programme
'Almost A Dodo'. Cindy
Buxton's footage became the
source for the only
scientific paper on the
shoebill written by Leslie
Brown, world authority on
water birds and birds of
prey. The great white
pelican Cindy is holding was
a pet of the Benguelu
Warden.

Whales became the subject of two one-hour *Survivals*. 'The Passing of Leviathan' was centred on the Southern right whale, the subject of prolonged study by whale experts Roger and Katy Payne in the Bay of Valdes, Patagonia. Des and Jen Bartlett camped with them there throughout one entire season when the whales visit Valdes to breed and rear young. Above, Des Bartlett reaches out to touch the jaws of an adult right whale. The white 'growths' are not barnacles but the whale's equivalent of facial hairs. A later Special, 'Humpbacks, The Gentle Giants' again involved the Paynes as advisers, though this time the filming, both underwater in Hawaii, and on the feeding grounds in Glacier Bay, Alaska, was by American Al Giddings. Some of the most sensational animal scenes ever filmed were those of the Humpbacks 'bubble-netting' krill in Glacier Bay. To do this they blow a ring of bubbles starting fifty feet down and spiralling upwards. They then surface vertically, in the middle of the bubble ring, mouth wide open, to engulf the shrimplike krill.

macro-photography and designer of much of OSF's specialized optical and mechanical camera equipment; John Paling, freshwater biologist; John Cooke, one of the world's leading authorities on spiders; David Thompson, small mammals man; Ian Moar who graduated to specialized filming from building camera equipment in OSF's well-equipped workshop. The nearly missed opportunity concerned Peter Parks.

Peter has developed incredible techniques for filming microscopic organisms against a dark ground. Though unreal in some ways, since the technique never shows you a minute creature from the marine plankton swarms, say, in its true watery setting, dark-ground photography does enable you to watch the subject in macro-detail, vivid colour and total sharpness of focus. Plankton, in fact all small aquatic organisms, are one of Peter's loves. Just as Gerald had showed me his stickleback footage when we first met, so did Peter Parks present me with an eighteen minute film he had shot on a small parasitic creature called *Argulus*. *Argulus* is a freshwater crustacean. It is often wrongly called the fish louse. Peter's film was certainly amazing. The dark-ground technique enabled one to see individual blood corpuscles pulsing around in the arteries not only of the victim but inside *Argulus* itself, an animal barely an eighth of an inch long.

I did not think the TV audience was ready for *Argulus*. Five years later I saw the footage again, plus some additional material Peter had shot of the little fiend swimming around looking for and finding a host. I wondered how I could have missed the fact that *Argulus* had a definite comic personality, almost a cartoon quality. It even looked amusing in macro close-up with its moon-face and two sucker discs that appeared rather like eyes painted on a boy's kite. It was this persona that would make it entertaining, even attractive to a mass TV audience. Having been charmed and amused by its irritating behaviour, the audience would then be hooked – *Argulus* specializes in hooking and making suckers out of its acquaintances – into admiring the marvellous equipment evolution has given it and accepting the really rather horrific and deadly nature of its way of life. Its victims do not find *Argulus* amusing. It can bleed them literally white until they lose condition and often die.

I told Peter of my new feelings for his little 'louse'. If he could shoot one or two more scenes, I said, it would make a wonderful *Survival*. Peter surprised me by becoming quite angry. Not because I wanted additional shooting but because I had turned *Argulus* down years before and had now done a complete turnabout. 'You never seem to know your own mind,' he said.

There was a certain amount of truth in the accusation. A programme-maker constantly changes his ground and is bound to do so over a span of five, let alone fifteen years. Tastes of audiences change. In

6

the natural history field, audiences are steadily becoming more sophisticated, demanding to be shown more in depth. I doubt if *Argulus* would have gone over in *Survival*'s early days. It is hard to tell. Perhaps the change is merely in oneself which, in the producer or writer of a long-running series, is no bad thing. All that matters is that the producer knows his mind *now*. *Argulus* did not win an award, possibly simply because there wasn't a suitable event around in which to enter it. It did, however, get a great reception, viewers doing that rare thing, writing in to praise it. Sir John Woolf, producer of, amongst other smash-hit successes, *Oliver* and *Day of the Jackal*, thought it was the 'best *Survival* for many years'.

Oh well, you do occasionally win one.

Normally, as I have pointed out, viewers only write to tell us if they don't like something or if we have made a mistake. We reply to all of them but file only a few. One of the thickest files resulted from a general and fairly undistinguished programme about insects called 'Creatures from Another World'. In this there was a sequence involving a spider. Spiders, as any schoolboy knows, are not insects but arachnids. Nearly every schoolboy and girl in Britain wrote to tell us so. For example:

> Dear Sirs,
> I am writing to you on behalf of my school friends and myself. We are all very disgusted with your programme *Survival* on which you talked about insects. At school we have learned about insects. We all know that a spider belongs to a group called arachnids and is only a distant relation to the insect.
> If you examined first an insect then a spider you would notice the differences. All insects have three parts to their bodies but the spider has only two. Spiders have not got antennae, all insects have. Insects have six jointed legs while the spider has eight jointed legs.
> We all hope you will amend your mistake at the beginning of your next programme.
> Yours truly,
> Catherine Waters, Form 2 Biology, Stalham Secondary School, Stalham, Norwich

We sometimes get quite touching letters from schoolchildren, too. For instance,

> Dear Mr Willock,
> I know it is wrong to kill wild animals for there [*sic*] skins. We are collecting pictures of animals. Is there any more ways I can help to save the animals? If there is any way please let me know.

We are finding out interesting things about them. We have made a picture of a game reserve.

Yours sincerely,

Nigel Doe (6), Infant Class 5, Tower Hill Primary School, Farnborough, Hants.

We always hoped that wildlife was basically a non-political subject, but, alas, not always so. We made, as we thought, a fairly innocent early *Survival* called 'Cloud Over Paradise', about the plight of wildlife in modern Sri-Lanka – formerly Ceylon. This involved some ancient history about the Tamil invasion in the distant past. We immediately found ourselves embroiled in violent, nationalist passions (with copies to the *Daily Express* and *Daily Telegraph*):

Gentlemen,

Why did the Ceylonese commentator, called Shalini, indulge in these palpable falsehoods and half-truths? It is because she felt confident that the contemporary Western viewers were ignorant of the ancient history of Ceylon and secondly she wished to justify the wicked persecution of the Ceylon Tamils by the present-day Pan-Sinhala Buddhist Government, a disgraceful fact that is known the world over. It might interest you to know that this Pan-Sinhala Buddhist Government, like the devil quoting the scriptures to suit his own convenience, has conveniently interpreted the rule of Democracy bestowed on the island by the benevolent British, as the despotic rule of a racial majority (Sinhala) over a helpless racial (Tamil) minority and not as the rule of a right thinking majority over a rightly defeated minority as the British constitutional experts anticipated.

To which I somewhat testily replied:

While we entirely sympathize with your views, we can only stress that *Survival* is primarily a wildlife programme and we keep as clear as we possibly can of politics and religion.

The sequences which seem to have caused you anxiety in the film, were, of course, historical. Where we are talking about something that happened a thousand years ago, we certainly check our facts historically. A thousand years is a long time. If we all had such long memories, I suppose we English would still refuse to go to France for our holidays because of what William the Conqueror did at Hastings in 1066!

I am afraid we can only express regret that you were disturbed.

But my favourite viewer's letter of all time is the following:

Dear Sir,

I have pleasure to introduce you myself, one of the producer of indian films in india. The main aim of to write to you is that I wanted to know weather you are interested in buying documentry film or not?

I am having a film of snakes romance and actually it is snakes intercorse film. The film is in 35mm and in Eastman color and the length of the film is about 300 feet and as well as the length of snakes is about 9 feet to 11 feet long. This is a very unique piece and you will rarely find this type of scene as specially snakes usually do not have their romance in front of anybody, but we luckly got this shot while we were shooting for our picture in the forest of Maharashtra one of the state of India. If you are interested in buying this film then please quote your offer. I had some offers in India but they wanted for Only India rights so that was not workable as I wants to give it for whole world right. So far I have not given rights for any part of the world.

Running a wildlife unit is rather like supplying and trying to control a specialized fighting force in constant and close contact with the enemy, and often operating far behind the enemy's lines. Popski's Private Army and the Long Range Desert Group of the Second World War spring to mind. Your troops are an élite but a highly eccentric force with demands to match. It all starts off nice and tidy back at base, with stores up to establishment, plan cut and fairly well dried and all the appropriate forms filled in. The procedure for requisitioning more ammunition and new equipment in the field is all laid down. Base must be radioed or at least telephoned, cabled or telexed if major expenditure above budget is likely. To sort all this out is the job of Mike Hay, *Survival*'s general manager and technical expert who has been a documentary cameraman himself in Africa and knows some of the problems the field force is up against. And so outlandish requests come in to office from all over the world. Dieter Plage in the Danakil Desert of Ethiopia wants to hire the only chopper that desiccated wilderness has ever seen. It's on a mining survey job and will only be available for two days. It'll be expensive, around £1,000, and there is no allowance in what is laughingly called the budget for such an extra. The chopper will enable Dieter to shoot some fantastic aerials of the salt lake at Karum four hundred feet below sea level. What is a poor base wallah to do except say 'yes'? Still, it's nice to have been asked.

Late one evening, Roger Payne, with whom Des Bartlett is shooting a whale Special in Patagonia, phones from Buenos Aires, or is it Boston? Anyway it sounds like Buenos Aires. He and Des are building a submarine. What was that again? Well, not actually a submarine, more of a submersible made of a ship's boiler. It's the first Hay or I have heard of it. It's apparently essential for filming southern right whales underwater and it needs two special windows that a firm in California is prepared to sell at the bargain price of only $1,200. It's an offer *Survival* can't possibly refuse and so, of course, doesn't.

The fact is that it is almost impossible to refuse any reasonable request from your commanders in the field, though it is possible to put different constructions on the word 'reasonable'. To say 'no' to the chopper or the submersible's windows or the remote-controlled model aircraft that will carry a camera or the vehicle that will get you across the Namib Desert or the tents that resist everything from giant hailstones to safari ants is rather like telling a front-line commander that he can't have artillery support when the enemy is massing just beyond the next ridge. And so *Survival* has collected around the world a very strange assortment of hardware, vital and costly at the moment of purchase, but somehow unnecessary and largely unsaleable once it has discharged its original task.

One such piece of equipment was a Schleicher ASK 14 sailplane equipped with a small motor for take-off. Bernhard Grzimek, who has brought us so many good things, was responsible for bringing us the Schleicher! A scientist called Colin Pennycuick, who specialized in the dynamics of bird flight – he had already made pigeons fly while staying more or less in the same place inside a wind tunnel – intended to study the flight of vultures in the Rift Valley of Africa. Pennycuick was a power pilot as well as a highly accomplished glider pilot. He believed that the only way to study the use of flight by vultures was to fly with them. Before one could learn how and why vultures use thermals to travel across country or to spot a likely meal, one had to be able to fly with them. A sailplane in skilful hands was the only possible vehicle. Now it is one thing to recover a glider that has landed far from its operating field in Britain or Germany, but quite another to retrieve your sailplane from the African bush. There are no convenient roads. Rivers, swamps, and gulleys often intervene. Moreover there are few launching facilities such as towing aircraft and then only on established airfields. Hence the motor, an 8½ hp job weighing less than thirty pounds but powerful enough to get the Schleicher airborne from eighty yards of level ground and to help it cruise at a speed of around forty-six miles per hour when travelling under power to a chosen study area. Once the pilot decided to switch over to sail, he simply cut the engine and feathered the prop. The Schleicher, a thing of considerable elegance and beauty, then became a moderately high performance sailplane.

I confess that I had always been fascinated by the thought of combining glider and vultures. Years before I had seen a film called 'Silent Wings' made in South Africa by a glider pilot called Dick Reucassel. In this, Reucassel flew in formation with vultures, who obviously accepted his glider as another vulture, since they flew literally wingtip to wingtip with him. I had always wanted *Survival* to make a longer and more complete film on these lines. The combination of scientist and powered glider seemed the ideal opportunity. Bernhard Grzimek had, as usual, miraculously raised the funds to back Pennycuick's research project. He proposed to buy the glider with this money. *Survival* would be responsible for shipping it out, insuring, maintaining it and providing it with hangar accommodation. Colin Pennycuick was delighted with all this and accepted that we would be making a film of his researches. John Pearson, East African Airways captain now on Fokker Friendships and Comets, was the obvious man to do the air-to-air photography as well as the behaviour stuff with the vultures. Pennycuick in the Sleicher's cockpit would press the camera button that would obtain the really dramatic footage of the vultures flying alongside. So far, so good. The scale drawings of the Schleicher arrived from Germany. Mike Hay and John Pearson got down to studying camera positions and mounting and the way in which the formating vultures could actually be filmed.

What we had all overlooked was that Dick Reucassel's glider was a fairly elementary machine; when compared with the Schleicher it was a box-kite. There was plenty of room on the box-kite for cameras. The Schleicher was a very different proposition. The cockpit fitted the pilot more tightly than that of a fighter aircraft. When the Plexiglass canopy was closed there was even less room to move or manipulate anything other than the controls. As to fixing cameras to wingtips, as Dick Reucassel had done on his basic glider, there was no telling what it might do to airflow and performance. A light 16mm camera on a bracket alongside the cockpit was obviously possible but this would simply command a forward field of vision. No self-respecting vulture was going to fly in front of the machine. Did we mount the camera facing aft and hope that some obliging bird would decide to fly directly behind the tail? This was a possible arrangement but avian co-operation was by no means assured. Anyway there was no way of aiming the camera from the cockpit, or was there? Reucassel's best shots had been made looking out along the wings to vultures flying aft in close formation. How were we to achieve this, given the clean lines and tight cockpit of the Schleicher? Mike Hay came up with what looked like a brilliant answer. Since you can't very well change magazines on an externally mounted movie camera in mid-air, the camera we used would have to be capable of holding a four hundred foot magazine as opposed to the standard one hundred foot model. At the time, this meant an Arriflex, the king of 16mm cameras but a fairly bulky instrument. Mike's suggestion was to mount this behind the cockpit canopy facing aft. The lens would look directly into a prism which would have the effect of deflecting the light rays at right angles so that the camera would, in effect, be looking aft but seeing directly down the wing. As an added refinement, the prism would be movable so that the camera could, within limits, look in different directions. Now the fun, if that's what it was, started. As a pilot, John Pearson was naturally worried about what a camera mounted behind the canopy of anything as delicate as a sailplane might do to the airflow. In addition there might have to be some modification to the airframe to accommodate the camera. There was only one way to find out, to visit the Schleicher factory in Germany.

The designer of the ASK 14 was highly intrigued, helpful even, but he felt forced to point out that minor modifications to the airframe were one thing but moving the entire fuel tank, which was situated exactly where we proposed to mount the camera, was another. We were beaten. We would have to settle for one forward-looking camera on the port side of the cockpit. The rest of the aerial photography would have to be done from an accompanying light aircraft, a Supercub or something equally slow and manoeuvrable.

We eventually made our film. It was called 'Wings Over the Rift'. I have to admit that as far as aerial photography went, the wings belonged mainly to the Schleicher and to John Pearson's accompanying light aircraft. There were some remarkable vulture flight shots but these were mainly obtained from the precarious one thousand foot ledges of the Gol Mountains that lie between the Serengeti and the Rift Valley, also from a National Parks Supercub, an aircraft so light that a skilful pilot can actually soar it, engine dead, in the right conditions.

This was one operation that did not turn out exactly according to plan. Nevertheless, Colin Pennycuick came up with some remarkable scientific results as a by-product of the Grzimek-*Survival* glider. He published a paper, summarized by an article, 'The Soaring Flight of Vultures', in the *Scientific American*, which threw entirely new light on the use of flight by the six main species of African vultures as well as of other birds like the great white pelican and the marabou stork. He discovered, among other things, that in level glide a vulture is not such an efficient flying machine as the ASK 14. Over a given distance the bird loses more height than the glider. In soaring in a thermal, however, vultures have a considerable edge since they can climb closer to the centre of the thermal, in far tighter turns, than even the best sailplane and pilot. More important, Pennycuick discovered how vultures use thermals to travel across country in search of food. The Ruppel's griffons who nest in the cliffs of the Gol Mountains, for example, frequently soar up to 120 miles to the Serengeti, travelling from thermal to thermal until a flock signal of other vultures homing on a kill pinpoints a meal for them. He found that there are occasions, in the early morning, when vultures cannot fly at all! He also discovered the soaring power of birds other than vultures. 'On one occasion, on a day of exceptionally narrow thermals, I was out-climbed by a tawny eagle (which has a still lower wing-loading than the white-backed vulture) even though I had my engine running while the eagle was only gliding.'

So *Survival* at the end of the day came out of it all with less than the film it had hoped for. On the plus side it had, not for the first time, in company with Bernhard Grzimek, backed some well worthwhile research.

In the meantime, if anyone wants to buy an ASK 14 in almost mint condition . . . Pending finding another use for it, the Schleicher is being flown in a desert research project by another scientist friend of *Survival*, Hugh Lamprey, former Director of the Serengeti Research Institute, in the wild district north of Samburu in Kenya.

Chapter 8

Portrait of a Wildlife Cameraman

SOMETHING that we had hoped for since 1962 had suddenly
and unexpectedly happened. In early 1966 Armand Dennis ceased
wildlife film production. True to his word, Des Bartlett had stayed with
Armand until he retired. His last assignments for ADP had been in the
USA. That's where he was when he cabled saying that he was at last
free to join *Survival*. At the time he was filming a marine life programme in Miami which he had told me about and in which I was
keenly interested. I wrote to him asking for details about a unique
seahorse sequence. Des's reply was typical of many we were to receive
over the years. In fact Des Bartlett's shotlists, the precisely documented, roll-by-roll accounts of everything he films, are minor masterpieces of natural history observation. This first letter from Des reveals
his deep knowledge of wildlife and his complete single-mindedness in
filming it.

23 April 1966
Dear Colin,
    Many thanks for your detailed letter of the twentieth. I'll reply
straight away so as to clear up a few points.
    Male seahorses get pregnant because the females deposit the
eggs in an abdominal pouch of the males, where they are fertilized
and develop. With the larger species of seahorses this takes many
weeks, until the pouch greatly distends – over twice the thickness
of the body of the male seahorse. The opening to the pouch is
closed. The male seahorse goes through labour pains the same as a
female mammal. What we discovered, which does not seem to be
written up anywhere, is that the labour is not just a matter of
straining for a few hours to force the babies out of the pouch, but

something that goes on for days. In our case we wasted eight days
and nights watching the damn thing – staying up until 2 or 3 am,
and then setting the alarm for each hour until daybreak. And still
we missed the main event. Around 7 pm on a Friday the labour
began, and I set up cameras and lights. The first baby was not born
until 7 am on the Monday. I filmed no. 2 being born about 7.30 pm
on the Tuesday.

Then for about five days the labour spasms slacked off, but one
or two babies were born each day, and the pouch continued to
grow in size. Then around 7.30 am on the following Saturday all
the rest of the babies were born – within a matter of a few short
minutes. Julie raced in to say that there were babies everywhere.
I filmed the last two spasms, with the pouch opening wide, but
without any babies coming out.

We filmed the tiny babies around Poppa, etc., and have a nice
sequence – but not what it should be considering the time we spent
on the project. The film is back, and it is all quite nice, with fairly
good coverage in cine and stills – but we will always know that we
missed the main action. Perhaps we will always get it on the Great
Barrier Reef! We really searched for seahorses, without success,
when working on the Kenya coast. We know a lot more about
them now, and how to catch them.

As it turned out *Survival* never did get the seahorse material. Des
eventually quite properly decided that since the majority of the marine
footage had been shot while Armand Dennis Productions was still
operating, the seahorse 'birth' must be part of the package which ADP
was selling on the open market. Eventually ADP's library of Bartlett
footage, including the seahorse, went into a television series in opposition to *Survival* in the USA.

What concerned us more at that moment was what Des Bartlett's
first assignment for *Survival* should be. Des wanted to do a series on
the remarkable US Wildlife Refuge system. We were afraid that such a
series would be far too repetitive even when broken up in a series of
Survival programmes from other parts of the world by other cameramen. In the end we settled on one Refuge, the first set up in this
remarkable national system – Pelican Island off the coast of Florida.
The programme which contained some wonderful slow-motion diving
by brown pelicans was called 'Monument in the Mangroves'.

For the next year Des and Jen Bartlett were busy in the Wyoming
Rockies and at Wichita Mountain Refuge. The *Survivals* which came
from this period were all of vintage quality. They included: 'Wilderness
at Bay', the story of Yellowstone as one of the first pioneers into the

area, Osborne Russell, saw it and 'Jackson Hole', about the elk herds that rely on the town of Jackson for winter relief in the form of hay. Several things happened at Jackson and in the nearby Tetons that were to make a considerable mark on *Survival* in the coming years. One concerned a particularly beautiful beaver pond with the Teton peaks as its background. The Bartletts also met two young people, both of whom were to go on to film for *Survival*. The first, Jeff Foott, was a Teton guide and climber of world class. The second was an attractive and athletic Californian girl, Lee Lyon. Both had an obvious sympathy with, and knowledge of, wildlife. Both had the ambition to become wildlife photographers. Des's generous nature has always made him willing to teach others.

In this respect he is different from some other top-line operators. However, all the top-liners, and Lord knows there are few enough of them, exhibit some of the same characteristics.

In early 1968 my wife and I made a five thousand mile field trip with the three Bartletts – Des, Jen and twelve-year-old daughter Julie – across the American south-west. It was largely a reconnaissance for programmes to come. It was one of the field trips that we all try to make each year, usually in a different theatre and with a different wildlife cameraman. My memories of it are, of course, highly personal to the Bartletts but in general terms they offer some clue to the type of people these wildlife cameramen are.

With the exception of Alan Root, who is lucky enough to own a house on the shores of Lake Naivasha, Kenya, wildlife cameramen seldom have a permanent home. At the time we visited the Bartletts close to Tucson, Arizona, they had two temporary ones, an adobe cabin rented for one hundred dollars a month on a former dude ranch with a name like the title of a TV Western – Thunderhead Ranch; also a Land Rover which had travelled all the way from Africa with them and, with 130,000 miles on the clock was, in Des's words, 'just run in'.

I'll start with the Land Rover since it largely personifies the Bartletts' way of life. It is rather like a fighting vehicle since everything in it and on it is designed for operational use. A wildlife cameraman has to be able to get in and out of terrain normally only accessible to a tracked or half-tracked vehicle. Des's Land Rover has double springs. For reliable starting in cold conditions – in the Tetons they had just been filming at temperatures down to thirty-five degrees below zero – it has double batteries. It carries power tools for in-field repairs and there is a power point for electric drills, etc., under the dashboard. A large part of Des's success comes from meticulous planning and this extends to the tactical stowing of gear. Almost the entire carrying space of the vehicle is occupied by numbered marine plywood boxes that fit either in racks or one on top of the other with cabinet-maker's precision. They were, in fact, made for the Land Rover by a cabinet-maker. When Des slides one in or out it fits so closely there is a sigh of escaping air, much as you might get if pushing a piston into a cylinder. In these boxes are essential stores, including much of the £30,000 worth of camera equipment to be carried on our present recce trip of the south-western deserts.

Only on the top-right-hand side of the load is any space left. This is a long, narrow slot such as might accommodate a small human body. It contains a sleeping bag and a pillow. This is where a small human body (twelve-year-old Julie), can stretch out if she gets tired. On the roof rack are larger items, including an aluminium picnic table. Even this has a dual purpose. Its bright upper surface is capable of being used as a reflector in situations where extra light is required on a close subject.

At the start of any trip, and often during it, one must adapt totally to the Bartletts' pace. It is no good getting impatient because patience is not only the keynote to their own characters, it is one of their most important stocks in trade. Thus when Des says that you'll make an early start next day and to be up about six, what he means is that he and Jen will make an early start. The first three hours are frequently filled with organizational checks, loadings and reloadings to which you personally can contribute nothing and you will only do more harm than good if you do try to help by putting a box on a vehicle. It is certain to be the wrong box in the wrong place. This is an 'in' game and you shouldn't try to play it. Wander off into the desert and search for Indian artefacts or look for western banded geckos and horned toads. Or, if you must, stay in bed, though you'll only feel guilty if you do. The worst thing you can do is to fret. Des is never late for anything that matters. His time clock is run by such diverse springs and balances as snows, floods, droughts, nesting birds and migrating mammals. This trip we were taking together had no such pressures applied to it. The preliminary organization, though, was just as thorough.

Shortly before midday we are ready to leave. Because we are operating in civilized country and because there are five of us we take a second vehicle, a Chevy saloon which Des bought for $500 in Jackson Hole and which has now done nearly two hundred thousand trouble-free miles. This is the sort of transport that doesn't normally feature high on a wildlife cameraman's list of priorities. Nevertheless the Chevy has an amazing record of going places no respectable station wagon should be asked to go.

By now I'm fairly longing to see some wild America, but the first stop is not the desert but the Desert Museum outside Tucson. Des makes the excuse that he wants to consult Lewis Wayne Walker, one of the biologists there. What he actually wants is for *me* to meet Walker. I do so and we have a fascinating talk for two hours, not about the Painted Desert, the Mojave Desert, all of which I am dying to see, but about Baja California and the Sea of Cortez. This meeting illustrates another key piece in the successful cameraman's way of life. Des Bartlett and his peers, and through them *Survival* itself, only succeed because they enlist the total trust of scientists and experts like Wayne Walker. Des's notebook is filled with the addresses of people whose lifework is studying rattlesnakes and roadrunners, rhinos and rheas, men and women with whom he has worked in the past and who know that his film and *Survival*'s production of it will never misrepresent or sensationalize. And so Des feels, quite correctly, that two hours of a blistering Arizona afternoon are far from wasted if the man from London, who makes the films, becomes a face instead of just a name to the man in Tucson who supplies so much valuable help to the camera-man in the field. In fact this particular meeting was to pollinate some blossom that fell off the tree as fruit over a year later. Des then went to the Sea of Cortez and filmed the dramatic battle for nesting space between half a million elegant and royal terns and the Heerman's gulls on the island of Raza.

So it was mid-afternoon before we finally hit the road. For the next three weeks the days fell into a regular routine. Out in the desert surveying likely locations or filming all day long. Pack up in late after-noon and drive anything from two to four hundred miles for the night stop. Constantly, and not always with success, my wife and I had to fight the impatience that is a natural part of anyone's temperament except that of a wildlife cameraman and his wife. The south-west is one of the scenically most spectacular areas on earth with its mesas and canyons, eroded pinnacles and natural arches of weathered red sand-stone. I had got to the point at which I practically had to beg Des not to show me any more damned red rocks. Relentlessly, because he thought it was good for me and *Survival*, he drove me from Bryce Canyon which looks as though it is filled with thousands of intricately carved red chess-men (one pioneer, ignoring its overwhelming magnificence, described it accurately as 'a bad place to lose a cow in'), to Chiricahua Canyon where Cochise defied, and I now perfectly understand why, the US Cavalry (it's a bad place to ride in, let alone lose a horse in). Even my wife, who loves sightseeing and wild country, had had a surfeit of splendour. Yet amidst all this Des and Jen moved at the same heartbeat-of-nature pace, shooting stills and movie, waiting hours for the light to strike a certain buttress at a certain angle; deciding, just when one was sure they must have exhausted every possibility of a location, if not their stock of film, to walk back a mile into the wilderness to shoot the same scene from a different angle.

The Bartletts were right of course. When I once suggested towards the end of a long morning that we should perhaps soon be moving, Jen Bartlett paused before setting off with the camera tripod to walk another mile into the scrub for yet another shot and remonstrated mildly enough: 'What's the hurry? We may never be here again.' That's the point. Many photographic opportunities offer themselves just once. Miss that one time and you've missed them for ever.

If I have over-emphasized the nervous rigours of the trip I have also understated the considerable pleasures: the snowgeese at the southernmost part of their range at Bosque de L'Apache; five thousand sandhill cranes coming in to roost against the setting sun at Bitter Lakes Refuge, New Mexico; the full-blooded Navajo ranger who walked a mile off the road in the Painted Desert to see what we were doing there and bore the memorable name on his jacket 'R. Redsteer'. I shall never forget flying in a light aircraft three thousand feet below the rim of the Grand Canyon or finding that Monument Valley is everything that John Ford ever filmed it to be.

Quite a few of my memories of this trip concern the fascinating young lady, Julie Bartlett. When we looked for pronghorn antelope at Rosewell, New Mexico, it was she who spotted the herd at a great distance on the prairie long before any of the eagle-eyed adult naturalists, including her father.

When we moved to a new area, she not only knew the birds there but knew them by their scientific names. 'That's a *Phainopeplla nitens*,' she piped at one point on the Mexican border. And it *was*. I noticed that even her father didn't argue. And always at the close of the day, and sometimes in the back of the Chevy, when travelling, there were those school books to be studied.

When the desert trip was over, my wife had to return to England. Des and I flew up to Alaska which was to be his next theatre of operations. Strangely, as I sit writing this chapter, ten years later, I am aboard a ship, the *Lindblad Explorer*, on another Alaskan recce with Des and Jen Bartlett. Despite my impatience with their obsession with red rock in the south-west of the United States we have remained the closest friends. Possibly Des even recognizes that my nervous twitch adds something to his brilliant camerawork.

Chapter 9

The Ethiopian Adventure

WITH Dieter Plage I have had more adventures than with any other *Survival* cameraman. Dieter is Des Bartlett's opposite number. Dieter is a West German. Like many other excellent things he came to *Survival* through his compatriot Bernhard Grzimek. In 1968 *Survival* was at the point where expansion in production of first-class colour film had become an absolute essential. Bernhard Grzimek was impressed with the wildlife shooting Dieter had done for a case-hardened eccentric American producer in South Africa. We signed Dieter, who was then just turning thirty, and sent him to that most German of former German colonies, South-West Africa, now called Namibia. Dieter wisely pressed for an assistant. Des had his wife Jen, Alan Root his wife Joan. No wildlife cameraman could have asked for more able assistants in the field. Dieter was not similarly and fortunately equipped. He asked that he be allowed to take on the young South African called Rod Borland with whom he had worked for the American.

Dieter and Rod had hardly set up shop in Windhoek before Aubrey Buxton received a hysterical and outrageous cable declaring both men to be unreliable, unsuitable, dishonest and deceitful. This description supplied by Dieter's former American employer did not tally with our impression of the two young men at all. Nevertheless it was sufficient to make you wonder momentarily whether you were, at worst, going mad or, at best, had hired the wrong men. Fortunately it turned out to be the sender of the cable who had at least temporarily slipped his moorings. We decided to ignore this unsolicited character reference and assume that our judgement and that of Bernhard Grzimek had been right.

Dieter Plage and Des Bartlett have at the moment of writing filmed more half-hours and one-hour Specials than any other *Survival* cameramen. They achieve their results by methods that are in some ways as different as their temperaments. Where Des Bartlett is reserved to a point almost of shyness, Dieter is a mercurial extrovert. He loves performing, has a sense of humour that is more Anglo-American than German, can be plunged into a state of almost pyschosomatic gloom by personal setbacks but seldom by professional ones. Temperamentally, Dieter swoops where Des flies straight and level. Both are dedicated to a point of monomania. Both are what I refer to as camera-nuts. Muslims turn their prayer mats towards Mecca. I should not be surprised to learn that both Dieter and Des kneel down facing Munich night and morning for that is where the great god Arriflex lives. The faithful who have made the pilgrimage to Mecca wear a green cord in their head-dress. Dieter and Des have made so many pilgrimages to the Arriflex camera factory in Munich that they both wear in their lapels a small gold camera, presented by the Arriflex Company. This is given to few cameramen in the world and means that you are not only a member of a photographic élite but that you have spent a hell of a lot of money on cameras. Of the two Dieter is, I suspect, the greater camera fanatic. He is more apt to fall in love with the latest equipment.

If Dieter has one fault it is that he cannot switch off. He is liable to come down first thing in the morning and say: 'Ach' (I didn't believe Germans actually did say 'Ach' until I met Dieter), 'Ach, I have been thinking about shot 25 on Roll 114.' He has, too. Last thing before he went to sleep, first thing on waking up. For all I know he has been dreaming of Roll 114 in between. A few things *can* sidetrack him. Spike Milligan on TV for one. So can a good soccer match, a bad all-in wrestling match, almost any Western. Of course, these diversions only work when he is in so-called civilization. There are no television sets in the Sumatran rain forests, the Danakil Desert, or an island in the middle of a remote Ethiopian lake. I have operated with Dieter in all these places. Then you must be prepared for monomania undiluted. Suggest to him, plead with him, demand of him that he thinks and speaks of something other than the problems of the job in hand and he will say something like: 'If I wasn't such a bloody monomaniac, I wouldn't be so good at my job.' Alas, it is all too true. You have to be a bloody monomaniac to do the job at all.

It is difficult to say how Dieter Plage's and Des Bartlett's techniques differ. What I do know is this: show any of us concerned with making films at *Survival* two hundred feet of any cameraman's rushes and I can guarantee that we can tell you, without being given a clue, who shot them. Dieter's work tends to be nervous, opportunist, superb where action is concerned, frequently poetic. In terms of diplomacy and winning friends and influencing people, he is the equal of Des Bartlett, which is high praise indeed. Once the initial diplomatic groundwork has been done he is a more pragmatic operator. In military terms,

Two species of camera assistant. Above, the author assists Dieter Plage during a downpour in the Sumatran rain forest while filming 'Orangutan, Orphans of the Forest'. Below, Olip, one of the young orangs, being trained for return to the wild after early years spent in captivity, offers to help Dieter change camera magazines. Olip was totally fascinated by the camera and used to switch it on, apparently for the pleasure of hearing the motor run. He also ate the rubber eyepiece. Orangs are sometimes called 'the mechanical apes'. They seem to understand basic mechanical principles such as the use of levers.

Survival's earliest adventures in Africa were both 'firsts'. They were also last chances. 'S.O.S. Rhino' covered the highly exciting capture of Uganda's few surviving white rhinos. They were the first adult white rhinos to be caught and among the last rhinos to be lassoed. Soon afterwards drugging techniques, safer to men and animals, were perfected. In 1962, Aubrey Buxton went with Alan and Joan Root (seen here with him) to the remote northern Ugandan district of Karamoja. The resulting documentary became the last record of the Karamojong, the wild tribesmen of the region. Shortly afterwards they were suppressed and their way of life drastically altered by successive political regimes.

Dieter is a Rommel to Des's Montgomery. Fortunately for us, however, they are both on the same side. There will never be a photographic Alamein.

Dieter and Rod took off with a rush. For two years they hit a level of productivity seldom equalled by a *Survival* camera team. When the early German miners went looking for diamonds in South-West Africa, they walked towards the rising sun at dawn and towards the setting sun at the end of the day. That way the diamonds reflected the low light and were easy to pick up, which meant that the diamonds were lying on the surface ready for the picking. That's the way the stories were in South-West when Dieter and Rod began filming there. The vast land which contains Etosha National Park, the largest park in the world; the Skeleton Coast, a thousand miles of the loneliest and most treacherous coastline in the world; the Namib, the oldest desert in the world with the highest dunes in the world – South-West Africa was a naturalist camera team's dream land. Moreover it was photographically virgin country. No one had seriously attempted to film its riches. Now it seemed that Dieter Plage, perhaps because of his nationality – German is still the *lingua franca* in South-West – had the sole concession. He and Rod clicked with the Department of Conservation, with its director Barnabe de la Bat and with the rangers and vets of its parks organization.

Dieter and Rod got lucky with their very first story. The gemsbok, the southern race of the oryx, were offering unwelcome competition to the karakul farmers in the pre-Namib, the arid country that lies adjacent to the great desert itself. Karakul are an extremely valuable commodity. It is the young of these sheep that provide Persian lamb for expensive fur coats. Fairly naturally, the karakul farmers were not happy at seeing the sparse grazing of the pre-Namib disappearing down the throats of large invading dry-country antelope. When fences failed to keep the gemsbok (pronounced 'hemsbok') out of their pastures they reached for their rifles and shotguns. The Conservation Department's answer was to order its capture unit to catch as many gemsbok as possible and move them beyond temptation of trespassing to a reserve several hundred miles away. For this purpose they picked a courageous and cheerful maniac called Peter Flanagan.

Flanagan worked out a special technique for gemsbok capture. Because of the nearness of the great red dunes of the Namib – they rise up to twelve hundred feet – he couldn't rely on darting his antelope. A darted animal frequently runs hundreds of yards before it goes down. With the gemsbok there was therefore a considerable risk that these powerful animals, nearly as large as a pony, would run and keep running into the soft sand of the dunes where the capture vehicles

7

couldn't follow. If this happened then the drugged antelope could easily become lost and die before they could be given the vital antidote: Flanagan's answer was lunatic but simple. Chase the galloping animals across the level flats, called 'streets', between the dunes and catch them by their tails!

On the front of the catching Land Rovers Flanagan had built a tubular metal guard rail on to which an intrepid and agile man might cling while the vehicle, guided by Flanagan, bucketed at forty mph across country. The intrepid men picked for the job were bushmen and Ovambo tribesmen of the park staff. Flanagan immediately suggested that Dieter and Rod serve an apprenticeship up front. When they not only didn't fall off but successfully caught oryx, Flanagan decided they were acceptable.

Living up to Peter Flanagan's eccentric standards was exacting but exciting work. In camp Flanagan would sometimes be sitting at table when a fly or insect intruded on the scene, to his annoyance. Flanagan's answer was to draw his Smith and Wesson .44 and shoot it. Once he did so among the cups and saucers on the breakfast table. Another time, Flanagan decided to have a bath with a difference. He made his catching crew carry a tin bath plus water to the top of a large sand dune. There he performed his ablutions in a manner and style possibly unique since the days of the Pharoahs and maybe before that. Flanagan was hell to film because his volatile and extrovert nature demanded that he never wore the same clothes twice, even in one morning. Continuity therefore became a nightmare. And since the cut version of any single oryx catch is likely to be composed of an amalgam of several oryx catches, Flanagan presented considerable problems to our editors back in London. One second he'd be there in a crash helmet and bush jacket; the next he was seen wearing a camouflage smock and beret. Our film editors never did get the continuity right. Minor inconsistencies of dress, however, could be overlooked in the excitements of the finished film which was called 'First, Catch Your Unicorn'. Flanagan's grab-by-the-tail technique made for wonderful scenes of the powerful gemsbok, whose long straight horns have been known to impale lions, being wrestled to a standstill by their Ovambo captors, tranquillized and then loaded aboard a truck for eventual transfer to an area where they would be protected from their own excesses. It revealed, too, that Dieter had a masterly touch for capturing action and a lyrical eye for filming wild animals in an even wilder setting.

By the time I was able to visit Dieter Plage in Etosha and to cross a large part of the Namib Desert with Rod Borland and his wife, Moira, the team had made eight half-hour films in South-West Africa. Dieter was by then fully proven as a top-line wildlife cameraman. Rod Borland was ready to operate independently. The very first film that he made on his own was partly the result of my field trip to South-West. Called 'The Empty Desert' it was the story of how desert animals adapt to life in a wilderness of red sand where day temperatures often reach 130 F. and the only moisture comes in the form of the mist that blows in across the immense dunes from the Skeleton Coast. That mist is the result of the cold Benguela current that runs northward from the Antarctic meeting the super-heated air of the Namib. The towering red dunes of the desert itself are also, in a sense, a product of that remarkable current. The Benguela runs so strongly that it continually alters the outline of the coast, making it one of the most dangerous in the world to sailors. Ships wrecked twenty years ago are frequently to be found up to a mile inland. There is even the story, though I have never verified it, that the timbers of a Portuguese galleon lie entombed in sand several miles from the sea. The name 'Skeleton' is well applied to this coast.

The red sands of the Namib have been swept, grain by grain, out of the heart of Africa by the Orange River in the south. The Benguela has carried these deposits northward and the constant lacerating winds of the Coast have piled them up and blown them inland to form the thousand-foot red dunes of the Namib.

There is an amazing amount of life in this frightening and beautiful wilderness including: spiders that build trap-doors over their burrows with sand impregnated with silk; tok-tokky (tenebrionid) beetles whose wing cases are grooved and guttered to catch, condense and deliver to their mouths, when they tip themselves up on their long back legs, moisture from the Benguela fog; the golden mole, a creature that looks like furry apple dumpling and progresses underground in its search for beetle larvae, aided by a coat whose grain is adapted to assist forward movement through sand. Rod and I used to go out on the dunes at night, armed with a Tilley lamp, to collect what he called 'goodies'. Goodies included night-hunting palmatto geckos, dune crickets, Namib side-winding vipers and beetle larvae. It is a weird and exhilarating experience to stand in a small pool of bright white light on top of a twelve hundred foot pile of red sand knowing that you are the only two people in the world whose interests are bizarre enough to make you do such a thing. My favourite Namib animal character was a little shovel-nosed lizard called *Aporosaurus*. *Aporosaurus* hunts the slip-faces of the great dunes for insects and for seeds blown there, perhaps from hundreds of miles away, by the wind. The Namib dunes all run east to west. There is therefore a hot side and a cooler side. The slip-face, the concave, hard-packed peak of each dune is the hot face. It is also the most productive of food items for *Aporosaurus*. The trouble is that the lizard can't stand the heat for very long. So it has a repertoire of cooling devices when the going gets too hot for it. First it jacks its tail up clear of the sand. This enables it to lose a little heat to the surrounding air while it continues hunting. A seed or a beetle or two later, it goes to stage two and raises its entire body off the sand. Next it raises one foot, then another. The very last trick of all involves tail, body and opposing front and rear feet. After that it has only one course left to it if it doesn't want to fry. Cold-blooded reptiles have no heat-regulating systems. *Aporosaurus* retreats to the cool side of the dune top, where, after a time, it finds itself getting too cold again. So it lets belly, tail and all other appurtenances fall flat on the sand and warms up once more.

Having learned at first hand, after getting the vehicle bogged down in it, how utterly helpless man is in the Namib, I found these animal adaptations truly wonderful. So did the judges at the Monte Carlo television festival. They gave Rod's 'Empty Desert' the highest award of all, the *Prix du Prince*.

Dieter Plage had meantime moved to Ethiopia, leaving Rod to make his second solo film called 'Beachmaster', a splendidly detailed study of the fur seal colony at Cape Cross on the Skeleton Coast. It was in Ethiopia that my series of adventures in the field with Dieter really began.

Once again the sequence of events had been started by Aubrey Buxton. Aubrey has been quite influential in interesting Prince Philip in birds, though he does not take part in HRH's special hobby of bird photography. Aubrey, though an excellent watercolour artist, is by no means the world's greatest, or even second greatest, photographer. In fact when in 1968 he won the Royal Television Society's Silver Medal for 'outstanding work behind the camera', an unkind colleague was heard to remark: 'about a mile behind'. His ornithological association with Prince Philip made him a natural companion on the rare occasions that HRH managed to sneak away with Hasselblad and hide to foreign parts. In 1969 the invitation came to join a royal birding safari to Ethiopia. During this trip the party visited a little-known lake in the Ethiopian Rift Valley called Shala, as well as the Awash National Park on the borders of the Danakil Desert. What Aubrey saw and learned convinced him that there were two great *Survival* stories here. In 1970 I joined Dieter Plage in Addis Ababa to follow them up. My wife once again came with me. Ever since I took her on her first trip to Africa in 1962, I have never been able to shake her off.

Aubrey and Prince Philip had been initiated into the mysteries of Lake Shala by two well-known ornithologists, Leslie Brown from Kenya and Emil Urban, then head of the Zoology Department at Addis University. Until these two made their discovery, it had been a mystery where the great white pelicans of the northern part of the Rift Valley nested. There was known to be a pelican colony on an island in Lake Rukwa in Tanzania but this nowhere near accounted for the entire Rift Valley population. There had to be another nesting colony somewhere in the north. It was an Ethiopian naturalist who first made the discovery that Shala was being frequented by large numbers of pelicans. The name itself should have provided a clue. In Galla, the local tongue, the word 'shala' means pelican. And yet no one, until Urban and Brown followed up the Ethiopian's lead, had tumbled to the significance of the name. Shala seemed such an unlikely nesting locale for thousands of large fish-eating birds with hungry young to feed. It is a soda lake, admittedly of fairly low concentration. Nevertheless it is sufficiently alkaline to discourage all but the smallest species of freshwater fish.

The lake itself is large, about thirty miles long, with steep mountains to the south that drop sheer to the water's edge and continue dropping to the lake bed eight hundred feet beneath the surface. There are several small islands to the west but no one visits them for at least two good reasons. Since there are no fish worth catching in Shala, there are no native boats – Africans do not go boating for fun. Also, winds that come whipping down out of the mountains make the lake exceedingly dangerous.

From the most accessible end of Shala, the nearest island lies twelve miles down the lake. Such is the heat haze that it is impossible to see the island let alone anything on it. Two years before we arrived on the scene, Leslie Brown and Emil Urban had set out to reach this island in a cockleshell of a metal boat belonging to the Game Department. At considerable risk they made it and kept on making it. They were excited enough by the revelation that the twenty-acre flat-topped volcanic island held for them to accept any hazard. At one end of the island, on a plateau less than two acres in extent, they found up to five thousand pairs of great white pelicans nesting and raising their grotesque grey young. The main mystery had been solved but almost as great a one remained. Where were ten thousand pelicans finding the three to four pounds of fish each bird needed daily to feed itself and its young? Certainly not in fishless Shala. Ten miles away to the north, beyond an intervening ridge of scrub-covered hills, rising three thousand feet above Shala, lies another lake called Abiata and Abiata, a freshwater lake, is so full of fish you can almost walk on them. Pelicans will travel fifty miles or more to find fish, but over a mountain range? How the pelicans solved the air transportation problem completed the story. As Leslie Brown and Emil Urban watched, they saw the huge birds form up on the water in squadrons. The first party flew out into the middle of the lake and marshalled themselves on the water around nine in the morning, just as the air around the shore was starting to heat up. There they waited until they detected a thermal – a rising current of hot air – building up on the shore in the direction of Abiata. Sometimes a dust devil might indicate the thermal but mostly they appeared to rely on the remarkable sense of observation that soaring birds employ in these matters. Despite their unwieldy appearance when grounded, pelicans, when it comes to soaring, are almost in the same class as vultures and marabou storks. Once the pelican squadron was over the shore and had found the thermal, it soared and soared in huge circles until, with barely a flap of its communal wings, it topped the peak and could see Abiata beyond. All it had to do then was to set its wings and glide down to the distant lake. Throughout the day, squadron followed squadron by the same route. At Abiata, the adult pelicans stayed fishing for up to twenty-four hours. Then, with a crop full of pre-digested fish, they caught the return thermal back to the island in Lake Shala where their hungry young awaited them.

When my wife and I joined Dieter in Addis he was well into this story and operating, since Rod Borland was filming independently in South-West Africa, entirely on his own. Dieter's life-style when filming is to say the least, spartan. Home comforts play very little part in his field operation. Though he hits the fleshpots when he is in town – there is hardly a steak tartare left for miles – when in the field, film, cameras and tape-recorders live in the utmost luxury; humans and their creature comforts tend to take second place. We quickly learned that he had been living eleven miles out on Lake Shala with the aid of a tarpaulin under which he slept, and a tin trunk which contained his food supplies. My wife swallowed at this but brightened a little when she learned that he had put up a two-man tent on the island as a gala celebration of her visit. Even with the tent it was a stark life on the island, but an experience neither of us will easily forget. We made the journey out to the island in a rubber boat. Rubber boats will go almost anywhere at any speed a powerful outboard cares to push them – except when there is a thousand pound load of stores aboard and the outboard develops recurrent electrical trouble. Then a journey that should take a bare fifty minutes can easily last two and a half hours. Shala lies at over six thousand feet. The atmosphere is just sufficiently thinned to allow a fair amount of unfiltered ultra-violet to penetrate. The reflection from the clear surface of the lake compounds this. The ultra-violet light has extraordinary effects on the human body. In Dieter's case it caused him to break out in severe cold sores around the mouth. By the time my wife reached the island on that slow boat to Shala, her ankles had swollen to over twice their normal size.

No wonder the pelicans were never seen from the shore. Not until we were within half a mile of the island was a faint white blur discernible on a small plateau at the southern end. The whole island resembled an aircraft carrier. The 'flight deck', about two hundred yards long and accommodating the pelican colony, was at the bow. At the stern, the aft third of the island dropped in one single step about twenty feet to a lower deck level. Close to the step was a single acacia tree, our only shade. Under this the tin trunk containing food and cooking gear was parked. Twenty yards away on a comparatively level plateau, stood a very small orange tent, our home.

To reach the pelican colony it was necessary, in order not to alarm the birds, to creep along, bent double, behind a crumbly lava cliff. One thing is evident from the great white pelican's selection of this remote offshore island as a nesting site. The birds require absolute solitude and privacy for their domestic life. Dieter had his film cameras set up in a wooden hide, set into the lava face and built by Leslie Brown and Emil Urban at the end of their first nesting season. Pelican Island is, of course, deserted by pelicans for three-quarters of the year, the birds then dispersing all over the Rift Valley lakes.

The stench along that cliff was enough to put anyone off pelicans for life. The guano produced by fish-eating birds is notoriously high in nitrogen, phosphates and odour. The heat in the hide – and remember, Dieter had been keeping a twelve-hour watch inside it for days on end – was about equal to that in the stokehold of a coal-burning freighter in the Red Sea in August. But the sight that met the eyes when the canvas curtains of the hide were parted more than compensated. Three feet away, the nearest of the comical great birds conducted their family life.

The terminology with which Dieter described the scene was Leslie Brown's. Great white pelicans develop a fatty knob above their bills four or five days before coming into breeding condition. These were the 'knobbers', pink-faced knobbers being females, yellow-faced ones the males. Courtship routines included a ridiculously dignified gait on the part of the male. This was the 'strutting walk'. Just in front of the cameras, groups of half-grown grey youngsters gathered in pods to await the return of their parents, perhaps not until tomorrow, with a cargo of Abiata fish aboard for them. There were the predators, too. Egyptian vultures attempting to steal eggs and sometimes succeeding; sacred ibis from their own nesting colony on a nearby islet consisting of columns of basalt, scavenging fragments of broken eggs; fish eagles and tawny eagles trying for any titbit they could get. Both these noble birds are capable of scavenging.

I sat several hours in the hide with Dieter, marvelling at the patience of anyone who could keep that sort of vigil up hour after hour for days on end. I remarked that he seldom seemed to use the second camera.

He told me that he had set this up largely for Leslie Brown's benefit. Leslie had visited the island quite frequently to advise Dieter and to point out finer aspects of pelican behaviour. Leslie is violent in his enthusiasms and tends to irascibility when his recommendations are ignored. It is a common assumption among scientists and wildlife experts that anything the eye can see the camera can immediately film. Sometimes this is actually the case, especially when the action in question is repeated at length or frequently enough. More often, though, the knobbers have finished knobbing, the strutters ended strutting, before focus, aperture, or even direction can be applied to the camera. Had Dieter shot everything that Leslie demanded he would needlessly have burned up about ten thousand feet of additional film. He therefore kept the second camera unloaded when Leslie was with him in the hide and pressed the button when commanded – to produce a satisfying, if sterile, whirr.

Despite Dieter's protestations that he made the most marvellous potato salad, he seldom had time to boil a spud, let alone slice it. The one time he got round to it he made a washing-up bowl full, enough to last for a week. So my wife catered while we were on the island. Once again she demonstrated her remarkable ability to change from Surrey housewife to experienced safari hand. We fed on steaks and fried eggs and bathed in the lake. The water was so sodary that soap lathered beautifully. The only problem was that when you emerged you had to rub down with a towel immediately or you became instantly coated in white. At night, the sleeping was, to say the least, lumpy. Volcanic ash and tufty grass does not make the best mattress. When the wind was in the wrong direction, which was from all directions, a living, buzzing, blanket of lake-fly settled over the island. Then there was a pair of spur-winged plovers, aggressive birds at the best of times, evidently equipped for night-flying, who resented the tent as an intruder on their nesting territory. Dieter, who had courteously moved thirty yards away to sleep in the open, had chosen an area previously used by nesting pelicans. By the morning he was heavily infested with pelican ticks. Despite all these minor irritations it was a joy to sit there in the moonlight, yet as isolated as if on the moon, looking across eleven miles of water at 'earth'. The first night we talked about lighting a fire, but the island rock held the heat and Dieter argued that a fire would attract the lake-fly. We all secretly knew that each felt that it would reveal our isolation to the rest of the world – not that the rest of the world would be looking. Far away, 'on earth', there was evidence of life. On the distant shore, a fire winked in the darkness, maybe a Galla village but more likely a bush fire.

So the filming of the colony itself presented few difficulties. It was all there before your very eyes. Birds at the nest, however, even birds as large, comic and numerous as the pelicans, have only a limited viewer interest, though dedicated ornithologists will tell you differently. We do not make *Survival* for dedicated ornithologists but for 140 million people of all nationalities throughout the world! The assembly of the squadrons on the lake, the flight over the mountains, the arrival at Abiata and the actual fishing at Abiata – no one knew exactly where the pelicans did fish at Abiata – were all important elements of the story yet to be covered. All presented their special problems.

One spectacular sequence that could be filmed from the island was the return of the birds from Abiata with a load of fish in their crops. This started around eleven in the morning and continued until about four in the afternoon, a period that coincided with the best thermalling conditions over the mountain. Often the birds made a very steep approach, coming in over our tent at the 'stern' of their aircraft carrier. Then, they partially folded their wings and descended like bombs and with a whistle to match. Having made this spectacular slide down through the sky, they then opened their wings at a full-flap setting, lowered their paddles as air-brakes and levelled off to turn back into wind over the colony. There parents and young unfailingly picked each other out, no matter how many milling grey youngsters there might be waiting to chase the returning adults for food. There was invariably a rather charming aftermath to the return of each flight of pelicans. After they had landed, the island was treated to a gentle snowfall of feathers torn from the birds' breasts by the violence of their descent.

To film the still missing aspects of the story called for some ingenuity. The thermalling ascent of the mountain could only be filmed by climbing the mountain itself, no easy task burdened down with camera, film, tripod, food and water. Filming the pelican's eye view of the ascent and descent meant that a helicopter had to be hired and flown from Addis. At Abiata, Dieter had eventually discovered with Emil Urban's assistance, that the pelicans caught their fish among the dead trees of an acacia woodland killed when the lake level rose in one of the cyclical high water periods such lakes have. In one way this was a great plus since the drowned trees formed a bird city with cormorants and darters nesting in the branches, pink-backed pelicans roosting there, kingfishers, herons, egrets and ducks providing constant counterpoint to the activities of the great white pelicans themselves. To film this scene, and especially the communal fishing by the pelicans, meant transporting, first, the boat to Abiata, twenty miles by rough track from Shala, then finding timber and cutting reeds, finally building a series of tree hides in what promised to be the most likely pelican fishing areas. All this Dieter accomplished practically single-handed. None of this, however, matched for improvisation the way in which he solved the problem of close-up filming the pelicans assembling on the water.

Though the pelicans would be extremely shy of a man in a wet-suit swimming towards them, Dieter reasoned that they would accept a reasonable floating replica of themselves. With the aid of Emil Urban and his zoology department, Dieter obtained a stuffed pelican. Having removed most of the stuffing from this, he inserted a movie camera inside the bird and mounted the whole affair on an inflated motor tyre. Pushing this strange contraption in front of him, Dieter was able to approach to within a yard of swimming birds. One fully grown youngster even swam up to the camera 'bird' and begged to be fed!

Dieter spent nearly fifty hours immersed in the sodary waters of Shala. Despite the fact that he wore a wet-suit, the caustic action of the soda eventually removed, though not all at one time, most of his skin.

The resulting hour Special, 'Pelican Flyway', was a success, in our eyes at least. To be honest, despite all the love, care and hard work that had gone into it, it was too long for its subject-matter. As an experiment, we made a half-hour called 'Airlift' from the superabundant 'out-takes' which is film language for unused material. I am tempted to say that the half-hour was the better picture. In terms of earning its keep in overseas sales it was certainly more remunerative. But these are not considerations a wildlife film cameraman can, or should, take into account, when he is sweating his guts out alone on a highly odorous island in the middle of a soda lake. To him, as to the rest of us, this picture just has to be the most important one ever made. He wouldn't do the job if he didn't believe exactly that.

Dieter had a far harder time on his second Ethiopian assignment. This followed closely on 'Pelican Flyway'. The previous year Aubrey had been down to the Awash National Park and Tendaho which lies on the fringe of Danakil country. He had been impressed with the intransigence of the tribesmen, as have been the comparatively few people to visit that inhospitable land. The Danakil do not welcome *ferengi*, strangers. They proved their point by throwing stones at Aubrey when he tried to take some still pictures of their women. For the Danakil this is almost an expression of courtesy. Their more usual treatment of foreigners is to castrate them and wear their severed testicles, after drying of course, as trophies. Despite this, a handful of intrepid explorers had managed to penetrate Danakil country and emerge intact. One of the most remarkable of these was Wilfred Thesiger.

Until 1934, the geographers had no idea where the Awash, a large and powerful river that flows out of the Ethiopian highlands near Addis, ended up. All they knew was that it flowed down into the Danakil

Desert, as if making for the Red Sea somewhere near Djibouti, but never reached it. It simply disappeared. In an era when the aeroplane was a highly efficient survey instrument, this seems incredible. It is nevertheless true. Perhaps the idea of a forced landing in those hostile wastes made such a survey a less than attractive prospect. In 1934, Thesiger, a young man fresh from university, collected a caravan around him and, against all advice, set out to follow the Awash to its mysterious conclusion. He came near to being attacked several times, but reached the court of the Sultan who has absolute sway over the Danakil, or, as they prefer to be called, Afar. After facing considerable dangers and hardships, Thesiger and a handful of followers reached the end of the Awash River. He found that it simply disappeared into a huge sodary lake below sea level whence its waters evaporated as fast as and sometimes faster than, they flowed in. That lake is today known as Lake Abbaye.

Just as Aubrey had sensed several years before that a last opportunity was being present to film wild Karamoja, so he now correctly foresaw that the same situation applied to the Afars and their savagely beautiful Danakil Desert. There had been certain risks to be faced in filming the Karamojong. Alan Root had, however, got away with nothing more serious than being attacked by a witch. In Danakil country, the fact had to be faced that anyone working among the Afar might be sliced up, or, worse still, off.

We at *Survival* had several things going for us. An intrepid friend of Aubrey's, Brian MacDermot, had several times ventured into Danakil country. Brian (pronounced Bree-an) is a stockbroker with a penchant for exploring. He had followed Thesiger's trail to the Sultan's capital, Asaita, and had emerged in one piece. His summation was that if we could win the Sultan's support we might survive to make our film.

Aubrey admitted that there might be risks involved. He asked me to accompany Dieter from Lake Shala to make a recce and, if possible, to reach the Sultan. He suggested that I meet and discuss tactics with Brian MacDermot.

So we had one excellent source of up-to-date information on Danakil country available to us. We also had some very powerful commercial support. Aubrey had established close relations with the well-known international trading company Mitchell Cotts. Mitchell Cotts had very large cotton plantations at Tendaho in a kind of enclave on the edge of Danakil country. The Sultan, a highly commercial ruler, had cotton interests of his own and stood to benefit greatly from the success of the Mitchell Cotts enterprise. You might say that the Sultan was selling Mitchell Cotts protection. He kept his wild men under control in return for certain considerations. Without such co-operation Mitchell Cotts could not have operated. Without MC's ability to irrigate the desert and persuade it to burst into life, the Sultan could not have got richer. It was a nicely balanced arrangement.

My meeting with Brian MacDermot did not greatly reassure me that it was safe for a cameraman or men to work in Danakil country, for months on end, with or without the Sultan's protection, with or without Mitchell Cotts's support, with or without Brian himself as a guide.

Today I am rather ashamed of the note I wrote Aubrey after my conversations with MacDermot. Reading it I can detect that the temperature of my pedal extremities was well below blood heat.

> Aubrey,
>
> I had lunch with Brian to learn all I could about the practicalities of filming in Ethiopia. He is certainly a most impressive chap. As a result of our talk, might I make several comments which we could discuss.
>
> He is obviously enormously intrepid, far more so than I am. He's so intrepid that I think this question has to be asked about the Danakil operation: Just how good is he? Further, to what risks are we exposing a cameraman who may have to stay there for weeks or even a researcher who has to stay there for less? I can only answer for myself. Though I am more than willing to face a rhino horn where it hurts most, I do feel that castration, even at this late stage, is something I would rather do without. Brian plainly is not concerned about this, only about anthropological truth. It does seem to me that we have to get our own objectives in balance. They are basically making a marvellous film and getting good ratings. So what risks are the team exposing themselves to in order to achieve this? It seems to me that to walk in there with just Brian *may* be all right, in fact may be the only way of doing it. It may also be all wrong. You obviously have thought of all this. But I would like to feel that whoever is going there has a bit more than the know-how of one intrepid, and so far intact man, to ensure his Survival!
>
> It really does seem that whoever is going to film has got to be prepared to stick around for at least three months. Brian feels that the Sheikh's patience – provided he can find the Sheikh which seems a long shot, anyway – may last one more trip.

In the event, here we were, moving straight from the safety of Lake Shala, where the worst that could happen to you was that you might drown or get sunstroke, to a land where, for the male at least, a fate worse than death was practically a commonplace. MacDermot, who was not with us, had left me in London with one reassuring thought. 'The locals,' he said, 'are far keener on black balls than on white ones.'

Dieter had already made one trip to Tendaho. The prospects looked good. Mitchell Cotts were more than willing to help. Though they could give no guarantees of success, they would try to arrange an audience with the Sultan.

Dieter and I were a little worried about my wife's accompanying us. The Danakil are a Muslim people. Women are expected to keep in the background. The visit might even involve some danger. To all this my wife replied that, from what she had learned, the male members of the party were likely to be in considerably more trouble than she was.

Ours was no Thesiger epic. We flew in a Mitchell Cotts twin Aztec to Tendaho. The Danakil stood on the edge of the strip regarding us with fine-nosed autocratic Hamitic disdain. Viewing them from the tips of their long, curved castrating knives to the crowns of their fuzzy heads, it was easy to believe all you had been told about them. And these were relatively tame Danakil. As we were soon to find out, there is no such thing as a tame Danakil.

Tendaho with its vast acreage of irrigated desert blooming with cotton is a bit like a frontier outpost surrounded by Indians. A very thin skin of civilization protects the European management's houses, club and cotton jinnery from the hostiles all around. Europeans sleep with guns handy, just in case. Every now and again raiding parties of 'Indians' break into the settlement. Raiding takes the form of driving their goats and camels into the crops to browse and graze. If this happens too often the manager sends a message to the Sultan in his desert capital, Asaita, some half an hour's flying time away. The day before we arrived, the Sultan's police chief, the *Feterari*, had paid a punitive visit. We met him, a hawklike man with brilliants in the frames of his glasses and a long-barrelled revolver stuck in his belt. He seemed a very kind, cultured sort of Danakil. His penal system, we soon learned, made the methods of Richard III or even Himmler seem comparatively mild. Brian MacDermot had told me of his reputation. Serious wrongdoers were incarcerated in a dungeon dug out of the rock beneath Asaita from which they never emerged alive. Lesser miscreants, it was said, were hung head-down over a pit of burning pepper or had their legs flayed by being rubbed with wetted roughened planks. These had struck me as the pardonable exaggerations of a traveller's tales until the plantation manager gave me his account of a recent disciplinary visit by the *Feterari*. He had required that the manager drive him and his strong-arm men round the plantation after dark in a Land Rover. When they came across a party of Danakil grazing their camels among the crops, the *Feterari* ordered his 'police' to seize one at random. One of his legs was then bound between two short poles and a third stave inserted crossways. This was then levered about until the sinews twisted, the bones grated and, in one or two cases, actually broke. The manager had no choice but to sit through this performance as if it didn't trouble him in the least. Rough justice of this kind worked, for a time. After a month or so the Danakil were back in the plantations again.

In the end my wife came to Asaita. We had been told what to expect of our audience with the Sultan. We would find him sitting at the end of a plain deal table in his palace. On the table would be an alarm clock, pre-set to measure the length of audience the Sultan had decided to grant us. Once the alarm went off, the audience was over. Dieter and I had warned my wife what to expect. She would be considered less than the dust. She would be expected to walk well behind her lords and masters – us. Above all, she must take no photographs. The whole deal looked like a triumph for Men's Lib.

We flew in the Aztec and landed on the desert outside a sizeable cluster of rectangular yellow buildings, with the minaret of a mosque at the centre. This was the Sultan's capital, Asaita. Surprisingly, a battered pick-up truck came out to meet us. We drove into town. The main street was a modified lava flow. I had the impression I was entering Omdurman at the time of General Gordon. On the outskirts we passed an area of level ground covered with cairns made of lava rocks. This was how the Danakil buried their dead, presumably because they couldn't dig them in. I was reminded irresistibly of Boot Hill at Tombstone. Though murder and mutilation were almost a career among the Danakil warriors, they were directed always at the outsider and particularly against their identical-looking neighbours, the Issas.* Among their own clans there appeared to be comradeship and even gentleness. In Asaita we witnessed hand-kissing among friends, both male and female, when they met. However, I had the very distinct feeling that no one was going to kiss my hand. The feeling increased as we waited in a mud shack fifty yards from the Sultan's palace. This it turned out was the anteroom of Asaita's leading and possibly only brothel. From the traffic that passed through during our forty-minute wait, I found this easy to believe, not that the customers were Danakil. They had no need, for they seemed to possess some of the most beautiful women I have seen in Africa and most other places besides. No, the house was used by *ferengi* men from the high plateau, imported to work in the Sultan's own personal cotton plantations. That these despised outsiders were able to survive at all in Danakil country was a tribute to the Sultan's absolute power. Any castration among the cotton-picking labour force would undoubtedly have resulted in the offender's being hung upside down in the pepper pit, or worse. As the minutes ticked by,

* If you look on the map, you will see the adjacent areas described as the Territory of the Issas and the Afars. 'Our' Danakil were Afars.

Dieter and I began to feel the passing Danakil were regarding us from the waist downwards with increasing interest. We reassured ourselves by taking it out on my wife and reminding her to walk well in our rear when we were finally admitted to the presence. At last, the interpreter, lent to us by Mitchell Cotts, told us that we were on.

For an all-powerful and exceedingly rich man, the Sultan did not possess an over-imposing palace. Protected by a six-foot wall, a pair of iron gates and a bodyguard armed with ancient rifles of many armies, the palace was a squat white building more reminiscent of a warehouse than a seat of government. The bodyguard seemed composed of dark-skinned buccaneers whom Henry Morgan might have turned down as being a little too rough for the job. They were, as it turned out, mostly related to the Sultan, about as good a life insurance policy as you could get in Danakil country.

The plans we had for my wife went wrong from the outset. She did, as commanded, walk behind us through the courtyard. She was, however, admitted to the council room. Worse than that, the Sultan greeted her graciously.

We sat down. There was the alarm clock, its face turned towards the Sultan. There was no telling how long we'd got. The Sultan overflowed the end of the table. Even without his voluminous white robe he'd have been a mountain of a man. We began our dialogue, through our interpreter and with a good deal of flowery flattery. I heard myself talking but couldn't believe it was me speaking. I felt as though my lines were being written for me and that I was playing a part, perhaps in an episode of a TV series about big business negotiating with an unnamed Arab potentate for the oil rights. In fact what we were really talking about was permission to film in this highly lethal country with some assurance that we wouldn't get chopped up.

'Please tell His Excellency the Sultan that he has a truly exciting' (understatement of the millennium) 'country here.'

Long pause till this is encoded into Afar.

Much chubby smiling from His Excellency and a cascade of words about half the length of the Koran.

Shorter pause while this is decoded into English.

'His Excellency thanks you and wishes you to feel welcome.'

Somehow we kept this verbal knock-up going for about ten minutes. I began to worry about the alarm clock. Would it go off while we were still tiptoeing through the conversational tulips?

We next exchanged lengthy compliments about our respective countries including such insincerities as: 'Please tell the Sultan we expect to see him in London one day.' (Later, I discovered that this might, indeed, have come about. Mitchell Cotts had already flown him to Nairobi in their Aztec and were seriously considering a diplomatic pilgrimage to Claridges.)

The Sultan gallantly addressed extravagant compliments to my wife, so much so that I wondered whether he was considering her as a possible addition to his harem. This took another five minutes, after which the Sultan clapped his hands and summoned a bowing servant. Would we like coffee? We reacted with only partially assumed delight. Perhaps coffee was the signal for really getting down to business. Coffee arrived in small half-gourds. It was heavily flavoured with ginger. Beyond and behind this, however, was an even more distinctive yet not immediately identifiable flavour. It was only later that I discovered what gave the coffee its special edge. The Sultan's kitchen staff often scoured out their crocks with camel urine.

That alarm clock never did go off. In the final ten minutes we got it all sorted out with unexpected despatch. The Sultan actually wanted the outside world to know about his country. I believe the fact that Mitchell Cotts had widened his outlook by foreign travel was largely responsible for our good fortune. Not only did he approve of our proposition but he guaranteed Dieter a safe-conduct and detailed his nephew to keep him company wherever he went in the Kingdom of the Afars. The Sultan's assumption was that wherever his nephew went, there, in effect, the Sultan went and, since no one dared touch the Sultan, no one would dare lay a finger on Dieter. This turned out very nearly to be the case with one or two highly unpleasant exceptions. Alas, the Sultan's nephew could not always be in attendance.

There were bigger surprises yet. When the audience was over, the Sultan led my wife out into the courtyard where the villainous body-guard at once prostrated themselves. At this point she confounded all male chauvinist theories by producing a camera and asking the Sultan whether he would permit a picture to be taken of this historic meeting. That's how the only still picture of the Sultan of the Afars came to be taken.

I said that this was Dieter Plage's hardest assignment. Many projects later I still believe this to be true. We should never have asked him to operate alone in the Danakil Depression. Depression, of course, refers to the fact that the country lies in the northern end of the Great Rift Valley of Africa before the valley becomes the Red Sea. Some of the Depression in the area of the salt lake called Karum, where Dieter filmed the Danakil salt-cutters, is four hundred feet below sea level with an infernal temperature to match. Depression also sums up Dieter's state of mind at the end of three solitary months in this wilderness. The hostility of the warrior nomads was almost a tangible thing. Sometimes, despite the presence of the Sultan's nephew, the Danakil men refused to be filmed or to let their women be filmed and threw rocks as a preliminary form of discouragement. The basic hostility to strangers of these beautiful and, among themselves, carefree and happy people is sometimes explained by their need to keep others away from their slender water resources. There exist elaborate rituals concerning who may use the infrequent water-holes and in what pecking order. It is even said that the taking of testicles as trophies is a practical as well as symbolic way of indicating that the opposition will be more acceptable if there are fewer of them.

Dieter Plage was threatened many times during the long weeks it took him to shoot all the film needed for a one-hour Special. He came nearest to a very unpleasant end when filming, unescorted, warriors at a thermal pool which sent up roaring clouds of steam from the desert. Dieter wanted a shot zooming in on the steam just as it parted to reveal a particularly hostile Danakil face. He got his shot but the owner of the face took grave exception to the liberty and, with two or three friends, proposed to throw cameraman and camera into the boiling water. Fortunately tribesmen who knew Dieter and were friendly to him arrived and the opposition withdrew.

My plan was that Dieter should shoot, as far as circumstances allowed, in a way that would best illustrate the remarkable journey of discovery made by Wilfred Thesiger in 1934.

Wilfred Thesiger agreed to be filmed on one of his twice-yearly visits to London. The rest of the year he spends making a walking safari in some remote part, often the Northern Frontier District of Kenya. But when in London his daily routine includes a stroll from his mother's London residence to the Explorers Club. For this promenade he wears the uniform of the complete patrician clubman, with bowler hat from Lock's and carrying rolled umbrella. We filmed him thus for the opening of 'The Forbidden Desert of the Danakil', walking down St James's Street, pausing to look through the famous hatter's window. We then cut from his neat black shoes at pavement level as he walked to his club to the naked footsteps of a Danakil walking with his cattle to a water-hole.

That film and the conditions under which it was shot sum up Dieter Plage's single-mindedness and endurance. *Survival* was especially pleased for his sake that it was a success throughout the world and, most of all, on American network television.

As with the Karamojong, Aubrey Buxton's premonition had been right. The Afar and their way of life have since been virtually obliterated. The Ethiopian revolution deposed the Sultan who fled to Muslim friends across the Red Sea. Four hundred Araf were massacred by government forces from Addis in one battle. The Sultan's palace is

8

today full of holes made by machine guns, tanks and bazookas. There are telephone poles in the market square at Asaita. The Danakil, probably the most hostile people in Africa, certainly one of the most handsome and, in some strange way, the most attractive, must be placed on the list of endangered human sub-species. It is no consolation to them, though great satisfaction to us, that some of their ways have been preserved on film.

Chapter 10

Meanwhile in Park Lane

PEOPLE often ask us how wildlife cameramen succeed in getting their remarkable pictures of animals in action. There are no magic answers and the clues are scattered throughout this book. High on the list of the qualities they need is patience, patience along with physical endurance and ability to ignore hardships and dangers such as a mamba sharing one's hide, as happened to Dieter Plage in the Okavango Swamps, Botswana. But many other kinds of excellent film cameramen share these qualities, among them newsreel operators working in trouble spots. What is special, therefore, about a naturalist movie photographer?

A wildlife cameraman would get nowhere if he did not understand the habits of the creature which is his subject. Not only must he know when and where it can be expected to hunt or display, nest or rear its young, but he must be able to film it so that its behaviour remains entirely natural. Shots of spooked animals may be exciting, but they are only too evidently shots of creatures that have been alarmed. It follows then that he, or she, must be an experienced practical field naturalist. The cameraman cannot be an expert on every wildlife subject, any more than can the writer or producer of the wildlife programme. But once he understands the ground rules of animal behaviour and ecology it is relatively easy to move from one wildlife situation to another. Provided he, and the programme, maintain faith with scientists and other experts at all times, the latter are usually willing to give the expert advice necessary and even to reveal the results of field knowledge that may have taken them years to acquire. Often, and quite rightly, the scientists require a fee for their assistance, but *Survival* never quibbles at that. Why should one expect to pick anyone's brains for nothing?

The chance of the unusual scene when it comes is unlikely to be repeated. Equipment needs to be faultlessly maintained and backed up by reserve equipment in equally good shape, by no means easy to achieve in conditions of sun, dust, humidity, drenching rain or below zero frost. Specialized equipment plays a part, but not too often. When filming the Special 'Tiger, Tiger' in the jungles of Chitawan, Nepal, Dieter Plage obtained remarkable scenes of tigers on a kill in total darkness by using a device called an image-intensifier which enables an ordinary camera lens to 'see' on the darkest night. The need for such fancy equipment is rare. The normal gear, a full range of wide-angle and telephoto lenses, including motorized zoom lenses, is all that is usually required, though, I have said elsewhere, there may be as much as £40,000 invested in the outfit.

So, in the end, there is no substitute for wildlife knowledge, technical film expertise, the capacity for taking pains and sheer personal organization.

Though everything begins and ends with the wildlife cameramen in the field, there is a lot more to making a natural history film than shooting the footage. Without the skill and technique of the team back at base, the cameraman's work would remain simply a pile of exposed film. It is said that no one ever looks at the credits on a film except the people who appear on them. To the latter that forty seconds when their names come up at the end is the most important footage of all. There's some truth in this. Credits on TV films are usually mercifully short but all the people concerned with the production better be there – or else.

Survival is a team job. Many of our editors have worked with us almost from the beginning but, of course, there are changes from time to time. So in considering what happens to make a natural history film back at base, I will refer to the rôles as they appear on the credits rather than to individual people.

In the *Survival* unit it is the writer's job to shape the show. His name is the first one to come up on end credits. In close collaboration with the cameraman he will have started the project off with a story treatment. This sets down the ideal, or at least probable, story shape, describing highlights, special episodes that the team hopes to cover. The writer knows only too well that it is impossible to write a complete scenario for a wildlife film.

The moment the first processed rushes arrive, the writer views the camera original to judge it from a story and content viewpoint. The technical manager or his assistant joins this session to look for camera or stock faults, exposure or camera operation problems. A cameraman sitting on a hot rock in the middle of a desert wants technical information almost more than story and contents guidance.

As he views the camera original on a viewing machine called a

Steenbeck, guaranteed not to scratch or damage this precious source material, the writer selects the sections he wants printed. The coloured work-print that the labs produce from the selection is the material with which he and the editors will eventually work in cutting the film. Selection is necessary because of the high shooting ratios and the cost of printing every single foot that is shot. If he is lucky, the writer, who, of course, is a naturalist as well as a film-maker, is helped by detailed shotlists supplied by the cameraman – if the latter has had time. This is easier if the cameraman has a wife or assistant. Imagine, though, a day spent at 130°F. in the Danakil Desert, followed by the need to type out, in a sand-blasted tent, the details, scene by scene, roll by roll, of five thousand feet of recently exposed film.

Naturally, in making his selection the writer is often wrong. He misses some key piece of action or fails to print a sequence that will later prove valuable or even vital. It has been known for a writer to reject a scene to get which the cameraman risked his neck!

What happens to rejected material, which perhaps amounts to as much as one third of the whole? It is reviewed at least once before the picture is finally cut. If, as often happens in the case of a one-hour Special, the cameramen returns to Britain to advise in the final stages of cutting, then these 'out-takes', as they are called, are combed through several times. All the shots which the cameraman loves best and which have so far been omitted are printed up at great cost. Some of them even get into the finished picture!

These thousands upon thousands of feet that are not used in the original production eventually find their way into the library where they are logged, catalogued and stored to be sold as stock shots or used in future productions. At the moment of writing, the *Survival* library amounts to at least four million feet, much of which is material that can never be repeated.

So the writer and the technicians report back on the rushes to the cameraman by cable, telex, letter, or, if all else fails, by putting a note in a bottle. The cameraman, probably justifiably, complains that no one ever tells him anything in time. Communications, or lack of them, are the bugbear of our business.

On a one-hour project, rushes may easily build up over a period of a year. All the time the writer is storing away memories of the material, doing the research, making suggestions to the cameraman. In the case of a major project he is likely to visit the cameraman in the field. Finally, the moment comes when both writer and cameraman are convinced they've got the story. It is ready for the film editor.

The writer's task now is to produce an editing treatment. *Survival*'s film editors are first-class craftsmen but they are not, nor are they supposed to be, naturalists. The editing treatment from which they work must describe sequence by sequence, shot by shot if necessary, how they will cut the picture. Of course, the editor exercises his own creative skill inside this general framework. A half-hour *Survival* film actually runs for around twenty-five minutes to allow time for commercials. The cut film is about 920 feet long and may contain anything between 200 and 350 individual shots or cuts made by the editor.

Writer and editor confer as often as necessary during the cutting process, which may take anything up to three weeks. At the end of that time, the editor comes up with a rough-cut, which is, with luck, anything from five to ten minutes over length. This is the time for the writer to see where he went wrong, to rearrange scenes, switch sequences, bring in additional material, or just occasionally, decide that he made a mistake and that there isn't a complete story after all. The latter should never happen – though it has to be admitted that it occasionally does. Since *Survival* is a complex operation working to strict deadlines in order to produce up to twenty-five half-hours and six one-hour Specials a year, such a miscalculation is a disaster.

When writer, editor and producer (writer and producer are sometimes the same person) are satisfied, they have a fine-cut. The writer sits down with the cutting copy of a picture he may have wet-nursed for as long as a year and writes his commentary. Many people think that this is all that 'writing' a film involves. It involves all the creative processes I have described so far. The actual words of the commentary, though crucial, are merely the coat of paint the writer applies to the house he and the picture editor have painstakingly built. I personally find that by this stage I have lived with the picture so long – in company, it is true, with perhaps half a dozen other projects in various stages of construction – that when I sit down to write the commentary the words are practically ready to spill out on paper. All the research has long ago been done, all the information received from the camera team been absorbed, most of the scenes or shots that suggest commentary lines have already occurred to me. After that it is like completing a fascinating video-audio jigsaw in which eye and ear must be attuned to the rival needs and impact of picture, words, sound effects and music.

When he is happy with the result – and by now he is usually working against the clock – the writer goes into the studio and records his own commentary to picture. This is of great practical benefit to a number of people including the producer. The writer also learns a great deal from the exercise, for example where his commentary is too full, too scanty, not explicit enough, over-explicit, fails to hit picture, will clash with music or obliterate an important sound effect. This pilot commentary enables him to go back and take the bumps out of his work.

Now the finalized colour cutting copy is sent to the labs for a black and white 'dupe' of the entire picture to be made overnight. The dupe is what the dubbing editor will work with. His job is to lay sound effects from first frame to last. Natural history cameramen do not shoot 'synch', or synchronized, sound. Their film is 'mute'. Therefore each sound, from the rustle of a blade of grass to the roar of a lion, has to be laid separately to picture. This means creating a complete and separate effects track which exactly matches the action. To do this for a film involving human action is painstaking enough. With a wildlife film there are added complications. It is not enough to tell an editor that a certain sequence demands an atmosphere that includes the calls of, say, curlew, mallard and snipe. Birds tend to make different noises at different seasons. The call made by a curlew in the breeding season on a Scottish hillside is by no means the same as the sound it makes when feeding on a winter estuary. There is the danger, too, that a given recording will contain some additional natural sound that could not possibly occur in the scene in question. Once again it is the writer's or researcher's job to make sure that the dubbing editor is correctly advised. Sometimes it means shopping round the world for an effect. Wildlife camera teams provide as many of the appropriate natural effects as possible, but there are inevitably gaps. The camera rather than the sound-recorder always has first claim on their attention. Sometimes the writer has to ensure that some effects are left out. Editors can't be blamed for believing that every time an animal opens its mouth it makes a noise. Animals, on the whole, are pretty silent and call, bark, grunt or whistle for specific purposes. Some of the best wing-flap sounds in the wildlife film business have been made by dubbing editors vigorously shaking raincoats in recording studios. Alas, most birds are silent flappers, even at take-off. The wildlife experts in the unit have had to ask sound editors to remove enough wing-flaps to fill a cutting room or equip several vultures for life.

The dubbing editor is also concerned with the writer and producer when it comes to music. I have already covered this aspect in some detail. At an early stage, the writer and producer must make up their minds whether the picture needs music and if so whether it should be specially composed and recorded, or should they use library music? If the latter, then this calls for collaboration with one of the librarians from the big commercial music companies. These specialists are musicians themselves and enormously knowledgeable. The whole range of classics is usually available. Most of the best film and TV composers have written and recorded for the music libraries, themes, even whole works, to suit almost any mood and action. A skilful music editor can often adapt these by cutting bars or even whole passages. This rarely does the job as well as music specially written to fit picture, but it sometimes works brilliantly even for a Special. The resounding and emotive 'big theme' music used in 'The Passing of Leviathan', *Survival*'s whale Special narrated by Orson Welles, came from a library disc.

While dubbing editor and composer are doing their work, a narrator will have been chosen and the commentary recorded. With regular *Survival* narrators this is usually recorded to picture. The narrator speaks the commentary while the picture is being run. With a few minor adjustments made later by the dubbing editor, the commentary should fit exactly. With modern 'rock-and-roll' recording equipment it is easy to erase 'fluffs' or re-record unsatisfactory passages as you go along. The sound recordist simply rolls picture and synchronized magnetic tape back and then wipes the old stuff as he re-records.

None of this happens by accident. It all calls for a great deal of co-ordination and staff work. That's the job of the general manager and his assistants. So is the contracting of artists, musicians and studios and so on. All this is covered by the credit 'Production Supervised by . . .'

One operation that never appears on the credits is that of the neg-cutter. The moment the colour cutting copy is finalized, and about the time the dubbing editor gets his black and white dupe made from this, the cutting copy is sent to the neg-cutter along with all the cans of camera original containing material for the project. This may mean anything from ten to thirty or more cans, each one of which contains two eight-hundred-foot rolls of original. Some of these cans may not have been shot for this actual film. The writer may have culled one or two scenes from the backlog of four million feet in the *Survival* library. Any single eight-hundred-foot roll can contain just one shot, perhaps

Cameraman swims with forty-foot humpback whale in the clear waters off Hawaii. The one-hour Special, 'Humpbacks: The Gentle Giants', portrayed the life of the humpback whale in its tropical breeding waters as well as on the feeding grounds off Alaska. The humpbacks are often known as the singing whales. The film analysed the pattern and meaning of the songs that they sing only on the warm water breeding grounds. The song is almost certainly to do with mating and the sounds are made only by the males.

Overleaf: An Afar tribesman of the Danakil desert of Ethiopia silhouetted by Lee Lyon's camera against the sun that makes the region one of the hottest and driest on earth. Lee acted as Dieter's assistant during the latter part of the hazardous Danakil filming. As a girl she was probably in far less danger from the fiercely hostile Danakil, since their distrust of intruders and their desire to take 'trophies' from their enemies is directed almost entirely against the male rather than the female.

only three feet long, that the writer has insisted on in his editing treatment. To find individual shots on such tiny stuff as 16mm film sounds impossible. So it would be but for the fact that at frequent intervals the edge of 16mm film is marked with minute key numbers. None of these numbers is ever repeated by Kodak who manufacture the film. Even so, finding a shot by the key numbers would be quite impossible but for the fact that the *Survial* film librarians log every camera roll by its key numbers when it first arrives from the labs. Despite the key number system, the neg-cutter still has to match the editor's cuts, to the frame, by eye.

All of these technical operations, of course, are standard to any film production and not just a wildlife one. So is the dubbing session at which all the tracks – commentary, natural effects and music – are balanced against each other and a final mixed track produced. A music and effects track, without the narrator, is also made at the same time. This is for foreign versions where a narrator's voice will later be added in the language of the country concerned.

From the moment the last foot of film is received until the first transmission copy comes from the laboratory occupies a gestation period of at least six weeks. And that, minus a crisis or two, for which no one gets a credit, is how a *Survival* programme is born.

Previous page: Kasimir, the dominant male gorilla, 'in command' of the group of twenty-two mountain gorillas who were the subject of 'Gorilla', filmed by Dieter Plage. At first Kasimir charged the camera repeatedly but gradually came to accept Plage as being part of Adrien Deschryver's own gorilla 'family.' There is little doubt that Kasimir saw Deschryver, the founder of Kahuzi-Biega National Park in Zaire, as another gorilla like himself, albeit an inferior one. Kasimir's broken, stump-like teeth showed that he was at least thirty years old. He died soon after the filming was completed.

'Orangutan, Orphans of the Forest' portrayed the work of two attractive Swiss scientists, Regina Frey and Monica Borner, and their successful attempts to rehabilitate captive orangs at Bohorok in Sumatra and return them to the wild in a forest reserve. The location was made difficult by the intense humidity of the rain forest. At the end of three months, the camera team's tent and clothes had rotted. Mildew had even begun to appear between the elements of the camera lenses. The rewards were scenes like this of the most attractive and peaceful of the great apes.

Chapter 11

Beaver Special

UNTIL 1968, the one-hour Special had not played much part in our planning. When it had occurred, as in 'The Enchanted Isles' or 'Karamoja' it had been because the subject merited the full-length treatment, the best reason of all for making a one-hour production. Now we found ourselves increasingly interested in the one-hour format, first for our prime commitment to ITV and secondly for overseas sales.

For both purposes we had an immediate front-runner. Des and Jen Bartlett were filming beavers in the Teton Mountains of Wyoming. Their footage was something very special. Much of it had been shot underwater in a crystal-clear beaver pond. Clear *and* cold! Sometimes Des had to break the ice before he could swim underwater with the beavers. Even when wearing a cold-water wet-suit, he got so frozen that Jen had to revive him with massage and sweet sherry whenever he surfaced! The footage was far too good – and costly – to throw away in one half-hour. Our aim was to make a one-hour Special for Britain that could follow up the success of 'The Enchanted Isles' as a US network sale. Aubrey and I flew to New York to sell the idea.

Our allies at J. Walter Thompson in New York were impressed. The fun and character of the beaver material caught their imagination. They could see how this one might work out. Beavers were empathetic. People could identify with them. They were enthusiastic about the beaver as a solid, industrious, *useful* (as indeed it is) animal with which a solid, industrious, useful company like Quaker Oats (who had sponsored 'The Enchanted Isles') would be pleased to be associated.

A vital meeting with the top Quaker men was set up for three days' time in Chicago. Aubrey, who had been in New York for the initial discussions, had to return home. Jack Ball of J. Walter Thompson was to come to hold my hand. In the meantime I flew down to Thunderhead Ranch, Tucson, with Des, to work out in the peace of the Arizona Desert how a beaver Special should go.

Two days later I flew direct to Chicago. We had a brief, dynamic meeting in the J. Walter Thompson offices with the dynamic Quaker executives. They certainly empathized with the beavers. Bill Hylan of JWT, drove me direct from that meeting to the airport. The plane was about closing its doors as we arrived but Pan Am generously held it for me while I checked in. When I boarded the 707 I was under the impression that we had sold a beaver Special.

Des Bartlett started filming beavers straight away. He had to. It was now May. All the additional material would need to be in our cutting rooms by the end of October if we were to be ready for a US network transmission in mid-January. It was an ambitious schedule. Des and I had agreed that we would follow the year-round complete story of a pair of beavers from the moment they were born in a beaver lodge, through the time they were driven away from their home pond by their parents as two-year-olds, until they paired, built a lodge and dam and had kits of their own. This meant that Des had to cover all aspects of the beaver year, including over-wintering, which meant more filming under the ice, predation, or anyway attempted predation, by grizzly bear, eviction of two-year-olds by parents, dam-building and repair – to name but a few of the outstanding sequences needed to complete the story. Since time was so limited, it meant that the Bartletts would have to film from Alaska to Wyoming in order to cover all the seasons. It also meant that they were going to have to acquire quite a large cast of beaver stars and understudies. Most of the new material, such as dam-building and repair, cutting and storing food, entering the lodge under the ice, would be shot in the wild as it happened. All the close stuff of the central beaver characters could best be obtained by filming tame beavers. I have discussed earlier the purist arguments against this. My own reaction is that, since one beaver looks exactly like another and since we would not be trying to persuade the featured players to do anything other than they would do in the wild, there could be no possible objection to it.

I then did something I had never done before and which has made me shudder ever since. I gave the two main beaver characters names. As I thought about the story I started mentally to label the male beaver 'Castor' after the beaver's scientific name, *Castor castoreum*. After this it was but a short if fatal step to look for a name for his mate. I hit upon an Indian word for beaver – Amik.

Amazingly, the filming went to schedule. Des even shot a grizzly trying to break into a beaver lodge. I am not particularly ashamed to say that I knew this grizzly quite well. This enormous and comparatively docile creature was called Willie and belonged to a friend of the Bartletts called Dick Robinson – another bit of 'controlled' shooting that was more than counterbalanced by the incredible wild scenes the film contained. Des was due to come to England for the final production stages to pick up any last minute errors. I sent him a draft commentary script and got this reply: 'So far I have read your story about thirty times, and so know it off by heart. It may shock you to know Colin that you have written a perfect Disney script: you could not have done better if you had been working for Disney for twenty years.'

I felt aggrieved at the time. Today I am in no mood to disagree. It was true. Though all the information in the beaver special was authentic, I have always felt since that we had definitely crossed the anthropomorphic boundary.

Later in the same letter came some fascinating information about the sort of controlled shooting necessary to complete the project.

> It took me seven and a half days to make the suitable lodge interior, using beaver-cut logs, grass and mud and the beaver-made bedding of stripped wood. It also included the water plunge. Over the whole thing I made a plywood blind, filming through a hole in a black cloth to get the candid shots of the beavers inside the lodge. We started with our original pair, then switched to two similar beavers with two tiny four-day-old kits. We got a mass of nursing scenes, Colin, plus the little chaps diving into the water for a swim and learning how to dive and leave the lodge. If they stayed too long in the water, mum, or dad, would pick them up in her mouth – supporting their weight with both hands – and carry the kit up into the lodge to dry off. Later I did other scenes with six-week-old kits to show them growing up. Also did the original family where the big old momma has five tiny fourteen-day-old kits. This should come at the start of the story where the two-year-old is driven out to start life on his own.

'The World of the Beaver' had one more stage to pass through. With 'The Enchanted Isles', little conversion, beyond a change of narrator's voice, had been needed for the States. Now, with the guidance of our new colleague Jack Ball and with all the considerable muscle of J. Walter Thompson, New York, aiding us, we were in for the full treatment. We discovered that the show had to have a big-name narrator, not because it needed a star actor to give a boost to the production but because any Special needs a well-known name to make it promotable. The key journal in this respect is a small magazine called *TV Guide*. This contains details of all main TV programmes and has an influence quite disproportionate to its size. Make the cover of *TV Guide* or merit a one-page feature inside and you are half-way to commanding a very large audience. But we in London soon learned we had little chance of picking the right narrator for an American network show. For 'World of the Beaver', J. Walter

Thompson and Quaker picked Henry Fonda. Apart from being a fine actor with a delightful and recognizable voice, our American allies saw him as having the right folksy, down-to-earth image for the beaver. Maybe the fact that he once played Abraham Lincoln, who, of course, wore a beaver hat, had something to do with it. The beaver hat and Abraham Lincoln – much to my surprise – eventually played a prominent part in the film commentary.

Winston Churchill, I believe, described America and Britain as 'two great cultures separated by a common language'. His epigram certainly applies to TV documentaries. The narration as written for the United Kingdom and other English-speaking countries is not necessarily understandable in the United States. Take the word 'route'. As pronounced in Britain, this means to an American something that grows at the base of a tree. As pronounced in America, 'route' means a serious reverse in battle – to the British.

Aside from mere words, there are whole phrases, modes of expression and thought that just do not translate. There are also subtle differences of approach and emphasis, not to mention changes of programme format, that demand a separate, or anyway different, commentary. All of which means that you need an American translator, or writer. The writer recommended to us from J. Walter Thompson was a very bright young man called Frank Gannon. Frank had already written several books of a political or historical nature that had been critically acclaimed. He had also carried out historical research for Randolph Churchill. He was about to spend a sabbatical year seconded to the Nixon administration at the White House. Frank is, at this moment, I am sure, working on one hell of a book about the Watergate days. Knowing his talents, I am certain it will be widely praised for its political and human insight. I have to add, though, that Frank is a self-confessed non-naturalist. I had given him a lead with my Castor and Amik characterization of the beavers. Frank simply compounded the felony with lines like: 'I think it was Abraham Lincoln who said that the beaver has everything that a man needs to live a happy life: intelligence, ingenuity, a peaceful nature and a good set of teeth.'

Henry Fonda's narration was recorded in the USA. These days we would insist on the narrator recording an alternative version, whole or in part, for Britain and the rest of the world. Henry Fonda spoke the narration with great style. Just the same, I would be happy even now to record a straighter, less folksy version than the one for which Frank Gannon and I were jointly culpable. Nevertheless, 'The World of the Beaver' was a great success on US network television. It earned that rare accolade for a wildlife Special, a re-run, or repeat. We had achieved our second US network showing.

Chapter 12

Flight of the Snowgeese

FROM the moment I started planning this book I decided to tell in detail the story of how one *Survival* Special was made. There can be no other choice than 'Snowgoose'.

Both Aubrey and I have an obsession with wildfowl. Both of us had for a long time been fascinated by snowgeese. My interest in snowgeese as a *Survival* subject was stirred in 1969 when Des Bartlett visited the Sacramento Refuge in California and filmed masses of snowgeese at the southern end of their range on the Pacific flyway. Des knew my fanatical interest in the geese. We began to talk to each other about a goose migration Special.

There was nothing very original about the basic idea. We had discussed it many times in *Survival* with other migratory birds in mind, notably European storks. The idea was this: we would treat the birds like an airline. Everywhere they called in, some fresh drama would overtake the 'passengers', dramas that they could expect to meet in the natural order of things. At one stop-over, hunters might claim some of their number; at another, scientists would rocket-net a batch; at yet another, ice and snow would force them onwards.

We studied flyways. Despite the fact that Des already had experience of the Pacific flyway, he plumped for the central flyway from Hudson Bay to the Mississippi Delta, mainly because the Arctic breeding grounds, difficult to reach at the best of times, were slightly more accessible on that route. The many good friends Des had won in the American and Canadian wildlife services now came to his help. One of these advised Des that the breeding colony which he could best reach was one in the region of the McConnell River, half-way up the west shore of Hudson Bay. One of the advantages of this situation was that another good scientist friend of the Bartletts, Charlie MacInnes of the University of Western Ontario, had a study base there which included a wooden hut where he housed the half dozen students who spent spring and summer on the tundra with him. It was the only dwelling for hundreds of miles. The Bartletts would have to live in tents, but Charlie would not only store their food for them but bulk-buy their supplies with his own.

One of the areas in which advice was most needed was that concerning the legal catching or collection of wild birds. On to our original migration story we had now grafted an additional element and one which I personally believed would make it a superb Special. The idea was that Des should collect a number of snowgoose goslings on the tundra, hand-rear them and band them with coloured rings so that they would be recognizable in flight. He would then bring them down the flyway with the wild skeins in order to film them flying free. As a goose man I should certainly have realized that the chances of finding and filming our banded geese among the thousands on the flyway would be very small.

The whole onus of preparation fell on the Bartletts. From their base at Thunderhead Ranch, Tucson, Arizona, they had to plan what amounted to a long-range military operation. To reach the breeding grounds, they'd first have to drive two and half thousand miles to The Pas, the last railhead in Canada. There they'd load their Land Rover and Chevy station wagon on box cars for freighting north to Churchill. At Churchill stores and camera team would rely on a single-engined Otter ski-plane to take them into the McConnell. The geese arrive on the McConnell River in late May and leave around the end of July. By that time they have, in the short Arctic spring and summer, reared a hundred thousand youngsters who must be ready to fly south with them.

The tundra around the McConnell River is not exactly a home from home. In May, the temperature is so low that a glass of water put down outside a tent freezes solid in a few minutes. Ski-planes can get in so long as the snow lasts. When it thaws, a long canoe journey is the only way in or out. The nearest town, Churchill, whose main street is raided in summer time by polar bears, is 150 miles away. Once you're in on the McConnell River, therefore, you're *in* and your supplies and stores had better be in with you.

With a normal film unit, a production manager back in London, or New York, or somewhere remote and comfortable, would be responsible for the logistics. But not with a wildlife camera team and especially not with the Bartletts. All the planning, provisioning, diplomacy was done by them and them alone, for the very good reason that they were the only people who knew what they'd need. They were also the only people they themselves would trust to see that it was all there. They'd need some extra hands up on the tundra so Des contacted his nephew

Les, who was working nine to five in a bank in Australia. Les needed little persuasion. Nor did the fourth member of the group, the beautiful Californian girl Lee Lyon. Des wanted someone who was sympathetic with animals to handle the young snowgeese he intended to collect and tame. Lee had a great love and feeling for the outdoors and wildlife. She had a cheerful, outgoing nature and great strength of character. She had accompanied the Bartletts on a previous expedition to Baja California from which two *Survivals*, 'The Sea of Cortez' and 'The Richest Sea in the World' had come. Aboard the Bartletts' boat in the Sea of Cortez (otherwise known as the Gulf of California) she'd shown a talent for still photography. Lee needed no persuasion either.

The expedition intended to take it easy on the long drive up the USA and Canada. In Ontario, while still 500 miles from The Pas, Des phoned Charlie MacInnes to report progress. Charlie had bad news. There was an exceptionally early thaw. Soon there wouldn't be enough snow on the tundra for the plane to land at the McConnell. Once it went, there would be no way of flying in the Bartletts and their equipment that season. Des had just twenty-four hours to make the railhead at The Pas. The relaxed journey was over. By driving in shifts, day and night, there was just a chance they could make the train. They eventually drove into the railway station and loaded the vehicles into box cars with half an hour to spare. Twenty-three hours and six hundred miles later they were in Churchill. There they worried about the number of trips the single Otter would have to make. The total weight of cameras, camping gear for four months and four people was 2,500 pounds. This meant that they would have to make it in two lifts. With luck, the pilot said, the snow would last that long.

As Des flew north in the Otter over the tundra he caught his first glimpse of the snowgeese flying north beneath him. Des and Jen Bartlett's story of those four months of isolation in the Canadian Arctic is best told from the letters they wrote me, some of which relied on irregular posting by Eskimos on dog sleds. The first to reach me was dated 7 June 1971.

Dear Colin,

At just below freezing the typewriter does not want to behave and I must admit there is a stiffness in my fingers also. Perhaps I need to clear a little rust from the brain also – in a tundra setting it is hard to tune in to other ways of life and trains from Walton-on-Thames to Waterloo and crowded underground stations . . .

Jen recently wrote a family letter: part of this covers things well and would give you our news and so I can be lazy and quote from her letter. So here goes:

The success of 'Gorilla'
depended entirely on the
skill, knowledge and
patience of Adrien
Deschryver, the originator
and founder of Kahuzi-Biega
National Park for mountain
gorillas in Zaire. Adrien
took Dieter Plage and his
assistant Lee Lyon into the
forest with him every single
day for six months to
obtain the film they needed.
In the centre picture Adrien
'talks' with Kasimir,
dominant silverbacked male
of a family group of
twenty-two gorillas.
Kasimir's silver back, the
sign of full adulthood, shows
clearly as he crosses a park
track.

To film the great white pelicans of Lake Shala, Ethiopia, at water level, Dieter Plage had to turn himself and his camera into a pelican. The disguise, borrowed from the zoology department of Addis Ababa University, floated on an inflated inner tube. Dieter's head went inside the dummy pelican. The device succeeded so well that young birds even came up to be fed. Though Dieter wore a wet suit, the soda content of Lake Shala removed most of his skin during the forty hours he spent in the water.

The first six days here were pretty cold, with nights near zero and the days not reaching freezing, and always an icy wind blowing at ten to twenty mph. Getting up in the mornings in a freezing tent isn't easy! But we have been plenty warm enough at night in our down sleeping bags – Des and I have a double 'mummy bag' with seventy-two ounces of goose-down filling; mighty cold to get into but it soon warms up. So we are pretty well set up for the cold, but won't be sorry when it warms up a bit more! Putting the tents up wasn't too difficult, as we didn't actually have to dig the snow away first because of the early thaw – the tent site was already just clear, but with snow all around. Main reason it is impossible to use tent pegs here is because of the permafrost and rocky ground. So our tent is tied to piles of rocks. It wasn't easy to gather them either even though there were plenty around, for they were all frozen to the ground! We haven't yet had a really strong wind (over thirty mph) but hope the tents will stand up to it . . .

The last few days we haven't even had to break the ice at the river's edge to wash our faces in the morning, but it will probably freeze a bit again in the next cold snap. Good to use a toothbrush that isn't frozen solid too! (The water on a toothbrush would freeze almost instantly when we first arrived, and a glass would freeze on a rock when you put it down: great fun!) . . .

The 'Snowgoose' filming is going well and incubation is now the order of the day. From one blind recently we filmed a sandhill crane raiding a nest and eating the eggs, which is quite a nugget even though it was filmed after it had clouded over and there was a very strong wind blowing. Fortunately Lee was with me at the time so she was able to hold the tent back at the side so that I could film at a very odd angle towards the back of the blind where the action was taking place – without the flapping of the canvas being conveyed to the camera. On the same day Les found a crane's nest and moved a blind over to this. So we are all set to film this as soon as the weather improves. In the past the cranes have been observed catching and eating ptarmigan young and so we may be able to film this if we are lucky, as well as more predation on the geese. Also the jaegers are now here and starting to raid the geese eggs (also herring gulls), which we plan to film on the first sunny day . . .

It is just a month ago today that we arrived in Churchill and only five weeks since we left Tucson. Hard to believe when so much has happened in that time. There is still a large snow bank out from our camp ridge, but the snow has now disappeared from the flat tundra. Hudson Bay is frozen solid and the delta area of the McConnell River is still under about three feet of ice. The first Arctic terns are

9

now here and will be nesting before too long. It is a very low lemming year, unfortunately. Two chaps are to come later this month, walking the thirty miles down from Eskimo Point. So they will bring in the mail. But when this letter goes out is anyone's guess.

Our very best wishes to you all at Anglia from the four of us,
Jen, Lee, Les and Des

As far as the outside world, including *Survival* was concerned, the Bartletts were now round the dark side of the moon. There was no way of communicating with us until the following September when this next letter came. By then the Bartletts had collected a number of orphaned wildfowl chicks and hand-reared them.

14 September 1971
Dear Colin,

We are now safely out of the McConnell River camp, facing the rigors of civilization at Churchill – which fortunately moves along at the leisurely pace of a frontier town. We remained extremely fit while camping on the tundra and hated to leave. However, we are all rather worn out and trying to catch up on sleep, eating fruit and fresh meat, etc. During the summer, when it never got completely dark, we averaged only four to five hours sleep a night: we would be writing up the film until 12.30 or 1 am and up at 5 am, returning to camp for dinner around 9.30 or 10 pm . . .

I've been able to do quite a bit of helicopter flying while the weather was fine. This covers the aerial scenes of the snowgeese flying across the tundra, along the shore of Hudson Bay, over Churchill – the first sign of man's activity – across the tree line and over the countless lakes dotting the forests. The birds are mainly north of here, feeding along the shore of Hudson Bay, and are likely to remain put until the weather turns really bad. Then some will fly 2,500 miles nonstop in thirty-six hours to arrive on the wintering grounds in Texas and Louisiana . . . The geese jump the Canadian prairie provinces on their way south, stopping off first in North Dakota, where we will once more film them in detail. With the aerial scenes I now have, the pilot had no hesitation in flying the chopper right into the flocks, with the geese breaking off on either side, easily out-manoeuvring the man-made machine . . .

Once we leave here there is no filming to be done in Canada. We now have responsibilities, namely eleven orphaned snowgeese, three blues, one Canadian goose, two greater scaup and one sandhill crane called Fred. So travelling becomes a problem, especially with both vehicles packed to the roof with gear and one towing a trailer – with the above-mentioned 'children'.

With this big family – and all the gear – you can see that travelling is no picnic. We cannot stay at motels as the 'kids' need exercise, a pond to freshen up on, etc., at each main daily stop – and it is the hunting season for geese everywhere we pass through! So our free-flying geese are a big responsibility: we will not be free of the hunting threat until January. Even in Churchill it took us quite a while to get fully organized with our big family. We camped in the Lambair Hangar for a number of days, then moved to set up camp on a lake seven miles east of town at a cabin belonging to the Roman Catholic Mission. So we are now organized . . .

But we are camped in prime polar bear country and therefore have to be prepared to have one in camp at any time of the day or night. All food gets put away in the cars overnight.

It becomes almost impossible to describe in a letter our time at the McConnell River camp. There has been no word from you whether or not you got my long letter from up there: it went out with Eskimos by canoe. I doubt if I have ever filmed a project before where past experience counts so much.

Right from the beginning we used the tame goslings to cut in with the wild action. From a blind we filmed the geese moving their families, only a day or two old, down the river and through the rapids. Wherever we went our geese went also. So I would film a family of snowgeese with four goslings moving into the river, with the little chaps hesitating on the bank before tumbling the foot down into the river: their actual point of plopping into the water would be hidden by the bank. We would then film four of our goslings on the same spot on the bank – with the camera now out in the river – as they plunged one at a time into the river. The action should therefore cut together perfectly: same setting, same lighting, etc.

While they were very small we carried them with us in a cardboard box, but they were soon able to follow along behind almost as fast as we could walk. At the McConnell they grew up having the run of the camp, sleeping outside before they were a month old. They learnt to fly without being caged, following us as before – or flying back to camp from a mile or more away if they got bored. They soon recognized our blinds when we were filming the loons – the last to nest – and would suddenly come flying in to land nearby, jabbering away to us for all they were worth.

We marked out and tidied up an improvised airstrip so that we could fly out with all the gear in a Twin Otter. The geese went into cages for the trip out by plane. Charlie MacInnes, Les and I stayed behind to drive the ARGO, our amphibious vehicle, the thirty miles up to Eskimo Point, as it could not fit in the door of the plane . . .

See you soon . . . With every good wish from the four of us,

Jen, Lee, Les and Des

For the next four months the Bartletts, accompanied by their family of orphaned geese, followed the snowgoose skeins down the central flyway. Meantime sixty thousand feet of film, all told, had reached us. I reported on it in detail to Des as it came through.

3 February 1972
Dear Colin,

Many thanks for your long letter of 24 January, dealing with 'Snowgoose'. It is good to know that you have been through the entire sixty thousand feet again, to refresh your ideas about it.

I've just checked through my camera records to see what you have not seen yet: the footage from De Soto Refuge in Iowa, Squaw Creek Refuge in Missouri, where we did them in a snow-storm, plus the sequences from Tucson – perhaps the most exciting footage of the whole project . . .

At the De Soto Refuge in western Iowa there were three hundred thousand geese when we were there and the population was at its peak. We concentrated on the birds using an oxbow of the old Missouri River as a resting and wash-up stop around 10 am, after their morning feed on farms as much as thirty miles away from the Refuge. We also used the radio-controlled camera under the snow-goose decoy to get intimate scenes amongst the flock. No way of knowing for sure how this turned out until the film is processed: a bird could have its backside over the lens for the entire hundred foot. I now hope to use a small video camera alongside the Arriflex to know what is happening in front of the lens and when to shoot. For the feeding scenes at De Soto we can use some from Sand Lake as everything looks the same.

The next point of call was Squaw Creek Refuge in Missouri, also with about three hundred thousand birds. Here we filmed the birds tumbling as they lost altitude over the pond in the Refuge. Also a snowstorm with the birds on the water. Winter was following them south. And perhaps our best long shots of migration – taken about thirty miles away – as long lines and 'V's' of geese moved over-head, probably travelling from De Soto direct to Texas and Louisiana. I'll go into this tumbling or side-slipping business in detail, plus enclosing a photo of one of our geese doing it alongside the Chevy while we are filming. The stills show that the geese go completely upside down, but their heads remain in a normal flying position in relation to the ground. This happens at Squaw Creek when the birds fly in to the Refuge from outlying areas, crossing surrounding hills . . .

Getting back to our family of geese in the story. As mentioned, it is a pair of adults with four goslings. However, you will notice that I continually built up the story line that one little fellow is always running late – he gets caught up in tiny bushes, has frightening adventures in the rapids, but in the end always catches up. The parents do wait for him, as you will see in the film. This idea is very important to develop in the cutting as it will get the audience involved with our family and immediately feel sorry for the little fellow constantly running late. It gives us a chance to use scenes where only three goslings show with the pair of adults – we then cut to a close-up of the little chap all by himself. Luckily enough, the family of geese having an encounter with the nesting sandhill cranes also had four goslings: guess it is the same little chap that gets tossed up in the air by the sandhill crane when he doesn't keep close enough to his parents . . .

Despite the wonderful footage Des had obtained, I still felt we were missing out somewhere. At the end of March, I wrote to Des about this.

29 March 1972
Dear Des,

I have just finished viewing the superb super-slow-motion footage and am looking forward to seeing the rest.

You ask me what else you should film and this is a fairly hard question to answer. It is easy to be wise by hindsight but I am beginning to feel that what we should have done was to have taken your tame family of geese and followed their story down the flyway, from the moment they were imprinted on the tundra, until their arrival with you and with the wild flocks at the end of the journey. We would then have had the excitement of the wild birds, as well as the exciting personal story of your own adventures. However, you may not agree about this and, anyway, none of us thought of it. But, if only we could tell that story, I am certain we would have a Special.

Despite the breathtaking footage, the making of a Special does have problems. As I outlined in my previous letter, these are:
a) the lack of continuity of your own involvement and –
b) the practical impossibility, which you yourself have pointed out, of following a family of geese down the entire route.

I don't think there is anything that can be done, at this stage, to remedy this; so I think all I can ask, in answer to your letter, is that you complete the journey down the flyway, to the Mississippi, so that we have an end to the story. Whatever happens, we do have a marvellous lot of footage and our problem is going to be to get the maximum out of it.

7 April 1972
Dear Colin,

As you say, it is easy to be wise by hindsight. None of us knew if the tame geese would work out as we hoped: it was rather a far-out scheme to train them to fly behind a speeding car and keep them as free-flying birds in areas that they did not know. But it certainly has worked out perfectly – better than our wildest dreams. I was tempted to film the tiny goslings catching mosquitoes off our legs, but as we did not plan to show the tame geese we stayed off that type of filming entirely. Then when we had trained them to fly behind the car at Tucson, it was too good a sequence to miss: it was far more interesting than just showing slow-motion scenes of snowgeese flying. So I covered this fully. Now on the Refuge here at Sand Lake it looks even better, and I plan to do some behind the scenes filming as well. Here we have a good long run near the marsh – 1.2 miles in length – and I plan to film it from another moving vehicle.

You feel certain that we would have a Special if only we could show the whole story with the tame geese and our moving down the flyway with them. Perhaps this is not altogether impossible. When we come to London we will leave our gear up here, rather than in Tucson. There is a new snowgoose nesting colony at Cape Churchill, which is doing quite well. We could drive to the train in Canada in one day, have one day on the train to Churchill and fly in to the snowgoose nesting colony in a half hour by helicopter from Churchill. The young goslings would be hatching during the last week of June, by which time we could easily be back from England. I feel sure I could get another permit for this, handing the goslings over to the Prairie Waterfowl Research Center at Jamestown when we are finished with them.

With the tame birds we would not need too much. Collecting the hatching eggs would be essential, as would be some cute scenes of raising the little goslings. We could do scenes of swimming with them, which would also be rather attractive – especially as they dive right underwater to swim quite a way before surfacing . . .

Please let me know as soon as possible if you want to go this route with the new baby goslings. I can then start making arrangements before we come over to England. In London we can work on the film together and write up a script for the finished Special which would include all the new scenes required.

In the meantime I'll film our tame geese with this end in view. We could even stage at the US Customs on the border. We told the customs man that we could have crossed the border without the geese and they would fly across from Canada to join us in the States – as their wild brothers and sisters were doing flying across the border. So when we had cleared customs I asked the man if he would like to see some of the geese fly and come back to us. He quickly assured us that he would. The customs men stopped all traffic and I let four of the geese out on the road. They did a beautiful flight, coming down over the customs building to land at our feet. It was really something. Even more funny was the fact that the man who had been so difficult to start with, ended up asking for my autograph. We nearly had a fit! . . .

Is there any chance that you can spare even a few days between now and the first week of May to join us? The whole thing would then fall into place in your mind!

> With every good wish to you all from us both,
> Jen and Des

The penny finally dropped when I read that paragraph about the scene on the Canadian/US border at the customs post. If only we could re-create this and everything that led up to it! Of course, it would mean the collection of a new set of goslings. If Des could go north to the tundra again to film the collection, imprinting, and general rearing of a new set of young birds, which he had omitted to film the previous spring because we had neither of us considered it necessary, then we were in business. For the first time I was convinced that, if we could get these additional scenes, we had not only a Special but a special Special.

I wrote to him about the development of this new line on 13 April.

Dear Des,

For the present, and until we see you, Les Parry will go ahead, editing the material into purely chronological sequences, namely: your journey north; the arrival of the geese; nesting; predation, and so on . . .

Now let's deal with the new thought which we both share enthusiastically: the question of the tame family of geese. Three basic questions arise in my mind immediately and I'm sure you can provide satisfactory answers. In terms of conservation, why should we have found it necessary to adopt a mixed family of a dozen or so geese? Secondly, what is our justification for taking them down the flyway? Thirdly, what do we do with them at the end? In the present climate of American conservation awareness, these are very important questions about which we must make up our minds. Straight away I can think of a few answers, which may not be the right ones. For instance, the geese are orphans, or maybe adopting them has a scientific purpose.

I prefer the orphan idea, perhaps starting with a family of orphans which you and Jen adopt, and then gradually collecting other strays as the nesting period goes along. Having got this 'family' it would be fairly natural to take them south, as they would have a strong attachment to you and no parents to lead them.

But the question still remains: what do you do when you get to Texas? Could they find their own way back, or do we have to present them to some reserve or other? It would be ideal if there was a chance of doing a *Born Free* and sending them back to the wild, to go north again with the wild skeins. But would they have a chance, and would we be justified in taking it? If not, what do we do? Give them a life of security on a reserve?

Next, we come to more immediate filming problems. First, the obvious one of continuity. If we have scenes of Jen inspecting a nest in the present footage, and mean to use this, then she must look the same in future footage. Or do we start again from scratch? Probably the latter. So what is the minimum one would require to film? I would say it is as follows:

1) The actual collection of the waifs and strays.
2) Imprinting them.
3) Rearing them, with various scenes, as you suggest: for instance, swimming with them.
4) Seeing at least a few shots of them at different stages in their life, until they reach flying stage.
5) How they were actually kept in camp.
6) How you travelled with them. The problems of crating them; releasing them at different stops; getting them back. In addition: the splendid scenes you suggest of them crossing the US border at the customs.

As far as the story goes, once you have found yourself saddled with them and more or less forced to take them south, then we tell their story against the background of all the wild material you have. What we need to show is your involvement with them and your anxiety each time you fly them wild and free. Will they come back? Will they get shot by hunters? – and so on.

Already it is looking fairly complicated. Although I share your view that, if we plan carefully, we can probably get away with half a dozen good new scenes.

29 April 1972
Dear Colin,

As you know we originally got the permit for the geese in the hope that we would be able to train them to fly behind the station wagon, but there was no way of knowing in advance if this would be possible. We did not want to raid whole snowgoose nests and so adopted the plan of picking up strays that would have been gobbled up by gulls or jaegers anyway. We would plan to film this type of collection of strays: it is best for the story – and it is actually what we did at the McConnell. As you know geese lay all the eggs before starting incubation: therefore all the goslings emerge about the same time. However, if a few of them wander away from the nest the parents will go off with them, leaving behind a gosling if it is still not quite out of the egg. The gulls and jaegers are ever waiting for such strays.

Having raised the strays we have become, whether we wanted to or not, the parents of the goslings. They are imprinted on us and wherever we go the goslings follow – we are now responsible for their safety and their future.

Around our camp at the McConnell the goslings were free to come and go as they pleased, learning to fly without ever being caged. They would at times fly off with wild snowgeese – once disappearing out of sight over the horizon, but a few hours later they were back in camp. If they were to be any use to us for the slow-motion flying scenes – the reason we collected them in the first place – they just had to remain free-flying, regardless of the risk. At the McConnell we were sure that they knew the area and felt reasonably sure that they would always return to camp. But when we left the McConnell each day would find the geese in a new area, totally unfamiliar to them, and it would certainly be easy for them to become disoriented in the strange surroundings. In order to keep fit it was important for them to fly at least every second day, which proved to be quite a strain on us while travelling . . . However, the geese behaved perfectly; although we did play it safe and only allow four or five to fly at the one time in a new area. And from Churchill, all the way down the flyway, we had hunting season to contend with. At De Soto we did lose four geese: in fact we lost five, but got one back two days later with a pellet wound in its breast. This was Clark Gable – and to this day he is the tamest one of them all: he was really pleased to be back. After this sad incident we restricted their flying until we could get back to Tucson, where there would not be any snowgoose hunting and we could fly them freely on the Thunderhead Ranch.

As you know we have been very concerned about where the geese will end up when our filming project is over. On my original permit I put down Johnny Lynch, with the US Fish and Wildlife Service in Louisiana, as he is breeding waterfowl down there. Another alternative was the Northern Prairie Waterfowl Research Center at Jamestown, North Dakota. This is now our choice: a vast area, plenty of ponds and they could remain free-flying. It is on the fly-way and the geese could revert to the wild should they ever have the inclination. Otherwise they will breed when they are two years old – joining other snows and blues already breeding at Jamestown.

In many ways our geese are already 'living free' as there is just no way for us to get them back when they fly off a few miles out of sight, as they often do. It is up to them whether or not they come back to land with us, as we cannot bring them back. Now that we have decided to film our tame snowgeese this is the one sequence I am hoping to film first, just as soon as the weather permits: driving over to where there are a few thousand wild geese and letting our geese out to have a fly. In other words deliberately giving them a chance to return to the wild flocks. This spring the weather has been terrible and it seems to be getting worse rather than better. We would particularly like to get this sequence in the bag in the States so as not to have to take our tame geese across the border into Canada. We can then arrange to do the customs border-crossing sequence later, without the need to get new permits, vet. certificates, etc. Our geese, of course, now have much more white than they did in October when we made the crossing into the States. However, you are probably not too concerned about this: better to restage the sequence with older birds than to miss it altogether. On the other hand, our new birds would be flying by mid-August and so we could film them 'crossing the border' then . . .

On his way north Des filmed the crucial scene at the customs post and sent me this account of it.

I would be very surprised if you are not greatly excited by some of the new sequences. It includes the Canadian–US Customs sequence, with our tame geese flying back into Canada – and actually disappearing out of sight inside Canada for ten minutes or more, with the customs men firmly convinced that the geese had gone forever heading north. But they did come back, landing with us right at the border post. We then flew them a second time, making sure of good film coverage. So it should be good, with both the Canadian and US flags fluttering wildly in the wind on a clear sunny day.

It was time to be thinking of missing shots that would be vital to the editing. I wrote back:

29 June 1972
Dear Des,

We are now getting our thoughts on 'Snowgoose' pretty well organized and, indeed, have a long rough-cut which only awaits your extra shooting. This rough-cut has enabled us to see certain vital continuity gaps in the story. I am certainly not suggesting any big exercises: in fact most of them can be done on any bit of suitable road, so long as it doesn't identify too closely with any special part of the long route south . . .

We need these in order to keep you and the tame geese in the picture from time to time, during the long sequences in which the wild geese are moving down the flyway. It would be marvellous if one could also have a shot or two of the geese inside their trailer, as if travelling; but I suppose this is not really practical . . .

Now we come to the most important scene of all. The picture just has to have a big finish, or else it falls flat after all the excitement, and the big finish must obviously be the release of the geese. I feel this must be done in an area where there are plenty of wild geese around on the ground and in the sky. We know that most, if not all of them, are going to settle down on a refuge – and the commentary must say so. But I feel, from the point of view of the picture, we have also to leave the audience on the question: 'Will some of them join up with their wild relatives and eventually go on migration with them?' So, whatever else, we do need shots of geese being released and flying off, with wild geese preferably in the sky somewhere near. And, of course, a romantic shot of yourselves looking up into the sky as they go. Please don't think I am suggesting falsifying the real nature of the event, but we do have to have something visually exciting, whatever the true facts may be, which we will give in commentary. Just to take the geese to a refuge and settle them down in pens, will be a complete anticlimax. How you solve this problem for us, I must leave to you. All I can do is to present it to you and tell you how essential a grand slam finish is . . .

The Bartletts were soon back at the new snowgoose nesting site north of Churchill, taking with them the tame geese they had collected the previous year.

The next letter I received solved one problem. Hand-reared snow-geese *do* return to the wild of their own accord! The letter contained a poignant account of how the first year's 'family' had made their decision and re-joined the wild flocks. Fortunately, however, the Bartletts were by then busy raising their second family.

Dear Colin,

With temperature down to 36°F., I am likely to make many mistakes in this letter, as my fingers are so stiff. The wind is right off the ice of Hudson Bay today, and it is quite foggy. A good day for letters if only one could keep warm: the central heating does not seem to work too well at the moment!

But we really do not have any complaints with the weather. It has been a fantastic summer for this part of the world and we have had more sunshine than cloud or fog . . . quite amazing. Hudson Bay is still frozen over, but is starting to break up with icebergs washed up on the beach at high tide when the winds are right. We had just filmed this a day or two before the tame geese returned to the wild flocks. We have heard from pilots and biologists that the McConnell River is still frozen over and the ground mainly snow-covered. So the snowgoose production for the McConnell is expected to be zero this year – as with other breeding grounds to the north. Perhaps we timed it right for the 'Snowgoose' Special – and I am certainly glad that we came in to this nesting colony this year. It has been perfect for our purpose.

This cold snap makes life hard for mosquitoes . . . the poor things must be dying by the thousand. They keep crashing into the walls and roof of the tent all night long, with a sound just like rain-drops. And how we miss them on the tundra when making 'a call of nature': the change from mosquitoes to icicles can be very quick up here!

I hope you received my hurried note of about a week ago. A plane came in unexpectedly on the fifth to take two scientists out from the other camp three miles away – and brought mail in to us, including your letter of 29 June. I was reading your letter around 9.30 am, but did not realize at the time that our tame geese had returned to the wild . . . they had wandered off around 4 am. It was not a universal decision on their part, as several kept coming over to the tent to jabber away to us – but we did not answer them as we wanted them to go away without chewing on the tent ropes. The others were calling from some distance away. They visited the tents a few times, before finally all going off. They were still away that morning when the plane arrived . . . with Fred flying back by himself when frightened by the plane. Normally, if some of the geese were not already flightless, they would all have flown in together. But we did not worry, as we expected the geese to wander in when they were ready. Hours later we decided that they were lost in the willows and went looking for them. But we got no answers to our calls. It is not easy to look for ten geese supposedly lost in the willows in flat tundra country, where any point of the compass looks the same.

As it was a sunny day we could not search indefinitely, but returned to camp to film the new goslings, which were already growing fast. However, for a few days we really trudged around for many miles looking for our poor lost geese. It seemed so ironic . . . they always came back to us when they could fly . . . and now to be lost when half of them were flightless . . . it seemed unbelievable. Jen was the first to wonder if a primitive instinct was stronger than the imprinting. Did they feel insecure around our camp while we were sleeping, and realize that there was safety in the open flats near the water at the coast? The wild geese were certainly down there in force. We came to believe this more and more . . . that they had returned to the wild of their own accord.

Since then Fred has given us more 'proof' that our geese have joined up with the wild geese at the coast. Around 4 am one morning he was calling a lot, with geese at the coast answering him. Then he took off, calling as he flew . . . we could hear it all from inside the tent . . . until he landed with the geese amid a great greeting from them. To us it was clear that Fred was lonely and had flown down to his friends the geese. So we got dressed and walked down to the coast too, fully expecting to find Fred with the geese and to be welcomed by them all. But it is such a vast, boulder-strewn area that we could not even pick up Fred through the binoculars. All the geese took to the water when we were still half a mile away. We called and got an answer from Fred down near the shoreline, but we still could not see him. We walked on down but still could not see him. Then we saw him land near the willows almost behind us. So we turned our backs on the geese and headed home. But before going twenty yards Fred landed alongside us, having flown from the shore somewhere . . . It was a pair of wild sandhill cranes back near the willows. They stayed close when we walked up with Fred, obviously fascinated by Fred. So we stopped to see what they would do . . . they circled us three times, getting closer all the time . . . until they were only fifteen yards away and still not afraid. Fred took no notice of them at all, except for an occasional glance, but continued to pick mosquitoes off our clothing. When we carried on walking the cranes still did not fly, but called to Fred – but without him answering. We had often thought that Fred thought he was human, not a crane, and it was interesting to check it out. On our way back Fred stopped to feed in a shallow pool and we carried on. Later he flew to catch up with us and the wild cranes called to him from the coast. Still later Les saw the three cranes walk right through camp, but the two wild ones walked off when he came out of the tent. They visited Fred again the next morning . . . and Fred has called to them a few times. Another morning when he flew down to the coast we wondered if he was visiting the geese or the wild cranes. On checking it out, Fred had been visiting the geese as he flew in from our left . . . we found the pair of wild cranes later on, well over to the right.

You cannot imagine how we missed the geese at first Colin . . . we were really lonely without them. They had been part of our lives for over a year . . . always very talkative . . . always into something . . . always very important. I really missed having to sweep up their poops every morning . . . If they miss us as much as we miss them, they must be back when they can fly. However, we certainly cannot be sure of ever seeing them again. They have returned to the wild of their own free will . . . your story is now complete, except for actual film coverage . . .

I'll leave this with you for now. And we will see what develops in the weeks ahead.

Once again letters arrived with spectacular irregularity. The next one showed that cold and wet were not the only unfriendly elements to be dealt with on the tundra.

15 August 1972
Dear Colin,

We are set to fly out to Churchill on the eleventh, putting the cars on the train on the thirteenth and ourselves on the passenger train on Tuesday the fifteenth. So perhaps there is just time for you to reach us at Churchill before we leave, otherwise use the Sand Lake address once more.

You will be pleased to know that by the time you get this letter the new tundra film is also on its way to you, having left Churchill on 6 or 7 August. If this letter gets out, then the film will also get out and be on its way to you. Also included are three new tapes – with one on the banding drive to follow, unless the wind dies down first and we can finish it off on the young geese. We have had days of wind in the thirty to forty mph range lately, making life rather unpleasant. Also lots of fog, rain and temperatures in the thirties all day and night! Good fun for summer camping! One sure loses a lot of sleep with the constant flapping of the tents. And we have had many polar bear visitors at night also, which is inclined to keep one awake. We have a sow with two cubs in sight at the present time, but although she has been around for three days now, she has come no closer (as far as we know) than two hundred yards of the tents. Jen first spotted her through binoculars swimming up the coast, with the two cubs following in the water. A week earlier I had filmed her from the helicopter some miles south of the Cape. But at the moment she seems to like our area: there was another bear here too yesterday. The first afternoon when she swam ashore with her cubs the light was not too bad and I was able to take about 130 feet of her with the cubs: at one point all three black noses were up in the air at the same time sniffing, as they caught our scent.

So far we have not filmed any of the polar bears around the tents, as they seem to come only after we are in bed. We had one just outside last night, so can now honestly say that we have been within a foot of a wild polar bear . . . they breathe with a strange snuffling sound, but are otherwise very silent walking on the tundra.

As you can well imagine it was not too easy to get to sleep after all that excitement . . . every flap of the tent was the bear back again . . . or was it? However, we must have both gone to sleep as the bear did wake us up around 1 am: his dark silhouette loomed large over our heads on the canvas tent wall only a foot away – he was shaking the tent as he tried to push into the narrow opening under the flaps to the front part of our tent. We sleep in the nude and with a polar bear so close it does make you feel a little exposed! As we had no firecrackers we could only shout to scare the bear . . . I thought that I shouted so loud that it would wake the dead, but it did not panic the bear too much. He backed out of the hole and slowly walked along the side, turning the corner to brush along the end of the tent still within the guy ropes . . . his outline showing perfectly clearly as a dark shadow on the canvas. We yelled again . . . and he carried on his merry way. Once his shadow left the end of the tent we had no way of knowing where he was . . . his big feet made no sound on the mossy tundra . . . Later Jen and I both remarked about his snuffling breathing . . . it was the only sound we heard from him.

There was no comment from Les and we found out next day that he had slept through everything, so had the helicopter pilot. But they had both had a night out on the tundra the previous night . . . with about six others from Queens . . . when fog came in before the helicopter could ferry them all back to the base camp . . . about twelve miles from where they landed. I slept at the other camp and Jen looked after the geese here . . . hoping that a polar bear would not come while she was on her own.

Bob and Dave left the following day, taking out four of the Queens University people in the freight canoe. For our protection they gave us three thunderflashes . . . A few nights later Les got a chance to use one. We had only just gone to bed when a polar bear brushed along the side of Les's tent – and we could hear it from inside our tents, it was such a calm night. When Les looked out it was between our tents. So this time it was his turn to shout . . . and throw the thunderflash . . . Luckily this was a younger bear and he scared quite easily. Or so we thought, but he was still around next day – when the female and her two cubs showed up. So we have four bears – if we count the cubs – within a few hundred yards of camp . . .

We have waited for our geese perhaps long enough. If they are not back by the eleventh they will have to fly south. The current shipment of film will let you get on with the editing. Once we get to The Pas we can film the travelling shots . . . and then the geese riding inside the trailer. The filming will then be finished, unless you still want the big release scene.

14 August 1972
Dear Des,

Your most exciting letter about the polar bears has just arrived. It sounds a little too thrilling. We have made tremendous progress with 'Snowgoose' and I think it is going to work out marvellously. Once we get your final scenes we shall have the picture in pretty good shape.

. . . We have managed to get a very good final scene from some of your earlier shooting where the geese are flying by a lake close to the road. We needn't actually say that the geese are going to join the wild flocks but can leave at a query; will they soon go? Of course, we know the answer now.

I have reproduced this correspondence in detail because perhaps better than anything it reveals the difficulties of making a wildlife film in the field and of 'controlling' it from base. It also, I hope, shows that such an exchange would not be possible if we did not know each

Many *Survival* wildlife camera teams consist of husband wife partnerships. Housekeeping and catering in the field calls for a high degree of adaptability. Top, Joan Root cooks the evening meal watched by dandified Karamojong warriors. When filming 'The Enchanted Isles' in the Galapagos Islands, the mocking birds were a continual problem, even taking their baths in the frying pan and stealing the food as it was prepared. But the enchanting thing about *Los Enchantados*, 'The Enchanted Isles', is that all the wildlife there is tame, having no cause to fear man.

The success of any wildlife filming operation depends on meticulous planning. When the Bartlett team set out to film 'The Flight of the Snowgeese', they knew that they would be out of touch for at least four months. Above, Des checks camera stores and equipment at his desert base near Tucson, Arizona, before driving to the far north of Canada. Below, on the Bartlett's way back south, customs men queried the right of the Bartlett's family of snow and blue geese to enter the United States by road. They later relented and the geese obligingly flew across the frontier. Bottom, Fred, the sandhill crane who thought he was a human being, rubbing himself down with a towel after a swim with the snowgeese.

other extremely well; after working together for a long time, we are more or less able to gauge each other's thought processes, and we need to be.

We now had all the footage. All we had to do was to make the film. Even with 120,000 feet of priceless footage in the can, there were problems. The first was the sheer bulk of film. In many ways, it is easier to cut a film that is adequately though economically covered. A ratio of around sixty to one imposes a tremendous organizational load both on the film library and on the editor. Fortunately Les Parry, *Survival*'s senior editor, had been working on the project and keeping pace with it for some time. It was the tundra footage that was vastly overweight. This was only to be expected since Des had spent the whole of one Arctic summer there and part of the next. A great deal was going on all around him which he might never have the opportunity to film again. So he filmed it whether it was a whimbrel nesting or a lone caribou trotting past his camp. Much of this found its way into the first long, long cut. Then I threw it all out. Anything, no matter how fascinating from a naturalist's viewpoint, that leads away from the main story-line is to be deplored. If a polar bear raids a snowgoose nest, excellent: if the same bear goes for a swim in a tundra lake all by itself, forget it and lots of other goodies besides. If we were to make economic sense of two years' filming that had produced well over a hundred thousand feet of 'out-takes', then, later on, I would have to find a way of making some half-hours out of the 'Snowgoose' by-product.*

Despite the discarding process, the tundra section was, in the first rough-cut, greatly over length. Even with the new 'imprinting' scenes that dealt with the collection and rearing of the second family of orphans, in places the film still dragged. This meant that more variety would have to be found later in the story in order to allow us to trim the tundra scenes. This is where Fred came in.

Fred entered entirely unexpectedly. Fred, the sandhill crane adopted as a chick during the Bartletts' first summer in the Arctic, had featured spasmodically in Des's letters. It was not until we viewed the second summer's rushes from the Arctic that we realized that a powerful bit-part player had joined the scenario. Fred not only obligingly caught black flies and mosquitoes off Des's and Jen's clothing while they filmed, but swam behind a canoe and inexplicably dried himself off on a towel. Later when the whole menagerie was travelling south for the second time down the flyway, he even took his daily exercise flying behind Les Bartlett's bicycle. Des had shot the bicycle scenes in super-slow motion.

---

* In fact we made four half-hours, 'Land of the Loon', 'Arctic Summer', 'On the Trail of the Snowgoose', 'Central Flyway'.

10

The final problem was a tricky one. The slow-motion footage of the geese in flight was everything that Des had claimed for it. Shot against a clear sky background, it gave the impression that you were actually flying wingtip to wingtip with the geese as part of their skein.

It was on the strength of this slow-motion footage, which Aubrey had shown in New York during one of his business visits, that all doubts about the network sale of 'Snowgoose' were finally removed. Jack Ball of our New York office was enormously impressed with these sequences and was prepared to gamble on a network deal. We were fully committed from that moment on.

As Des had described in one of his letters, he had also filmed the method by which these miraculously beautiful shots were obtained. He had trained the geese to fly alongside his Chevy station wagon while he sat on the tailboard filming them. He had covered the entire process. These scenes would build into an exciting and highly unusual sequence, just the sort of thing we needed towards the end of the film. But if we used them, then the game would well and truly have been given away. Viewers would guess how we had obtained the slow-motion, apparently high-in-the-sky shots with which the film opened. My instincts were all against revealing Des's secret. Counter-arguments were that the viewer would accept the early slow-motion flight scenes in which airborne snowgeese filled the screen at face value and would not necessarily associate them with the give-away that came much later. I even argued this way, though I never fully convinced myself. There was also the instinctive feeling that you should never reveal trade secrets. Apart from that, did people really want to know how it was done? Wouldn't the magic of those aerial scenes be destroyed for them? Our American friends had no doubts. They urged us to use the station wagon sequence. I've never heard anyone complain, so perhaps they were right. But to this day I still have my doubts whether it was the right decision.

'Snowgoose' obviously cried out for music and big music at that. We even talked about Marty Paich and Nelson Riddle. That big! We discussed the possibilities of a ballad and a singer. Glen Campbell, a good choice with his country boy image and pleasant voice, became frontrunner. Time, as it usually does in the film business, was running out. Neither Paich nor Riddle was able to write a theme in the time. So Farlan Meyers, head of the Los Angeles office of J. Walter Thompson and a professional composer, gallantly stepped into the breach. Aubrey and I waited with much apprehension. What if his composition turned out to be awful? It might create a diplomatic incident on a par with the Boston Tea Party.

One afternoon in December, with only a week to go before the music had to be recorded, an audition tape arrived from Farlan. I remember that Aubrey and I guiltily sneaked it away from the editor, Les Parry, and rushed upstairs to play it secretly in my office. The effect was devastating. Farlan would be the first to admit that he has not got the greatest voice since Sinatra. There he was, a bit like Rod McKuen with laryngitis, croaking away to his own accompaniment. To our strained ears, the tune sounded just about all right, but a bit thin and rather banal. It was the old trap being sprung once again: non-musicians simply cannot imagine what a theme picked out on a piano will sound like once the arrangers have been to work on it. Deeply apprehensive, Aubrey and I tried it on Les Parry, who cautiously gave it as his opinion that it would sound a lot better when it had been orchestrated.

So we called in one of *Survival*'s regular composers and best arrangers, Sam Sklair. Les and I told him that the Americans wanted a really big, lush sound. To my surprise, Sam said that he thought it would sound terrific, a little reminiscent of *Born Free* perhaps, but then, what wasn't reminiscent of something else?

Buoyed up by the expert's opinion, we told Farlan that we were vastly enthusiastic and learned that he himself was so enthusiastic that he had booked Glen Campbell not only to sing the ballad but to speak the commentary of the American version. What ballad? We asked. The one that our then American scriptwriter, Ken Thoren, was even at that moment writing, he told us.

While we were waiting for Thoren's lyric a new complication arose. We were expecting Des and Jen Bartlett in London to check over the final cut of the film to ensure we hadn't missed anything, also to help the dubbing editor lay the sound. A few crucial days at the end of a very tight schedule had been set aside for this. Completely uncharacteristically neither Bartlett turned up on the set date. A letter came instead.

15 December 1972
Dear Colin,

Thought I'd give you a running report from New York on how things are going in case it races us to London.

We are having family problems – Fred is seriously ill and Jen stayed at Sand Lake to look after him. He caught a virus infection last Friday afternoon and we did not expect him to last through the night. We kept him going over the weekend but half expected him to pass away at any time. On Sunday he picked up and rallied and we started to hope that he would make it. We began to get water into him at last. But by Monday morning the poor chap was way down. We took him in to the vet as a last resort. He gave him two shots and we were to continue giving him injections twice a day.

Before we could get him back to Sand Lake, Jen said he had gone. But he was still feebly breathing when we got him home. We sure did not expect him to live through the next night so we had both packed and were expecting to catch the plane to New York in the morning.

Fred lasted the night but I missed the plane. Jen is staying on to look after him. We were able to get some dog food into him. Later Jen caught grasshoppers for him which he could swallow if she put them well down his beak. He is still improving but can't stand up but this could be the effect of the big hypodermic needles going into his muscles. We are hoping he will soon be okay so that Jen can join me in England.

See you soon,
Des

Fred miraculously recovered. Both Bartletts arrived in London with just enough time to play their vital part with the sound-tracks of the film.

At the moment of writing Fred, the sandhill crane, is still living with the Refuge Manager at Sand Lake, still partially convinced he is a person. He may even owe his recovery to this imprinting factor. Des swears that the only thing that kept Fred going through the long, dark crisis nights of his illness was that he and Jen called out to the bird, at regular intervals, 'Are you all right Fred?', thus sustaining him in his struggle.

Shortly after the Bartletts showed up in London the snowgoose lyric arrived from Ken Thoren. It was called 'Fly high, Fly free'.

It arrived in unalterable form, a recording with backing by Glen Campbell. Once again we non-musicians were proven wrong. It was obviously a winner. Schmaltzy? Yes, but acceptably so. It contained some sentiments, perhaps, that did not entirely accord with the migrational drives of the lesser snowgoose.

> Fly high, fly free
> Fly home, fly south to me . . .
>
> Fleeing from the northland,
> Down across the States,
> Heading for the southland
> That's where my love waits,
> That's where my love waits . . .

Or again:

> So it's up, high above the clouds . . .

Any ornithologist knows that migrating birds can't operate in or above cloud. They are not equipped for instrument flying. These, however, were captious criticisms. The song, particularly when supported by Sam Sklair's rich orchestration, was a real heart-tugger and contributed greatly to the emotional effect of the film.

Glen Campbell's song was not only what the picture needed, it was also acceptable to an audience of any nationality. His spoken commentary was not. That Arkansas accent is part of America but not part of Britain. So, at the last minute, we had a problem. The show was needed for a special Boxing Day presentation on British network television. Campbell was just not possible as narrator. Was there any reason, though, why we should not use a different voice? After all, raindrops had fallen on Butch Cassidy's bowler hat and Paul Newman hadn't sung a note. Peter Scott, *Survival*'s scientific adviser, was the obvious choice. In timbre his voice is not so far from Glen Campbell's anyway. Peter accepted the invitation at once, especially since Glen Campbell had recently sung at a fund-raising occasion for the World Wildlife Fund of which Peter was then chairman. The marriage of voices and music worked perfectly.

There was still one hazard for 'Snowgoose' to cross in its long journey from the tundra to the TV screen. This concerned the title. There was an obvious danger that a simple title involving the word 'Snowgoose' might clash, or become confused, with Paul Gallico's 'Snowgoose' and more particularly with the Richard Harris production made by the BBC. In the United States, where the laws concerning titles are more complex than in Europe, confusion might lead to litigation. For Britain we decided to call the film 'The Flight of the Snowgeese'. American titles being what they are, our transatlantic allies added the word 'incredible', which wasn't in itself amazing. It would have been incredible if they hadn't.

So at last, after two years of shooting, we had it. Perhaps because of my wildfowl orientation, 'Snowgoose' has always been my favourite *Survival*. I find it strangely moving. I have even seen hardened naturalists leave the auditorium quietly wiping a tear from the corner of the eye. Some of them may have made a ritual complaint about the use of the music and that song. None of the latter would admit, I think, that the music plays a powerful part in activating the tug at the heartstrings which the film undoubtedly gives.

Chapter 13

Safari by Balloon

ALAN ROOT, as was predictable, had come back to *Survival*, but on different terms. He was now conceiving, writing and photographing his own wildlife Specials, which *Survival* co-produced with him. Alan was now set to begin the epic he had plainly had in mind since his earliest connections with *Survival*. The annual wildebeest migration on the plains of Serengeti is arguably the greatest single wildlife spectacle in the world. Driven by the need to find water and fresh grazing, up to one million animals, perhaps three-quarters of them wildebeest, perform an annual long march that describes a complete though irregular circle of over two thousand miles. On the way, they mate, give birth, die, are killed by predators, fall victim to disasters both natural and of their own making. Each year they produce about a quarter of a million young. Each year enough survive to ensure the spectacle is repeated the following year. As fossilized wildebeest horns found in Olduvai Gorge show, the cycle has been repeated for at least one million years.

It was a subject of epic proportions, Despite the fact that the migration turned full circle in one year, it was obvious that not even a filmmaker possessed of Alan Root's demoniac energy could hope to capture it all in one season. In fact it took the best part of three. After the success of his two one-hour Specials 'Mzima Springs' and 'Baobab Tree', both of which were networked in America, Alan could now enjoy the wildlife cameraman's supreme luxury. He could take his time to do the best possible job. The Serengeti is at least three days' drive from the Roots' home at Naivasha. In a light aircraft it is about an hour and a half. Alan could therefore commute to the point at which his own knowledge or local information told him that something particularly interesting was happening. He could be back in camp ready to film the herds in just over the time it takes many people to reach their offices.

On several occasions I was lucky enough to join him in camp. On a good many occasions I was foolhardy enough to fly with him. A whole chapter could be written about Alan Root's flying experiences. The fact that it is not a chapter of serious accidents is tribute to the fact that he is a pilot of remarkable judgement. He flies as naturally as birds fly. Not everyone, however, wishes to fly as low or as close to cliffs and trees as birds fly. It is a matter of taste. I confess that I enjoy the experience though I fully appreciate that a good many others would rather take the longer route by Land Rover.

A brief diversion, then, to describe some of the more publishable aerial incidents involving the Red Baron of the Serengeti. He has hit vultures and survived. The Maasai once speared his parked Cessna to see what it was made of. The spears narrowly missed a fuel tank and partially severed a rather vital electric cable. He did not discover this until he had landed safely at Wilson airport, Nairobi.

Twice in one day, while flying the fifty odd miles between Naivasha and Wilson, he developed engine trouble. The first time he got down safely on a main road and called up Wilson to report his position. Wilson sent out a mechanic who ministered to his engine and declared it to be sound. Traffic was then stopped while Alan took off. Five minutes later, when over a built-up suburb of Nairobi, the engine cut again. Alan hadn't attained much height and had about five seconds to make his decision. Below him was a short section of straight road between two sharp bends. The straight lay alongside a shoe factory. Alan was fully committed to a landing when he saw across the road a high tension cable supplying power to the factory. Alan decided to pass over this and did so only to see another cable directly ahead. By now his air speed was falling off sharply. He had no option but to fly under this one. When all seemed set for a touch-down, a motor cyclist suddenly roared out of the shoe factory and on to the main road just ahead of him. Alan had just enough speed left to lift the Cessna's nose slightly. The motor cyclist, in Alan's words, 'could see I meant business and threw himself flat.' The aircraft's wheels passed inches over the recumbent cyclist's head. Alan was down, once again without a scratch to himself or plane, and, in this case, cyclist.

Just south of Alan's home at Naivasha is a spectacular gorge called 'Hell's Gate'. Alan often uses this as a low level short cut home. On the other side of the lake lives another demon birdman, Iain Douglas-Hamilton, the scientist who, as I shall later recount, starred with his wife Oria in *Survival*'s 'The Family that Lives with Elephants'. Iain uses the gorge as a short cut also.

While roaring within feet of the basalt walls of the gorge, a nervous passenger – and which one isn't? – asked: 'What happens if you meet someone coming the other way?' To which Alan replied: 'There *is* another chap called Douglas-Hamilton who sometimes comes through here. We've got a special arrangement worked out in case we meet in the narrow part. Now, let me see. Iain goes up and I go down . . . No, wait a minute. I go up and Iain goes down. Or is it the other way round . . .? By which time nervous passenger had dissolved into a blob of sweat and Alan was out of the gorge.

Such things are done for effect, of course, as is the aerobatic that is sometimes performed for a special passenger's benefit just north of Naivasha. Between that lake and Lake Elementeita are some piles of lava known as the Eburru volcanics. Two small hills stick up with a deep V-shaped cleft, like the notch in the backsight of a rifle, between them. The slot is far deeper than the wingspan of a Cessna monoplane but not as wide. Alan tends to fly, apparently absentmindedly, flat out at the top of the cleft and just below it. At the last moment, when the passenger is certain the wings are about to be ripped off, he flips the Cessna into a vertical bank. Naturally, he only does this with passengers he thinks can stand it. None of them can. One thing can be asserted about Alan's flying. When close to the ground, which is a lot of the time, he flies very fast and that is the best recipe for staying alive.

His low-flying once earned him royal displeasure. Alan once had a safari business in partnership with Richard Leakey, the palaentologist whose early hominid finds at Koobi Fora, on the east shore of Lake Rudolf (now Lake Turkana) have already pre-dated those of his famous father, Louis, at Olduvai Gorge by a million years. Alan and Richard are both what might be described as forceful, outgoing personalities. Richard flies his own plane also and has a strip at Koobi Fora. When Prince Philip was his guest there on one occasion, Alan dropped in by air. Unfortunately HRH was photographing birds when Alan arrived on the scene, flat-out at nought feet as usual and buzzed the sandspit where the royal photographer was in action. Accidental, of course, but the subject of some right royal language.

To Alan Root everything is a challenge. When flying south down Lake Turkana with BBC producer Tony Smith aboard, Alan looked down and saw aircraft wheel tracks on the unfriendly volcanic surface of uninhabited South Island. Alan was upset that anyone should have made the first-ever landing on that blighted spot since this was a pleasure he had intended to reserve for himself. So he landed also, arguing that where one light aircraft had been he could follow. Braking hard on touch-down, however, he found himself running out of island and finally stopped with a yard or two to spare. The previous landing had been made by a Supercub which can land or take off in a far shorter distance than his own Cessna. In the hot, windless air there was little chance of getting off again – unless Tony Smith agreed to disembark with all the camera gear. Alan's proposal was that, thus lightened, he take off and look for a better strip. Tony watched him depart with apprehension. There is no fresh water on South Island and the lake itself is, of course, brackish. He had to assume that if Alan couldn't get down again he'd somehow send a boat for him. But that might take a considerable time, possibly even several days. However, with his usual combination of luck and skill Alan found a longer landing strip and was just able to take off again with passenger.

This by no means exhausts Alan Root's adventures with flying machines. There is one further aerial saga that needs to be related since it eventually became the subject of a *Survival* Special.

In 1968 Alan first became exposed to ballooning. The man responsible was none other than the so-nearly-marooned Tony Smith. In that year Tony Smith conceived a marvellous adventure and asked Alan Root along to film it. Tony set out to cross East Africa in a hydrogen-filled balloon called 'Jambo'. The journey was successfully recorded by Alan Root on film for the BBC and in Tony Smith's book *Throw Out Two Hands*. From that moment on, Alan became a balloon addict. Filling a balloon in the African bush with hydrogen each time it has to be inflated after a descent is both costly and highly inconvenient. Fortunately, the hot-air balloon was rapidly coming into the ascendant. Alan learned to fly one, returned to England to obtain his balloon licence and bought his own hot-air balloon which he christened 'Lengai'.

'Lengai' was soon sailing gracefully over Naivasha and, of course, the Serengeti where its value as a camera platform immediately became apparent, though in one way it was probably not so effective as the hydrogen-filled 'Jambo'. The burner of a hot-air balloon makes an appalling noise that can be compared with the roar of one hundred blow-lamps. At low altitude, wild animals do not appreciate this, though of course lengthy periods of shooting can, in the right conditions, be obtained before it is necessary to 'burn' to gain height. Some fine scenes were shot by the Roots before the first 'Lengai' was reduced to fragments, but not, as might have been expected, in the air.

After flying is over for the day, the nylon envelope is simply bundled up and stuffed into a large wicker basket carried on a trailer. While towing home to Alan's camp on the Serengeti, a few feet of balloon escaped from the basket and caught on a thorn bush. The envelope paid out behind like an opening parachute and clutched at every acacia thorn along the way. The situation did not reveal itself until a couple of miles later by which time Alan Root was the owner of what he later described as 'the most expensive set of nylon handkerchiefs in Tanzania'.

So another 'Lengai' was purchased. By the time it had arrived Alan was working on a grand ballooning scheme. He was determined to be the first man to cross the summit of Kilimanjaro, Africa's highest mountain, by hot-air balloon. He also came up with the suggestion that, together with *Survival*, he make a Special about the joys and perils of ballooning in East Africa.

Alan first proposed this idea to me at Embakasi, Nairobi's airport, as I was about to catch the plane home after my wife and I had camped with him on the Serengeti. We had both also been ballooning and so he knew that I was under the spell. Back at base in London, the idea quickly took hold. We agreed to the purchase of a larger, twin-burner balloon for air-to-air filming. The enterprise took off with Alan in charge of flying operations and two of *Survival*'s leading cameramen, Dieter Plage and Alan's old friend Bob Campbell, shooting the wildlife adventures. In addition, Anglia film director Forbes Taylor set out from England with a crew to film the non-wildlife scenes.

The result, called 'Safari by Balloon', was networked successfully in America and, of course, in Britain too, with David Niven speaking the narration for both versions. It is purely my personal opinion and, let's face it, Alan has never failed to give *me* his personal opinion about the films I produce – that it was not a total success. To make a film about such an entertaining and idiosyncratic personality as Alan, calls for a cool, amused, objective look by someone outside the action. There were some good jokes, some beautiful photography, but for me, at least, it never quite gelled. Even the great adventure, the climax of the first balloon flight over Kilimanjaro, did not score as it should have done. To make up for that deficiency I propose to recount the full story of that flight as Alan told it to me shortly afterwards.

The staffwork necessary before the flight was considerable. To start with, the meteorologists could only give broad indications of what wind and weather conditions were likely to be above Kilimanjaro's twenty thousand foot summit. Their forecasts were designed for captains of jet aircraft operating at half that height again. Several light aircraft pilots had flown over and round the crater but even they could not guess how a balloon would fare in the up-currents or down-draughts that might exist there. Then there was the need to get clearance from air traffic control both in Kenya and Tanzania. The balloon would be operating in heavily used airspace. Suitable oxygen apparatus had to be found. What clothing would be necessary? Presumably it would be pretty cold above the famous snows of the mountain.

Alan set up camp at a place that would enable 'Lengai' to catch the prevailing winds that should take her across the crater once she had gained the necessary height. Test flights were made. Then it became a matter of sitting and waiting until the met. men said the wind was in the right direction and conditions at high altitudes seemed favourable. There had been a good deal of discussion as to whether Joan Root should accompany her husband or whether the balloon, with the extra butane gas cylinders needed for the flight, would be carrying enough weight already. The matter was resolved at the last minute in typically Root fashion when Alan suddenly grabbed Joan's hand and said: 'Come on, honey, you're coming too.' Joan Root went.

The upward flight was uneventful except at one point. When gaining height opposite the awesome lava cliff called Ruenzi that lies to the east of the summit, a freak gust of air suddenly blew out the pilot light of the burner. It was not the best of moments to be left without lift with the scarred face of Ruenzi rapidly drawing nearer. Alan looked for the matches. As a protection against dampness in the atmosphere, Joan had wrapped them in a length of polythene. This took some time to unwrap. By then the balloon was beginning to descend. Mercifully, a match was struck in time for the burner to roar out its message of good cheer. Not only was Ruenzi left safely below and astern but 'Lengai' eventually passed almost exactly above the crater. There two friends in a light aircraft, Ian Parker and Alaister Graham, were waiting to film its triumphal passage.

Even over the summit, the Roots found they did not need the warm clothing they had brought with them. The explanation was that, since the balloon moved at the speed of the surrounding air, there was no wind to chill them. They breathed through their oxygen masks comparatively seldom, though they might have been in better shape to face the ordeal that was to follow had they used oxygen more frequently.

Their troubles began when they tried to descend. At lower altitudes the wind died out on them completely. They were going nowhere. They were having to burn precious gas just to stay in one place. That one place was not a healthy one in which to land. They remained 'anchored' in still air above a tortured pattern of lava ravines and thick rain forest. Alan then recalled that a jet-stream had been forecast at twenty-two thousand feet. If he risked some of his precious butane gas to burn to reach this, it would blow him out of danger. Up he went and found the wind he sought.

The real trouble came not from the winds or the mountain but from the human reception committee that awaited them. They were now well into Tanzania. Farmland lay below intersected by roads and tracks. Along one of these the Roots spotted Land Rovers racing to meet them and guessed from the size and composition of the convoy that it consisted of Tanzania's often over-zealous police. Meantime the trail rope, the long, thick hawser that a balloon drops to slow its progress before bumping down, had to be lowered. Alan lowered it and then saw that, somehow, a granny knot had become tied in the end. If this knot caught in a fence or tree as it dragged, it could cause them to tilt and fall from a great height. He was now very tired but managed to haul the rope aboard again and undo the knot. By this time he didn't feel like carefully lowering the heavy rope once again, and so he kicked it out of the basket. The rope snaked out and hit him so hard in the small of the back that it knocked him partly over the side and would have done so completely had he not been wearing, surprisingly for Alan, a safety harness. He struggled back, helped by Joan, only to find that his glasses had been knocked off. Alan is shortsighted; so is Joan. So, not for the first time, he borrowed hers. Even through the slightly distorted view that these gave him, he saw that the police convoy was racing their own recovery vehicle to touch-down. 'Unload the cameras,' he ordered Joan. 'Put some unexposed film in them. Whatever you do, hide the stuff we've taken.' Alan knew the Tanzania authorities and guessed that local officials might well believe them to be spies, if not from outer space, then from some unfriendly power.

While she did as he told her, he myopically supervised the landing. Unfortunately, the view through his wife's glasses suggested that they were a lot closer to the ground than they actually were. Alan pulled the ripcord to dump the balloon. It dumped, throwing them both heavily out of the basket. As they lay there, Alan heard the bolt of a Tommy gun cock. The police clustered aggressively round him. Meantime their own recovery crew had come up. Gasping for breath and pretending to be hurt, Joan crawled towards their car. Hiding the film under her she smuggled it into the vehicle.

Alan was now under arrest. In fact they both were. But the film which would otherwise surely have been confiscated was safely hidden.

In a totally exhausted state, Alan and Joan were held by the police and questioned for seven hours.

'Do you know anyone in Tanzania?'

'President Julius Nyerere,' Alan said, which was quite true.

'We don't believe you. Do you know anyone else?'

'Frank Poppleton, head of the Wildlife College at Mweka,' which was also true. Alan provided a stream of impeccable witnesses to his non-espionage status. Eventually they were released almost as inexplicably as they had been arrested.

Alan Root will continue to push his luck. I only hope he doesn't push it too far. Shortly after he finished the balloon film, he returned to Mzima Springs, the scene of one of his first TV epics. With him were Joan and cameraman Martin Bell who had served on the balloon adventure with Forbes Taylor, Dieter Plage and Bob Campbell. Alan wanted some more underwater footage of hippos to add to a longer version of 'Balloon Safari'. The idea was that the camera should look up through the surface and see the balloon hovering above the hippo pool. Alan, Joan and Martin were in the water together. They had persuaded an old bull hippo to retreat into a bay in the reeds. Here is Alan's account of the incident:

We were diving in Mzima Springs together with cameraman Martin Bell to get a few more linking shots we needed in order to add some Mzima footage to a lengthened balloon film. All had been going well and the hippos were quite co-operative. On this morning however one bull was a bit up-tight. He was a second-ranking bull and they are never as relaxed as the one at the top. You can see this particularly clearly in advertising agencies but it happens in nature too. Anyway we met him in the water and he moved off rapidly, stirring up a lot of muck so that we could not see. Rather than swim through the murk and risk bumping into something we simply lay in the water waiting for it to clear. (We were wearing aqualungs.) We did not realize that the bull had stopped about twenty feet away and was now staring and snorting at the spot where our bubbles were coming to the surface. Also occasionally one of our tanks would appear and this obviously disturbed him. Had we been in clear water, where he could have lowered his head and seen what we were, I have no doubt that he would have moved away, and certainly we would have been able to see his mounting tension and moved the other way. As it was, only the people watching from the bank were aware of what was building up.

When he charged he made the typical upwards and sideways scything motion, mouth wide open, and Joan was first in line. At the time she remembers nothing except that she was hit a tremendous blow – but somehow a soft, slow-motion blow like being hit by an E-type marshmallow. It seems that the hippo got his nose under her and threw her up and out of the water. As she was in mid-flight one of the hippo's canines pierced the rubber of her face mask just below her right eye and smashed the glass. (To put her face mask on and stick your finger through that hole is as chilling a feeling as you could ever want.)

Having flung Joan aside he turned on me and took a bite at my backside. Here I should explain that he still could not really see us, he was just making great slashing sweeps of his jaws as he ran towards us. His canines made two neatly incised holes through my swim trunks, taking only a sliver of skin from my right buttock. (This nicely balances the leopard bites on the other side, but unfortunately like them it will be a small scar and hardly worth showing.) But the blow rolled me over on to my back and the next thing I knew he had my right leg in his mouth. And I really did *know* it. I was vividly aware of every detail of what was happening. No pain, just a numbness and dull feelings of tearing and crushing but no pain at all. He got my leg right into his mouth, so that the left-hand canines were slicing through the calf, while my foot and ankle were between his right-hand molars. Fortunately they do not chew as a cat would, but just open and close their jaws enough to get a nice scissoring action of the canines. So at least my foot and ankle were only cut and badly bruised. My calf was bitten right through and chomped three or four times, fortunately all more or less in the same place. The hippo then shook me like a rat. I apparently appeared above water a few times and I was certainly scraped along the bottom too as my trunks were full of sand and debris. My most vivid recollection here is deciding that my leg had had it and the feel of the hippo's whiskers on the back of my thigh as I was shaken about. He then dropped me and went off.

I had lost my mouthpiece and had water in my mask, but I still had air in my lungs and I stayed down a while. I knew that if the hippo was still there and I surfaced I would be attacked again. I had to surface though, and the hippo had gone. Joan was standing about twenty feet away in waist-high water. She didn't know I had been bitten and I didn't know she had been thrown. Martin Bell's head appeared about fifteen feet behind me – all he knew was that there had been a hell of a commotion and that something was wrong. In dream-like slow motion I emptied the water from my goggles, found my demand valve, cleared it and put it in my mouth. Somehow, though I knew I had been bitten, I could not come to grips with the reality of it. Then I reached down and felt the floating mush that was my leg and called out, 'Christ I've been bitten.' Joan gave a wail and came wading towards me, but I yelled at her to get out of the water and she turned back to the bank. I lowered myself to swim for the shore, but I was swimming through blood and not doing too well when something clamped on to my wrist. It was so fierce and tight I thought it was the hippo again, but it was Martin, and he towed me across that pool with all the power of a nuclear submarine.

We were concerned now about a ten-foot crocodile who had spent a lot of time over the past week methodically stalking us as we worked. We had met him in the water and faced him down a couple of times, but he had been getting bolder every day. I knew that as his fear of us decreased I would have to watch him carefully, but felt that for the moment we were OK as long as we behaved properly. Thrashing about on the surface and bleeding like a stuck pig did not come under the heading of proper behaviour, so it was a relief to get to the bank.

There I was bound up by an Italian doctor, part of a tourist group who saw the whole thing, stuck in the Range Rover where I lay drinking whisky on the way to Kilaguni Lodge, where we were able to amicably hi-jack a tourist plane. In less than three hours from the attack I was in the familiar homely surroundings of the casualty ward of the Nairobi Hospital.

Getting there was all the fun. In the next twenty-four hours I developed gangrene and became so odiferous that even some of my best friends told me. In fact all my best friends told me. I had some spectacular fevers – boy! I have had the sheets changed before when I was sweating, but never the mattress! And in between the sweats I needed an electric blanket to keep warm. Three days, seventeen pints of saline, eight pints of blood, many millions of units of intravenous penicillin and several cups of tea later I was declared OK and since then I have been on the mend.

As my surgeon put it, 'That hippo was as good an anatomist as I am,' and I must say that for all the random savagery of the attack the hippo really did do a neat job. There was a hole through my calf large enough to push a coke bottle through, and by the time the doctors had cut away the damaged tissue to clean the wound they had enough meat, as they put it, 'for a reasonable hamburger'. But the teeth smashed muscle only – no bone, no tendons, no arteries and no major nerves or veins. It is hard to conceive of passing through a bull hippo's jaws and having so little real damage. (They are still the leading herbivore in Africa when it comes to killing people – crocs lead the carnivore list.)

I have now been in hospital for two weeks, the leg is much improved and I am having a skin graft in a couple of days' time. If it takes I should be out ten days after that, though not walking for another week or so. Joan had a few bad days when the shock of her near-miss was compounded by my gangrene, but is now well and comes in every day to photograph the wound for the surgeons who are interested in just how it closes over. So that's about it – my bum is numb and I'm putting on too much weight but I'm going to be OK.

Chapter 14

Apes and Elephants

BETWEEN 1973 and 1975 I shared a number of adventures with Dieter Plage in pursuit of background for three *Survival* Specials. Rodney Borland had long since ceased to be Dieter's sidekick. He was now most successfully making *Survival* films on his own. Dieter badly needed another assistant. Des Bartlett had suggested that Lee Lyon, the Californian girl who had helped him with 'Snowgoose', was ideal for the job, especially since she was keen to move on from stills to movie. Dieter flew over to Tucson to meet Lee. The Bartletts took them on a brief tour of the south-west. At the end of the trip it was obvious to both that they would get on and work well together. Within a few weeks Lee had joined Dieter in South-West Africa. It was there that I first met her.

Less than four years later, tragedy was to overtake Lee. In that time she played a full part in *Survival*'s life, especially in two of the adventures I am about to describe, but first I must describe Lee.

At the time she joined Dieter, Lee was about twenty-five. She was a dark, handsome girl just this side of beautiful, though she could be that too, when she forsook jeans and dressed up. Lee claimed she had some Indian blood on her grandmother's side though I should not be surprised if there was a drop or two of Spanish somewhere as well. She had that glow of health that belongs to young girls brought up in the sun. She had courage. She also had great physical endurance. She had climbed in the Tetons and made the long slog to the top of Kilimanjaro for fun. Cold and heat did not worry her. Lee had a great sympathy for, and understanding of, wild animals. She was completely at home in the outdoors. Some people found her a shade strong-willed. Well, so she was, but you do not succeed as a naturalist cameraman unless you have a determination like the bow of an ice-breaker. She stayed with our family often and our young liked and admired her greatly. My wife and

I knew her shortcomings just as she knew ours. We had been on three safaris together and you don't travel in the wild without discovering each other's failings. Lee's were practically all covered by the term 'strength of character' and all that that implies. She was always kind, always in good spirits and had a delicious sense of humour. We loved her dearly and saw her as part of the family, not only *Survival*'s family but ours too, whenever she cared to join it.

Lee was operating as Dieter's assistant when we made 'The Family that Lives with Elephants'. The family in this instance was that of Iain Douglas-Hamilton and consisted of his wife Oria and their two small children Saba and Dudu.

Iain, whom I have previously mentioned as the other intrepid bird-man Alan Root constantly expected to meet in the narrow confines of the gorge at Hell's Gate, had become a world expert on elephants as a result of four years spent at Manyara, Tanzania, studying the problems of the herds in Lake Manyara National Park. Towards the completion of his study, Iain came to our offices through a mutual friend, the late Sir William (Billie) Collins. Collins were publishing Iain and Oria's book, eventually titled *Among the Elephants*. Collins were also handling the film rights for the authors. Some film already existed. It had been shot over a short period at Manyara by the French photographer Christian Zubert. It contained some very remarkable scenes, including an episode in which Iain's Land Rover was charged and partly demolished by a cross-tusked matriarch whom Iain had christened – all the elephants in his study had names for record purposes – Sarah. Good as it was, the footage didn't add up to more than quarter of a one-hour film. If we intended to make a Special of the Douglas-Hamiltons' study and adventures, then we would need to get into the field ourselves and start almost from scratch. Dieter and Lee Lyon were picked for the assignment. My wife and I were able to join them for a period following a stay in camp with the Roots on the Serengeti.

I was by no means certain how the two women would get on. Oria is several times larger than most forms of feminine life. She has an Italian father and a French mother. Her mother did not overstate the case when describing her two daughters (the other is Mirella Ricciardi, the well-known photographer whose book *Vanishing Africa* was also published by Collins). 'Darling,' Madame Ricciardi said to my wife, 'I do not have daughters. I have *dynamites*.'

I need not have worried about the juxtaposition of female personalities. If Oria is voluble, my Joan is Welsh. Both are warm, emotional, extremely outgoing. And anyway, dynamite does not necessarily explode when placed next to TNT. The situation needs a detonator. There was none present.

The safari got off to a lively start. Alan flew the four of us – his wife, Joan, came along too – from his camp at Lake Lagaja on the Serengeti where he had been filming the scenes for 'The Year of the Wildebeest' in which more than one thousand calves became separated from their mothers and drowned crossing the lake. His own Cessna was being rebuilt after a crash on the ground – no fault of Alan's. A mechanic had started up another plane without putting on the brakes or chocking the wheels first. This machine taxied across the apron on its own and severely mauled Alan's plane with its propeller. The insurers had supplied Alan with a little Minerva Rallye, a low-wing monoplane of extreme agility. It had automatic flaps and could leap from the ground like a gazelle or wallow safely along at less than fifty mph when required to do so for observation purposes. When fully laden, however, it was possessed of limited power. We had discovered this a few days earlier when, with four people and luggage on board, Alan had attempted to fly over the crater of Tanzania's only active volcano, the nine-thousand-foot Lengai. The Minerva had tried and tried but had finally refused at around eight thousand feet with the particularly evil-looking lava ribs of the mountain safely distant but seeming, to the aeronautically nervous, distressingly adjacent. My wife, when flying with Alan, comes under the heading of nervous passengers, perhaps understandably so. A few minutes before, we had been flying over the angry pink surface of Lake Natron so low that the stench of soda filled the cockpit. Even birds crash into Natron, fooled by the reflection of the mountains Lengai and Gelai on its pink mirror surface. Birds, skilful aviators that they are, do not possess a rate of climb indicator. A prudent pilot flying low over Natron watches this dial continuously to ensure that whatever he's doing he's not descending. Nothing that crashes into the caustic pink confection of which this unearthly lake is made emerges from it, least of all aircraft.

On our way to join the Douglas-Hamiltons, Alan flew round the Crater Highlands, past the huge green shoulder of Lemagrut and down to the shores of Eyeasi, another sodar lake at the tail end of the East African Rift. We sidled round a storm or two and watched the cloud-shadows tinting the slopes of the Highlands momentarily a deeper green before moving on to rinse them a vivid emerald in sunlight once more. It was an idyllic, uneventful flight until we reached the wall of the Rift Valley where it drops sheer six hundred feet to the narrow strip of forest along the shore of Lake Manyara that constitutes the park. There are a number of steep, narrow, water-cut ravines running down the Rift escarpment to the park. Iain's camp was situated at the end of one of these, close to the Ndala River. Alan now announced that we would fly along the rim of the Rift until we found Iain's ravine and then simply fly down it. Half-way down a ravine that became narrower and more winding, Alan said he thought he'd got the wrong one and that he'd never been down this gorge before. Some Sonjo tribesmen living in a hut whose roof was at ground level – a mode of construction originally intended as a defence against the warlike Maasai – dived for cover as we side-slipped over them as if they feared that the Maasai *Morani* were once again intending to blood their spears. After Alan had performed some wingtip-grazing banks, the ravine eventually opened out as Alan had known it must do. We then set out to find the Douglas-Hamiltons' camp. When we finally spotted their tents on a bank above the dried-out Ndala River, we proceeded to wake them up and drop a message. This was fairly standard stuff except to heads and stomachs unprepared for the pressure of moderate G-forces. When we landed at the Manyara strip, situated at the top of the escarpment, eleven miles from Iain's camp, my wife was white, gallant, but undeniably shaken. We were to meet the Douglas-Hamiltons at the Manyara Lodge. Transport, however, was a long time coming so Alan suggested that he and I take off and buzz the lodge. Once over the rim of the escarpment Alan dropped like a stooping peregrine. So abruptly did we disappear that Joan was convinced we had crashed. Fortunately Alan's Joan was there to reassure her. Alan then made a tight turn and zoomed up over the Rift edge so shatteringly that a man poised on the diving board of the lodge swimming pool fell in, possibly from fright but more likely in self-defence. We repeated the evolution to make sure the lodge had got the message. As our wheels cleared the roof by feet at the second pass, Alan observed with perfect truth: 'Joan wouldn't have liked that.'

Iain and Oria, Saba, Dudu, Dieter and Lee arrived half an hour later. Alan then took off for the Serengeti again, leaping into the clear, bumpy air above the strip like a jump-jet. Joan watched the Roots go with relief. Whatever we were to face with Iain and the elephants it couldn't be as nerve-racking as bush-flying with Alan.

An hour later, I was not so sure of this. Iain and Alan are of much the same stamp. What one does, the other has to do better or at least more extravagantly. One afternoon at Manyara, for example, they had a contest that involved creeping up behind elephants and pulling hairs from their tails. Each has a sense of drama. Both, at times, play for effect. Iain did not require us to remove hairs from the rear ends of his elephants. He did, however, want to see how we would react when presented threateningly with the front end.

If you have not seen the *Survival* Special 'The Family that Lives with Elephants', or read the Douglas-Hamiltons' book *Among the Elephants*, I should explain what is so remarkable about Iain's four-year study. Since man intruded on the scene, elephants have become their own worst enemies. The spread of towns, villages, farms, roads has meant that the traditional migration routes, often hundreds of miles long, which the herds travelled seasonally in search of food have been cut. Instead the elephants have been allotted ever-dwindling areas to themselves. The best preserved of these are national parks. A park, however, provides comparative safety from poaching (though this is by no means the case, as in Tsavo, Kenya, at the time of writing). With protection, the herds increase. Because they cannot move far outside the park, and are often legitimately shot as crop-raiders when they do, the elephants have to eat what the park provides. The strain invariably falls on the trees. The elephants eat the bark as well as leaves and shoots. When they've ring-barked the trees, the trees die. When the trees disappear, the entire eco-system changes. Woodland species such as giraffe, kudu and bushbuck suffer and may even disappear. The area gradually turns to savannah and is likely to fall victim to serious erosion. At Manyara, upwards of five hundred elephants live more or less permanently inside an area 30 miles by, at its widest, four miles. The *Acacia tortilis* woodlands of Manyara take a heavy toll as a result.

Before you can begin to suggest a cure – other than by more or less indiscriminate shooting –a number of puzzles must be solved, among them how rapidly the resident elephants breed, at what rate the herds are increasing, the food preferences of the herds at different seasons, the migrating pattern if any, outside the park, the composition of family groups as well as the age and sex of individual members. Where previous work of this sort had been carried out, the study was done mainly on dead elephants. Whole herds had been shot and the bodies of the 'cull' dissected. Admittedly this was done where elephants were superabundant and time in which to come up with some answers was extremely short.

Iain elected to study the Manyara herds without killing a single elephant, though on a few occasions, as with Sarah the cross-tusked matriarch, the elephants came close to killing him. To make a detailed study by purely pacific means, he had to persuade the elephants to accept him, both in an open vehicle and often on foot. That he did so was a remarkable feat of understanding and courage. By the time we made our film, Iain had given every single elephant a name and had completed a dossier on it which included its photograph, individual temperamental and physical characteristics, its height (calculated by an incredible piece of stereoscopic photographic apparatus), and, since there is a co-relation between height at the shoulder and age, its age, accurate to a year or so.

On that very first evening, Iain and Oria took us to see their elephants. I have been in close proximity to elephants many times. I admire them greatly and am overawed by them. I am always aware of the fact that, should they so wish, they can reach into an open vehicle and lift you out of it, or drive your head down into your shoulders with a single tap of their trunks should you in any way arouse their displeasure. Iain's Land Rover was the one which a year or two previously had been charged and pushed backwards by Sarah for thirty yards before it was stopped dead by hitting a tree. It was hard to detect that any significant repairs had been effected in the meantime. The steering wheel was still rhomboid in shape. The front was dented and holed. The screen had not been replaced. Moreover, it showed a marked reluctance to start. So I found my palms sweating slightly when Iain drove quietly into the middle of the first herd and switched off the engine. It was like being becalmed among a squadron of drifting battleships. The grey hulls loomed large and at times actually rubbed the battered bulkwarks of our vehicle. Meantime Iain consulted his card index system, registering a fresh tear in Calliope's ear, the new attachment of one of the calves to a nursemaid teenager. In between his observations, Iain would give soft-voiced instructions to Dieter in the rear-gunner's position, squatting on the tailboard, to train his tripod-mounted Arriflex on some interesting piece of behaviour. Gradually Joan and I relaxed, realizing that this young man really did know his elephants. We visited three herds and spent half an hour rubbing shoulders with each. Something in the way that Iain purposefully searched the area told me that we weren't through yet. Nor were we.

'Ah,' said Iain at last, with smug satisfaction, 'I want you to meet someone.'

In a small clearing in front of her herd of female relatives and young, stood one of the most impressive elephants I have ever seen. She did not stand for long. She came in a headlong charge, shaking the dust off her ears in clouds, flailing the bushes to splinters with her trunk and trumpeting at the top of her very considerable voice. This was no ordinary charge and yet, in the face of it, Iain had switched off the engine.

When scared I need something to occupy my mind. In a wildlife situation beyond my control, I dementedly take photographs. I got off about four shots in the time it took the elephant to cover perhaps forty yards. Behind me the cine camera was whirring away. In the back, too, Lee Lyon was shooting with a stills camera. It is a mark of the professional photographer that he or she recognizes the critical optimum split second at which to press the button. My four pictures were all good but only one was superb – Lee's. It has become the classic picture of a charging elephant.

The charge eventually stopped, six feet short of the Land Rover.

There the elephant shrieked again and tore at the bushes. Then she retreated to protect her herd.

'Now you've met Boadicea,' Iain said. He seemed satisfied with our reactions. 'She's the matriarch of Virgo's group. We'll find Virgo in a minute.'

Virgo stood a little way apart with two calves, one of them very young. Virgo was a small cow born with only one tusk. She was also Iain's favourite elephant. Over the years of his study, Iain had increasingly persuaded various groups to accept him among them, or anyway close to them, on foot. Boadicea's group, of which Virgo was part, was one in whose society he constantly mixed. Virgo, an elephant with an exceptionally trusting temperament, had come totally to accept his presence, so much so that she would come up to greet him and touch his hand with the tip of her trunk. She was equally gentle when Oria or the children were with Iain. At the end of his study, Iain had returned to Oxford for a whole year to write his thesis. When he returned to Manyara after this interval, largely to complete the film with *Survival*, Virgo, true to the legends concerning her kind, had not forgotten him. When Iain first spotted her after his return, he left his vehicle and advanced cautiously up the track to stand silently in the bush close to her. Almost at once Virgo approached and greeted him by touching his outstretched hand with her trunk. I myself was present on the occasion, filmed by Dieter, on which Iain stood on a fallen tree while Virgo brought both her calves up within feet of him as if to show off her children. And this with an animal that is said to be ultra-ferocious when escorting young! Perhaps Virgo was an exceptional elephant but then her friend was an equally exceptional scientist, not least because he was emotionally caught up with the object of his study.

What came out of the Douglas-Hamilton study except a thesis, a lot of new knowledge, a best-selling book and a highly successful film? The answer is some management proposals for the Tanzania National Parks, some of which they have acted upon. Through telemetry, radio-tracking both on foot and from his aircraft, Iain had mapped out the annual migration pattern of the Manyara herds. He discovered that the elephants could quite easily climb the steep wall of the Rift to reach the dense forest reserve that lay there high above the southern end of the park and that this migration was crucial if the pressure was to be taken off the *Acacia tortilis* woodland of the park itself. He made recommendations to secure access routes to the forest for the elephants. The Tanzanian authorities supported him and made this possible. He also tried to persuade the Parks to buy the Italian-owned farmland at the southern end of Manyara Park and even arranged to raise some of the necessary funds, a large part from *Survival*. Had this move succeeded, the elephants would no longer have had to risk death or wounding when they went crop-raiding on these farms. Unfortunately local politics concerning the priorities that can be accorded to wildlife and to farming intervened. The farms were never purchased even though the farmers expressed themselves willing to sell. Perhaps Iain's major accomplishment was that without killing a single elephant during his study he managed to produce convincing scientific arguments as to why the Manyara elephants did not need culling.

Iain and the colourful Oria, with her extravagant theories about bringing up Saba and Dudu like young elephants 'with lots of tactile touching', were delightful and exciting safari companions. We lived in a great though simple style that might be described as Afro-Italian, Oria's safari cook conjuring up *cordon noir* meals out of tins and local vegetables, including watercress that grew in the pure streams running down from the Rift. We had our moments, though. One night while eating under the corrugated iron roof of our al fresco dining room, five hundred buffalo decided to stampede just beyond the glare of the Tilley lamps. On another we left the camp deserted for an hour only to return and find that a pride of lions had been into our tents and pulled all the bedding out into the open. There were tooth and talon marks in the sheets and lion saliva was still wet on the linen. We assumed, hopefully, that the lions were just in playful mood and would not have come near the camp had it been occupied. It was a funny feeling going to bed that night, knowing that a lion had been there before you. Iain was slightly worried about the children and issued Dieter and me with a heavy tyre lever each though I am not, to this day, sure what we were supposed to do with them. Since our tent was the one nearest to the bank of the Ndala River, an ideal place from which a mischievous lion might launch a maraud, I placed a spare safari bed to act as a lion obstacle just behind our heads at the back of the tent. I was mindful of the fact that even though lions weren't supposed to do such things, Jane Goodall and Hugo van Lawick had recently watched lions demolish their unoccupied tent on the Serengeti. I expected Iain to laugh when I told him about my anti-lion precautions next morning. Instead he took it quite seriously and said that the bed hadn't been a bad idea.

We found the lions later the following day. They had killed a buffalo about half a mile from our camp. After the manner of Manyara lions, they were sleeping off their meal in a tree.

The following year Dieter was still in Africa, though he had moved southwards into what was new territory for *Survival*: Zaire, the former Belgian Congo. His compatriot Bernhard Grzimek was once more the contact that caused *Survival* to move Dieter and his now fully fledged assistant, Lee Lyon. Bernhard had met and, through the Frankfurt Zoological Society, was helping to finance a Belgian conservationist, Adrien Deschryver. Deschryver had once owned family plantations in Kivu Province on the slopes of Mount Kahuzi. Having survived the civil war in what amounted to a one-man campaign against the Simba rebels, Deschryver had decided to devote all his energies to protecting the pocket of mountain gorillas who lived around his family property. With half-pygmy trackers he had spent four years in the rain forests on the mountain, simply getting to know the gorillas there. This was no easy task. For a long time the gorillas showed no desire to get to know him. For weeks on end, all he got was an odd glimpse of a face among the leaves or an arm pulling down a branch for the owner to eat the leaves. Gradually, though, several family groups, and one group in particular, came to accept his presence. By the time *Survival* came on the scene, President Mobutu of Zaire had recognized Adrien Deschryver's work by gazetting the twin peaks on which the gorillas lived as Kahuzi-Biega National Park, Biega being the name of the second mountain.

Grzimek told *Survival* that Deschryver's was a natural story for us to cover. He wrote to Deschryver suggesting that he allow Dieter to film his work with the gorillas. He warned, though, that Deschryver was a naturally modest and reticent man and that, in common with many scientists and wardens doing an exacting and sometimes dangerous job

The world's most appealing animal? Certainly a candidate for the title. Bright, too! The California sea otter is one of a select group. Along with Man and a few other animals, it can use a tool. In the sea otter's case the tool consists of stones from the sea bed which it uses to crack open sea urchins and large molluscs called abalones. The fur trade made the sea otter almost extinct. Now the otter is on the increase, both in Alaskan waters and off the California coast near Monterey. Jeff Foott filmed the sea otter's life above and below water for 'Saga of the Sea Otter'.

Overleaf: Charles Darwin's theories on the origin of species were largely crystallized by his visit, in 1833, to the Galapagos Islands. The different ground finches – often called Darwin's finches – gave him an important clue to how different species evolve by adapting to different conditions. But Darwin did not see the most amazing finch of all. The woodpecker finch, another tool-user, is a bird which has learned to break off and use twigs and cactus spines to winkle grubs out of dead trees. Alan Root obtained remarkable footage of the bird in action, one of the highlights of 'The Enchanted Isles'. The film, which was introduced by HRH the Duke of Edinburgh, had a Royal Première.

in the field, he had already had one unfortunate encounter with a television crew. Grzimek had made the point that Dieter Plage was in no sense a TV 'crew'. He was a dedicated specialist used to hardships, risks and disappointments. The rest was up to Dieter.

Dieter and Lee Lyon flew down to meet Deschryver in Bukavu. They found him charming, remote and cautious. Because Bernhard Grzimek had backed him in his work, however, he agreed to take them both into the forests of Kahuzi-Biega to meet and shoot some film of his gorillas. It is a twenty-five-mile drive from Bukavu to the park. The first few journeys were made with the minimum of conversation that politeness required. Then Deschryver succeeded in introducing them both to Kasimir. It was the case of Boadicea all over again. Kasimir was the immense silverbacked male who dominated a group of twenty-two gorillas with which Deschryver had done a great deal of his observation. If Boadicea's charge is impressive, Kasimir's is shattering. After this immense animal had rushed at them, roaring and screaming, standing nearly six foot tall, mouth open and arms flailing, Deschryver looked round for the camera team, expecting to find them retreating prudently, only to see them both there still filming, with at least apparent unconcern. He realized now that he was dealing with something different.

Because of the extremely difficult conditions of light and half-light in the forest, Dieter was not, at first, optimistic. He promised himself that if he had twelve minutes of usable film in the can at the end of six weeks, he would persevere and try to shoot a complete gorilla half-hour. When

Previous page: 'Tiger, Tiger' probably ranks as the most difficult Special *Survival* has ever made. The project had to be completed within a year and tigers are not only nocturnal but notoriously unwilling to appear before the camera. The filming, by Dieter Plage and Mike Price, took place principally in Royal Chitawan National Park, Nepal, and in Dudwa National Park in the Northern Province of India. One of the most remarkable scenes was the one in which Mike Price found himself in an eyeball-to-eyeball confrontation with a tiger through the slit of his canvas hide. Night filming on kills was made possible by using an image intensifier.

'Rivers of No Return' told the epic story of the sockeye salmon forcing its way upriver to spawn against tremendous natural odds. Not one of the millions of salmon that run the Pacific rivers survives spawning to return to the sea. Bears are just one of the hazards the fish face on their way upriver. The bears congregate at well-known fishing spots and scoop the salmon out of the water. Jeff Foott who filmed the sockeye story shot this scene at one of the most famous fishing places on Alaska's McNeil River.

the first rushes reached London, *Survival* shared his unease. A lot of the material was too dark. Exposures, on account of the unreliable light penetrating the forest canopy, were uneven. Often the gorillas did not show up well, even when they were in fairly open locations. One gorilla looked very much like another. To untutored eyes it did not seem that gorillas did very much to catch the interest of the ordinary viewer. There were some fascinating scenes, however, and it was undeniable that, even when seen only fragmentarily, gorillas had a powerful presence. As to the scenes in which the big male, Kasimir, charged, they were heart-stopping. I reported cautiously that if the luck was with Dieter and Lee, they might yet give us an exciting half-hour.

Meantime a powerful chemistry was at work in the forests of Kahuzi-Biega. Adrien Deschryver, Dieter and Lee had formed a strong bond of friendship. Adrien's reticence had turned first into guarded co-operation and then to complete determination to see that his gorillas were fully documented on film. Dieter still had to overcome Adrien's reluctance to have his own work with the gorillas recorded but gradually this fell away too.

Every day for six months Adrien, Dieter and Lee walked in the forest together. Some days they walked for eight or nine hours before they made contact with Kasimir's family who had been chosen as the stars of the film. They walked carrying heavy camera equipment at altitudes of between 6,000 and 8,500 feet in heat, mist, tropical rain and even hail. At the end of it Dieter had lost two stone and Lee, who could hardly afford the luxury, one and a half stone. And right at the end they filmed an unplanned episode which could have proved fatal to at least one of them but which gave us one of the most dramatic scenes in the history of wildlife filming.

The way of it was this. As conservator in the new park, Adrien had complete authority over all mountain gorillas in the area. So when he heard that some European farmers were trying to rear a baby gorilla whose mother had been killed by poachers, he flew to the farm in his Bonanza monoplane and gently persuaded the foster parents that they must give the baby, a very small female, into his more expert keeping with the eventual aim of returning the orphan, when old enough, to the forest. The baby was christened Julie, after the Swahili word for gorilla, 'ngila'. The early stages of Julie's education, her introduction to wild foods, the first crawls in the forest with Adrien acting as foster mother were, of course, filmed by Dieter and Lee. Julie progressed so well that Adrien soon decided that he would carry her within range of Kasimir's family so that she could begin to adjust to the sights and sounds of her wild relatives.

They found Kasimir's group easily that day. Dieter and Lee set up to film Julie's reactions. However, it became clear very early in the encounter that things were not developing quite as planned. Julie began to cry very loudly, the wild gorillas responding by barking and screaming and pressing very close. Hannibal, the second most senior male who was normally on exceptionally good terms with Adrien, made an unusually noisy and potentially hostile demonstration. By this time there could be no question of a strategic withdrawal. The gorilla group was far too excited and was clustered all around. Even Adrien began to feel apprehensive. Something, he was certain, had to happen to break the build-up of anxiety and tension among the gorillas. Suddenly it happened. Kasimir came bursting out of the undergrowth directly at Adrien. He paused, making his most intimidating demonstration, at the range of a few feet. All the time the baby in Adrien's arms continued to cry loudly. Then Kasimir came straight for Adrien as if to take the baby from him. Afterwards Adrien said: 'At that moment I thought I was dead.' Understandably, he dropped the baby gorilla on the ground. Kasimir snatched her up and backed off, still barking with mouth wide open, yet keeping his eyes on Adrien all the time as if expecting an aggressive counter-move. Perhaps because of his concentration on Adrien, Kasimir dropped the baby after he had backed off a yard or two, but he picked her up again in one gigantic sweep of the paw. He retreated into the undergrowth and there in a small open space the family gathered round to inspect Julie.

Dieter had kept the camera running throughout the entire incident. It was still running when Lee Lyon stepped into the picture, white-faced and in tears. She could not fully explain the tears, she told me later. 'It was just release of tension and relief to find Adrien untouched. At one point I honestly didn't think any of us would escape alive.'

Julie, as anyone who saw the *Survival* Special 'Gorilla' will know, was totally accepted by the group. Sadly, though, her unplanned return to the forest proved premature. Had there been a lactating female in the family she would probably have survived the period of exceptionally wet, cold weather that struck the forests ten days later. Alas, she didn't have the stamina to survive the hailstorms and drenching rain.

My period in the gorilla forest came towards the final stages of the filming. Though I missed most of the exciting action, the experience was invaluable when it came to making the film. Unless you have been in close contact with wild gorillas you just cannot conceive their majesty and power. Until then I had always thought the elephant the most impressive animal in the world. The first time that Kasimir stood upright on his hind legs and charged I knew that I had been wrong. Nothing could match the presence of this creature. When he turned his back on you, it looked as broad as a full-sized billiard table. When he faced you it was the human, albeit sub-human, cast of countenance that made you feel uneasy and inadequate. Inevitably, though your knowledge of evolution told you it was not the case, he spoke to you of your own distant origins. By the time my wife and I walked with Adrien and the camera team in the forests of Kahuzi, Kasimir was almost too well behaved. He had come to accept Adrien as another gorilla leader. I am certain of that. One morning we moved through the undergrowth in close proximity to the group without catching more than an occasional glimpse of one of them, though their musky smell and barkings and uneasy breast-beatings were all around us. Adrien forecast that, sometime during the day, Kasimir would choose the ground on which to meet him. Sure enough, in late afternoon, he did so. Kasimir was reclining in a bed of nettles at the edge of a small open clearing. Nearby was one of his females called Broken-arm. When close to the gorillas, we moved in single file behind Adrien. You did exactly as you were told, making no sudden movements, avoiding staring the animals in the eye, failing to indulge the instinctive gesture of pointing. All these movements were liable to be taken by the animals as signs of aggression. In dense forest, Adrien communicated with Kasimir by coughing, as the gorillas themselves coughed when advertising their presence to each other, and by calling the great ape softly and reassuringly, thus: 'Kasimir, *du calme*, Kasimir', and when Kasimir barked irritably: 'Kasimir, *assez, assez*'. On this occasion there was no need for talk. Kasimir reclined in the nettle bed – a potentate holding court. In Adrien's wake, my wife and I advanced until we were standing within six feet of the great man himself. After half an hour during which he permitted us to take, using tactfully slow movements, a number of portraits, Kasimir turned his back on us. The audience was over. The great silverback silently led his family away to find a nesting place for the night.

Zaire is a far from reassuring place in which to work. Joan and I had received our baptism at the frontier. On the flight in we had landed at Rwanda's international airport at Kigali in our chartered Aztec in order to have visitors' visas stamped in our passports. This was only necessary because our pilot had to deposit us at Kamembe, a strip on the Rwanda side of the Zaire border where there were no such facilities. We would only be in Rwanda the ten minutes it took us to drive to the actual frontier at the river bridge. Neither of us had noticed that the immigration official at Kigali had only stamped one of our passports, my wife's. I was, therefore, technically, an illegal immigrant. At the tin shanty customs post on the Rwanda border, the duty officer was quick to point this out. I was illegally in Rwanda. What could I do about it? I could return to Kigali but, of course, the Aztec had by then taken off. There is one thing *not* to do in such circumstances and that is to argue. It is simply a question of how much. When the alternative is a visit to the local gaol, $40 US does not seem excessive.

The payment would have been higher had Adrien not been present but even he couldn't entirely beat the system: Dieter had warned us what to expect at the Zaire customs post which stood in one of those galvanized iron rondavels at the far end of the bridge. 'Don't protest, whatever they do, and let's hope for Joan's sake the woman isn't on duty. She'll pinch any cosmetics that take her fancy and may even insist on a body search.'

The woman, mercifully, wasn't on. Dieter exchanged polite jokes in French with the customs officer while that official verbally roughed up one of his countrymen who hadn't paid the excess 'duty' expected of him. Dieter made his contribution by presenting the officer with a pair of jeans he had bought specially in Nairobi. This presentation was to see Dieter through a very nasty situation in a few weeks' time and possibly even to save his life.

I describe the atmosphere in and around Bukavu as it impressed me because it makes believable what was to happen to Dieter when it finally became imperative for him to leave Zaire in a hurry. Just one illustration of the atmosphere prevailing: the third or fourth week in the month the police in Bukavu usually did not get paid. They were expected, therefore, to make up their own wages. In their white steel helmets and dark glasses they reminded me vividly of the *tons-tons macoute* of Papa Doc in Haiti as described by Graham Greene in *The Comedians*. They were certainly quite as sinister in appearance. If they stopped you because your headlights were switched on in broad daylight, when they weren't, you didn't argue but went through the motions of switching them off and paid the necessary fine. Even though all was outwardly calm, there was an indefinable menace in the Bukavu air. It was not hard to imagine that a few years before, during the civil war, three hundred bodies had lain rotting in the main street. But as far as Dieter and *Survival* were concerned, all seemed normal in our relationships with the authorities and with the National Parks in particular. We made our plans for a longer stay accordingly. There was no hint that anything was about to go wrong.

Survival's plans included the launching of Lee Lyon to shoot her first half-hours on her own, though still under Dieter's general guidance. We chose relatively easy, or at least self-contained, subjects, both of which I had surveyed on my visit. Both were situated in the magnificent Virunga, formerly Albert, National Park. This had the advantage of providing her with a stable base at Park HQ with assistance on hand if she needed it. On the reasonably good terrain of the park, she would also be able to get around, except perhaps to some of the remoter areas in the wettest part of the rainy season, in her Volkswagen Kombi. The first story was about Vitshumbi – 'the place of the salt' – a fishing settlement within the park on the shores of Lake Edward where the fishermen shared the village with thousands of pelicans and marabou storks and where 'tame' elephants strolled through the 'streets', rubbing their backsides against the huts. It was this total acceptance of wildlife by people, and vice versa, that made the village a good story.

The second half-hour concerned Virunga Park's huge hippo population, how the herds lived, reproduced, affected their environment and presented problems to the ecology.

Dieter himself was to tackle a volcano story. The Virunga volcanoes stretch in a line from Rwanda to the northern end of Lake Kivu in Zaire. The idea we worked out was a simple one. We would portray the volcano both as a destructive force and as a creative one. Creative in the sense that much of the early development of the earth itself was shaped by the gases, the water and matter spewed out by volcanoes. The second element would show the local adaptations of the animals that lived on the volcano. Dieter laid his plans to start filming on the active volcano in the Virunga chain, Nyirangongo.

Meantime he had an exceptionally close call. Bernhard Grzimek was on a goodwill visit to Zaire. He had asked Dieter whether he could find time to shoot some scenes of himself in a wildlife setting for his German TV programme. Dieter immediately thought of the semi-tame elephants in the village of Vitshumbi. The big bull there was especially co-operative. The schoolchildren pelted it with mud which it good-naturedly ignored and were even said to swing on its tusks. All this, however, took place within the confines of the village.

When Dieter took Bernhard Grzimek for his filming session, the elephant had temporarily moved out of the village to the swamps two or three hundred yards away on the edge of the lake.

There, it quickly became clear, it was a very different elephant. It no longer felt secure as it did among the fishermen's huts. It had once again assumed the suspicions and apprehensions of the real wild article. Dieter, however, judged that the bull was still a fair security risk and posed Bernhard in front of it for the scenes he required. Towards the end of the session the elephant became uneasy. Bernhard Grzimek retired behind Dieter but continued to take still photographs of the bull. The bull suddenly decided that he had posed quite long enough and, without giving the customary warning false charge, rushed Dieter with the obvious intention of flattening him.

Dieter instantly recognized that this was the moment to bail out. He had overlooked one fact. He was wearing a heavy battery belt to power his camera. The stout lead from this was, of course, plugged in to his camera. There was no time to unplug the lead or unfasten and drop the battery belt. Elephants move at a rate of acceleration quite incompatible with their bulk. Dieter turned and ran for his life and, in doing so, pulled over the Arriflex and the heavy tripod. It was this that saved him. The elephant paused when he reached the fallen camera and placed one foot on it, giving Dieter time to unfasten his belt. There was a lesson here for all our cameramen: when filming in a dangerous situation, never attach yourself to camera by battery belt and lead. Tragically it was a lesson that was not to be learned until it was too late.

So Lee, who had been present when the big bull charged Dieter, settled down to start filming her two stories in the Virunga Park. Dieter climbed to the top of Nyiragongo and began the unearthly experience of filming inside its crater. The crater itself is over half a mile wide. Once you have made the precipitous descent down its lava cliffs you are faced with a trembling floor, by far the larger part of which is solid yet fissured with thousands of vents from which sulphurous smoke emerges. Two or three hundred yards across this lies the pit itself where the molten magma seethes and rolls in glowing waves, throwing up breakers of scarlet fire, cascading down a huge sump apparently simply to be recycled into another part of the cauldron. During the three weeks in which Dieter lived inside the crater, he never got used to the sub-terranean roar. He described his location as like living on top of an underground station through which at least ten trains passed every minute. Living close to the crater was also extremely dangerous. The gases it produced were lethal. The wind had constantly to be watched for sudden changes which might bring with them deadly clouds of hydrochloric acid gas. Dieter had armed himself with a respirator. Despite this he inhaled more than was good for him and on one occasion passed out while filming. That he recovered at all, he claims, was entirely due to the fact that in his hallucinated, semi-conscious state the figure of Jack Ball, *Survival* Anglia's US President, appeared before him and offered him the most beautiful girl in New York if he would only make the effort to live. Dieter, who is as open to this sort of encouragement as the next man, perhaps more so, lived.

However, even while he filmed inside Nyiragongo's crater, equally primitive forces were at work on the plains below, in Goma at the north end of Lake Kivu to be precise. One day a messenger appeared fearfully on the wall of the crater. Dieter must return to Goma at once and surrender all the film he had shot in Zaire.

Accustomed to the confusions that arise in local officialdom, Dieter saw no course but to return to Goma and straighten the matter out. It must be a mistake. Mistake or not, he was not going to hand over a foot of the film he had shot at so much effort and risk. When he reached the office of the head of wildlife and tourism in Goma, he found that no mistake had been made. The official there meant what he said. Furthermore, he suggested, in best feature film tradition, which was all the more chilling, because of the place and manner in which the threat was delivered, that in Zaire they had ways of getting what they wanted.

Dieter strode out of the office and climbed into his Unimog, the remarkable four-wheel drive vehicle made by the Mercedes company. As he drove away, he saw a police car slip out behind him. Dieter drove flat out down the main street, swung right-handed and pulled into a vehicle workshop whose doors, he knew, were open at both ends. When the police car had shot by, he took the Unimog out of the rear workshop doors on to a back street and headed for the lakeside road leading to Bukavu, one hundred miles away.

He was now convinced that, for some reason he didn't understand, he was in bad trouble, the sort of trouble in which an accident might easily be arranged to prevent his leaving the country with his film. He banked on the fact that the road to Bukavu had been cut by recent rains and was certainly impassable to any normal vehicle. The Unimog with its twenty-odd gears, four-wheel drive and differential lock is no normal vehicle. The impassability of the road became evident as night fell. At one point he came across a group of heavy lorries bogged down and completely blocking the route. To the Unimog this presented little problem. One by one, Dieter winched them out. Communications between Goma and Bukavu are notoriously bad. Moreover he was gambling that whoever was gunning for him would reckon that it was impossible for anyone to drive to Bukavu in existing conditions.

When he arrived in Bukavu friends assured him that there was as yet no alarm out to stop him but that it might come at any moment. He started out for the border straight away. The customs post on the bridge presented the last obstacle. This was where the pair of jeans bought in Nairobi some weeks previously proved invaluable. The official to whom he had presented them was on duty and seemed genially disposed. This friendliness, Dieter realized, would disappear instantly, should a message be received that Dieter with his precious cargo of film was a runaway. The jeans, in fact, proved a tantalizing embarrassment. The friendly customs man was disposed to talk at length about the possibility of Dieter's obtaining other garments for him. While this interminable conversation was going on, the official excused himself to break off and deal with the problems of an African traveller. This occupied a further five minutes. At last, when Dieter was cleared to leave and

The Sultan of Aussa, Dedgazmatch Ali Mirrah, chief of the Afar people of the Danakil Desert of Ethiopia, poses for a rare photograph, taken by my wife, who expected to be treated by this Muslim potentate as less than the dust. Instead, she was made an honoured guest.

On the far left is the only English-speaking Danakil, our interpreter; on either side of the Sultan, his sons, showing the westernized influence of Cairo University. All are now exiled and many of the Danakil themselves have been slaughtered. Bottom: the real thing. The warriors over whom the Sultan ruled. The rifle probably no longer fires but there is no doubt about the sharpness of the castration knives they traditionally wear.

Top, the two faces of *Survival's* founder and producer. Aubrey Buxton on safari in northern Kenya; and, flanked by Des and Jen Bartlett and editor Les Parry at the 'Emmy' presentations by the National Academy of Television Arts and Sciences in New York. The Bartletts won the coveted 'Emmy' (Television's equivalent of the 'Oscar') for the photography; Les Parry, *Survival's* senior film editor, for the editing on 'The Incredible Flight of the Snowgeese'. Bottom, John Forsythe, star of many feature films and Broadway plays (and incidentally the 'voice' in the TV Series 'Charlie's Angels') who introduces the 'World of Survival' half-hour series in the United States. John held the peregrine falcon as a 'prop' while introducing a Survival programme about preventing birdstrikes on aircraft.

saying his adieux, a police motor cyclist pulled up outside. A few seconds later, one of the guards came crashing in and seized his rifle out of the rack. Both events were coincidental but Dieter was convinced that they marked the moment of a last-minute arrest.

He crossed the bridge, cleared the Rwanda customs post on the far side without further trouble and sat on the airstrip hoping and praying that the Aztec would come in that morning. While he waited he watched the nearby shore of Lake Kivu, marking the border. It was not unknown for police from Zaire to cross in order to retrieve those who had left under a cloud and in a hurry. In the event, the Aztec came in and Dieter reached London with his film thirty-six hours later.

We never did unravel the strands of local intrigue that led to this hurried exit. Plainly someone somewhere in high places thought that Dieter's filming was a threat to his own activities. The most likely theory was that a high official planned a private exploitation of the wildlife in Virunga Park and feared that *Survival*'s cameras would expose this. The vendetta was not, apparently, against Lee Lyon. She was permitted to remain. With Adrien Deschryver keeping an eye on her, she was undoubtedly safe but, frustratingly, she was not allowed to film in the National Parks. The whole Zaire operation had collapsed, apparently without logical explanation.

Had Dieter Plage panicked unnecessarily? The answer must be: not if he wished to save his film. Was he in danger of his life? We will never know the answer to that. Having spent some time in the strangely oppressive atmosphere of Kivu Province, I can readily understand that he felt that a convenient accident might have been arranged on his behalf. One has to remember that, though order and even law may exist in Kinshasa, Bukavu and Goma are fifteen hundred miles from the capital.

In London we did our best to clear the situation through diplomatic channels. Aubrey Buxton even arranged another royal première at the National Film Theatre for Dieter's magnificent 'Gorilla', at which Prince Philip presented a copy of the film, with French commentary, to the Zairois Ambassador. All seemed to be sweetness and light. We were assured that permission would be granted to finish off not only the volcano project but Lee Lyon's two stories in Virunga Park. For some reason that permission never filtered down to the local authorities at Goma. We never did get back into the Zaire parks.

It is inevitable that, from time to time, tropical illnesses catch up with members of the team. The Hospital for Tropical Diseases at St Pancras, London, receives regular visits from cameramen who are either suffering from, or fear they may be suffering from, the attentions of some exotic

12

bug. Bilharzia, the debilitating illness caused by the intrusion of a creature part of whose life-cycle is passed as guest of a certain water snail, is perhaps the most common. You have only to step into, or put a hand into, water infected with this pest to give the parasite an opportunity to burrow through the skin and attack vital organs, including the kidneys. Though one tries to keep clear of waters which are known to harbour the snail and which lie close to human habitation from which infection comes, it is extremely difficult to be careful all the time. Treatment used to be lengthy and unpleasant. Today, fortunately, it is comparatively simple and routine.

It might be expected that we hot-house flowers who spend most of the year in our offices and cutting-rooms in Park Lane would be highly vulnerable during our spasmodic trips into the bush. Not so. We never feel fitter than when on safari but invariably catch 'flu the moment we step on to the plane to come home. I had always been very lucky where health was concerned. However, on my most recent trip with Dieter Plage to Sumatra, the luck ran out. Something very nasty was lying in wait.

We were making a one-hour Special on orangutans and the work of two charming Swiss girl scientists, Monica Borner and Regina Frey, to rehabilitate and return to the bush orangs that had been kept in captivity. You may ask why this should be necessary. The reason is that there are remarkably few wild orangs left in the forests of Sumatra and Borneo, the only two places of the Far East in which these once widely distributed great apes still exist. Orangs have vanished through persecution, of course, but mainly because the primary rain forest in which they live is being felled at an appalling rate. The trees are coming down to make way for rice paddies and rubber plantations. A great deal of such felling may be necessary. But they are also being hacked down for a quick profit in timber with no thought to the effect such decimation may have on climate or soil, let alone on the animals who depend on the forests.

The Swiss girls ran a rehabilitation centre in the rain forest at a place north of Medan in Sumatra called Bohorok. The station, funded, by Bernhard Grzimek's efforts, through the Frankfurt Zoological Society, and helped by the Indonesian Government and the World Wildlife Fund, took in apes that had been illegally captured and taught them how to live wild again. When their guests could feed themselves on wild plants, make nests in the trees and generally show that they were fit for rehabilitation, the girls took them at least fifteen miles away from Bohorok, far enough to prevent them from making their way back home, and released them in the Gunung Leuser Forest Reserve.

Dieter's brief was, together with his assistant Mike Price, to cover the whole process of rehabilitation as well as the life of the truly wild orangs in the forest.

My wife and I joined the team towards the end of the filming. We had been warned that the forest was extremely humid. Even so, I wasn't quite prepared for the degree of moisture in the air beneath the two hundred foot high trees and among the ground cover of giant ferns and bamboos. We walked in from the point at which the road ran out. It wasn't a particularly long or strenuous walk and it was certainly a very beautiful one, passing through caves and along the side of streams, with leaf monkeys peering from trees and the occasional hysterical whoopings of excited siamangs – a species of gibbon – for background accompaniment. By the time we had crossed the Bohorok river by dug-out canoe and trooped up the hill to the wooden station which Monica and Regina had designed and persuaded local labour to build on their arrival in the forest three years previously, I was fairly warm. Regina instantly produced a large mug of steaming tea. After I had drunk it I sat there wondering if I was going to live. The tea seemed to be leaving my body via the pores almost as quickly as I swallowed it. I remember thinking: 'If it is like this all the time, I shall definitely succumb. I never did like Turkish baths.'

We quickly got used to the conditions even though our clothes smelled of mildew within a few days. Fungus even formed between the elements of the team's camera lenses. I wouldn't have been surprised to find my sleeping bag covered with mushrooms every morning. We slept in a tent on an air-bed, with an occasional Sumatra tiger padding around in the immediate vicinity. We would all have found the forest unbearably claustrophobic, I feel sure, had it not been for the fact that the rapids of the cold, clear Bohorok river ran into a deep forest pool only thirty yards away. Whenever things became too much you could body-surf down the rapids and end up exhausted in the pool below. These swims and the rain that fell after sundown when Dieter, Mike, Joan and I foregathered for a beer in our 'night club', a polythene and bamboo shelter, before trooping through the forest to eat at the station the remarkable meals produced by Regina and Monica out of nothing, were the highpoints of the day. It is perhaps indicative of the conditions that Dieter and I developed an unnatural appetite for pickled cucumbers. After we had demolished a half-gallon jar of same, we would practically fight each other for who was to have first drink of the brine. We drank an awful lot of pickled cucumber liquid. Our need for this unlikely beverage reached addictive proportions, so I can only assume that we were losing a great deal of body salt. I have never felt the same way about pickled cucumbers since, though at the time I came to understand that line in a Turgenev play: 'Eight thousand years of human civilization and we've never invented anything better than the pickled cucumber.'

Despite the fungus that grew on everything and the salt that leaked out of our bodies, we kept surprisingly fit and would, I think have continued to do so if it hadn't been for Rambong.

Rambong was one of the orangs due for rehabilitation. She was a very sad case. When rescued by Monica and Regina she had already spent several years in a small crate. Her incarceration by her owners – a number of well-off Indonesians illegally keep orangs as status symbols, having originally obtained them as babies – was comparable to keeping a six foot man in solitary confinement in a sweat-box in which it is impossible to stand upright. As a result Rambong had developed the sort of mental disorders which a human being might be expected to show after several years of this sort of confinement. In addition she obviously had lung and sinus complaints of a serious order. Rambong sat alone most of the day, pining, coughing and streaming at the nose, a picture of misery which it was difficult not to see in human terms. It would almost certainly have been a kindness, as well as a sensible hygienic precaution, to put poor Rambong down. This, I am sure, occurred to her Swiss guardians many times and yet, such was their dedication to the work of rehabilitating as many orangs as possible that they could not bring themselves to do so.

So Rambong daily hung around the feeding centre. At this point I must describe the centre and its importance in the daily life of Bohorok station. The centre consisted of several flat-topped cages high up in the forest above the river and the girls' living hut. The cages contained one or two orangs who were reckoned to be still too young to wander the forest at night on their own. The rest of the candidates for return to the wild, perhaps twenty or more in number, roamed the forest freely all day and returned to the feeding centre in the afternoon for a free hand-out of bananas and milk. This was distributed on the flat-topped roofs of the cages. Every day at around four in the afternoon we climbed up the steep trail to the cages carrying the food. On the long upward climb we were often met by orangs commuting in from the surrounding forest for their free feed. Sometimes the smarter or lazier ones intercepted us along the path like hitch-hikers thumbing a lift. Often we let them climb on board. I remember once seeing Dieter arrive with four apes clinging to him. Soon we got to know the names and highly individual personalities of all these young orangs. There was Olip who had a mechanical genius and liked to press the button on an Arriflex camera. (Eventually he ate the rubber eyepiece.) Ojong was bone-idle and a habitual hitch-hiker. Suka was a youngster who seemed destined to be a super-ape. A young male, Suka was in on every situation, causing alarm and despondency among his fellows on all possible occasions. Then there was Agam, whom Dieter called Robert Redford after some imagined resemblance (his hair seemed to part in the middle), and an excessively ugly and thuggish orang, Pesek, named by Dieter, because of his rugged appearance, 'the oil man'. Dieter saw him as part of the crew of an oil rig. A pair of dark brown orangs were known as 'the twins' because they always went round together, arms entwined, even in the depths of the forest. In fact they were in no way related and had been brought to Bohorok at different times from different places.

All these and many more orang characters turned up on schedule for a tea party at which Monica or Regina presided every day. The gathering was not only highly entertaining but vital to the two scientists' work. It was the one time they had to check on the different animals' growing independence; to decide at what point, possibly after six or more months' habituation, individuals were ready to be flown by chopper to a release point fifteen miles away so that they could begin a wild, free, forest life again.

Table manners at the tea party were tolerably good. Fighting seldom broke out, though there were tantrums and sulkings, extremely human to behold, often as the result of Suka's intrusion on the others' privacy or food supply, usually the latter. Rambong, of course, was part of the daily gathering, though, as always, she sat a little aside. Nevertheless the poor thing with her complexes, coughs and runny nose, was dangerously in contact not only with the other apes but with us. Since we handled the young orangs, or to be more accurate they handled us by climbing over us whether we liked it or not, we were all in an ideal situation in which to exchange germs with each other.

When the tea party was over and the last green banana eaten, then one by one the orangs disappeared back into the forest for the next twenty-four hours to re-acquire their wild style of living. Suka and one or two other youngsters were locked up in the cages for the night and Rambong just hung around.

When we eventually said goodbye to the Swiss girls and their attractive charges, all was well with the health of both the orangs and ourselves. The shooting was over. We were due to move back to Dieter's base in Katmandhu, Nepal, to begin work on a tiger Special. But first we had to fly to Singapore to buy equipment, including the eyepiece that Olip had eaten, and then on to pay a brief visit to Jakarta, capital of Indonesia.

Within twelve hours of leaving the forest I began to feel as though I had a bad attack of 'flu. There was nothing I could do about it except, literally, sweat it out. In that atmosphere it wasn't very difficult. By the time I reached Singapore I began to suspect that I had some nasty form of malaria, though I had, of course, been taking Paludrin daily as a preventative. Descending in the jet to Jakarta I thought my eardrums were going to burst. I got through the diplomatic talks in Jakarta somehow. Bangkok airport at two in the morning with Dieter bludgeoning the authorities to pass nearly a ton of equipment through in under an hour I remember as an opium-smoker might recall a hallucinatory dream. I rallied brightly at the first sight of the Himalayas from the air, relapsed into a state of fatalistic and feverish indifference during the three hours it took us to get out of Katmandhu airport. Two hours later I began to shake and go into a rigor with a temperature of around 104°F. Andrew Lawrie, the young scientist studying rhinos with whom Dieter and Mike had made a rhino film before leaving for Sumatra, was fortunately around to give my wife some advice. 'Don't for God's sake let anyone put him into hospital in Katmandhu. They use the same needle on every patient until it gets blunt. He'll never come out alive.'

This was possibly an exaggeration, but only a slight one. Andrew's brother had barely survived hospitalization there. Andrew and Joan scoured the town for a good doctor and came up with the best, the retired physician to the King of Nepal. He had been trained in Edinburgh and America. Dr Malan, I'm pretty sure, saved the day, though even he didn't know what I'd got. At first he thought it might be typhoid but tests proved negative. He filled me full of antibiotics until the inside of my mouth burst with ulcers. After ten days or so it became clear that I was going to live. Meantime, if nothing else, I learned how to harvest rice. A Nepalese family garnering and winnowing the crop was all I had to watch as I lay there wondering whether, like Mad Carew, I would merit a little wooden cross above the town. That I survived I owe not only to Andrew, my wife and Dr Malan, but to two good friends who lent me their houses in which to make up my mind whether I wanted to live or not. I watched the rice harvest from the home of Frank and Inge Poppleton. Frank had been head warden of the Ugandan Parks when I first met him in Uganda in 1961. Now he was UNO wildlife adviser to Nepal. Later in my recovery I was able to enjoy a distant view of the Himalayas from the house of Jim and Fiona Edwards. Lying sick in Jim's house was a survival course in itself. Jim Edwards runs two very successful travel operations, 'Mountain Travel' and 'Tiger Tops' in Chitawan National Park. Both cater for specialized and adventurous tourists who either want to meet rhinos and tigers on elephant back or else go trekking up to sixteen thousand feet in the Himalayas. The house, therefore, was like a caravanserai, continually full of climbers, Sherpas, in fact almost anyone who arrived in Katmandhu. The noise was stupendous.

At the end of about three weeks it was decided that the best thing I could do was to make a dash for England. Joan and Dieter thought I needed a little revitalization and rousing from my lethargy. My rehabilitation took the form of flying with Dieter in his Cessna 206 first down to Chitawan to look at rhinos from the air and then next day up the pass leading to Everest. I am still not sure whether these flights speeded or retarded my recovery. They were certainly spectacular, though I wasn't perhaps quite strong enough to cope with the vision of sheer rock walls apparently a wingtip away and the dead carcases of Royal Nepal Twin Otter passenger planes lying wrecked below us on the terrible mountain airstrip at Lukla.

Three days later I made it back to England and celebrated my return home by being sick in my own garden before I even reached the front door. It was plain that I wasn't quite cured of whatever it was that ailed me. Six weeks later I was still running a temperature every night.

The Hospital for Tropical Diseases, to which I reported soon after my return, was delighted with my suggestion that I had come in contact with a badly infected orangutan. Their interest in my case immediately perked up. Was it, they asked, possible that a swab could be got from the orang concerned? I told them that I thought this unlikely. Poor Rambong was either dead or back in the forest. They went along with the idea that she was the probable cause of my illness. People, they pointed out, could give diseases including polio and tuberculosis to orangs, so why shouldn't the reverse procedure apply? I saw no reason why they shouldn't be right.

The plague eventually went away as mysteriously as it arrived, leaving me two stone lighter. The orangs of Bohorok, alas, didn't come out of it so well. We heard later from Monica and Regina that the ebullient Suka and one of the twins, Cura, had become ill and had died. None of us will ever know whether the stricken Rambong was the cause of these disasters, but a note in the records of the Hospital for Tropical Diseases at least records that it is possible. As for me, I need no convincing.

Chapter 15

The Ladies

I HAVE written so far as if *Survival* is an all-male enterprise. It is very far from that. The women in *Survival*'s life are not only a very special breed, they are in many cases at least fifty per cent of the team in the field. They keep their men sane. They keep them going. All of them drive. Some of them fly. Most of them film. They house-keep and plan in the most impossible conditions. At various times in their careers they are expected to live, eat, work and sleep in deserts, rain forests, on mountain tops, on uninhabited islands. To say they are expected to do so suggests that their men demand it of them. From what I have already written of Jen Bartlett it will have become clear that the women wouldn't have it any other way.

In terms of time served, Jen Bartlett is undoubtedly *Survival*'s first lady, though Joan Root must run her close. Jen, the ex-Wimbledon tennis star, takes most of the still photographs in the Bartlett team. Jen is a wiry, handsome woman who when necessary carries the same load as her husband, about seventy pounds of equipment in a back-pack. She is reserved, sometimes almost enigmatic, so that it is hard, well as I know her, to gauge what her true feelings are about some fundamental matters. For example: will she ever tire of the nomad's life? She must now be in her late forties so it must occur to her, as it does to the male photographers, that she can't scale mountains and live in a tent for ever. Like any other woman she must, surely, have an urge to put down roots. One would imagine so and yet it is impossible to judge her values from my own comparatively staid and urban standpoint. She has the most important root of all: a daughter who is a triumph of upbringing. She has a family in her native Australia and the Bartletts have recently bought an apartment in the Bahamas. But will she ever feel happy without the freedom to come and go with apparently limitless space around her? For example, when she is in the English countryside, which I personally find the most lovely in the world, she is under-standably oppressed by the *smallness* of the fields, the claustrophobic effect of stone walls and hawthorn hedges. I sometimes feel that Des and Jen are indestructible and perhaps that is exactly what they are. Probably the answer is that, given the superb health and physical fitness they both possess, they will go on doing exactly what they are doing now at a pace which suits them both as they grow older. They both appreciate the comforts of civilization when they are available but in Jen, especially, I sense that she is always on her guard against becoming *too* comfortable. A warm fireside and a comfortable bed with all mod. cons. are beguiling things. But they must never become too beguiling. The tundra with its bleak wind, the desert with its oven temperatures is just outside the door waiting and beckoning. That, as far as she is concerned, is where life is lived and it never does for one second to forget it.

Joan Root grew up under the wide skies of Kenya. She is a gentle, shy and warm person who differs from Jen in one important respect. She and Alan have a permanent home on the shores of Lake Naivasha, fifty-odd miles up the Rift from Nairobi. Unless you built a house half-way up a mountain with all East Africa at your feet, there could be few more beautiful settings. The freshwater lake lays down its papyrus-fringed carpet of purple lotus lilies within fifty yards of the verandah. Bushbuck and dikdik, the tiny antelope little bigger than a hare, nibble the flowers. Occasionally hippos haul out in the shrubbery at night. Fish eagles call and sometimes nest overhead in the tops of the yellow-barked acacias. The house itself is a typical colonist's bungalow, not particularly beautiful. How can any construction with a corrugated iron roof be called beautiful? Yet it is right for its setting and cool and spacious inside. It was built by a settler who had walked all the way up from the Cape and decided when he reached this point that he wasn't going any further. He was right.

The interior of the house is, perhaps, a little short on comfort. Naivasha gets cold at night, for its altitude is just over six thousand feet, and there is sometimes frost on the grass in the mornings. There are nights when a blazing fire in the spacious fireplace which the old settler built to remind him of home would be a welcome addition. But a fire is never lit, partly because it would disturb the birds nesting in the chimney but mainly, I suspect, because fires in the grate are symbols of home and, literally, hearth. For such as the Roots, fires are something to cook on in the bush, to sit round under the stars when the evening meal is over. A proper fire is a camp fire. For the same reason, Joan Root, who has excellent taste and is in many ways highly domesticated, does not go to any lengths to decorate or furnish for comfort and relaxation. It is not, she will explain, that she doesn't care about such things. It is just that she and Alan are never home enough to bother. Also, she will add with some justice, that when you have possessions you become a target for thugs and thieves and the house is, after all, in an isolated position. Nevertheless, you suspect that, as with Jen Bartlett, there is a reluctance to become too settled.

A wildlife cameraman's wife has to be willing to share many of her husband's hazards. Joan Root has had her own share of mishaps. She was bitten by a scorpion on a wedding night spent under canvas in the bush. A two inch acacia thorn passed through the sole of her foot. Alan had to remove it with a pair of pliers. And, of course, there was the case of the hippo that bit off her face mask in Mzima Springs. She accepts these things. Less easy to accept, I feel sure, are the strains put on her nervous system by some of Alan's escapades. I have seen her sit in one of the rear seats of a light aircraft looking as though she wished she was somewhere, anywhere, else. Recently she has been learning to fly, perhaps in self-defence. Alan is a lucky man to have her. I'm sure he knows it. She is a superb organizer of African domestic staff, safari cooks, safaris and all the planning that goes into them. She is an excellent photographer and a natural handler of animals. Who else would encourage a caracel, an African lynx, to sleep on her bed, a young hippo called Sally to bask on her verandah, an aardvark known as Millions ('Aardvark a million miles for one of your smiles', Alan's joke based on Al Jolson) to dig up her grass and a striped hyena to romp on her sitting-room floor to entertain her guests? You could easily walk a million miles without finding another Joan Root.

Then there are the girls who actually film for *Survival*. Lucinda Buxton is a petite blonde who has lived down the fact that she's her father's daughter and brought some excellent *Survivals* in without the partnership in the field or, in the first instance, experience that many others enjoy.

Cindy obviously didn't fit into any of the ready-made young girl slots. She wasn't cut out for an office or indeed for working indoors. She had been brought up in the Norfolk countryside, bird-watching, sailing, riding and shooting. A friend and mentor from childhood was Ted Eales, warden of Blakeney Point National Trust Nature Reserve and, as I have described, one of the earliest naturalist cameramen for *Survival*.

When Cindy showed a strong interest in wildlife photography, her father, Aubrey Buxton, suggested she equip herself with a Bolex 16mm camera and attach herself for a course of tuition to Ted Eales. Ted stuck her in hides, showed her how to approach and film birds and taught her the basics of camera work. It was soon clear that she had a talent for the work as well as an iron determination to succeed.

Survival sent her to Kenya, to Lake Nakuru, to make a film about the million flamingoes then using the lake and the problems they faced. There she had the advice and help of John Hopcraft who lives by the lake shore and is one of the leading authorities on Nakuru. It is not easy for a girl wildlife photographer to operate in Africa. There are obvious dangers from large wild animals, though these are absent at Nakuru. But the real difficulty comes in getting things done and people to do things for you. No one who saw the small attractive blonde girl stumping about the mud flats of Nakuru, immuring herself for hours on end in baking hot sunken hides made from forty-gallon oil drums, could doubt that here was one memsahib who wasn't going to take no for an answer. 'Nakuru', Cindy's first film, was highly successful and contained one genuine wildlife 'nugget'. This was a fine sequence in which marabou storks made low level attacks on gangs of young, newly fledged flamingoes standing at the water's edge, panicking them until they could pounce on one slower and less aware than the rest. From 'Nakuru', Cindy went on to shoot a *Survival* which we called 'The Floating Worlds of Naivasha'. Here again there was a notable nugget, a sequence in which it was possible to see what went on inside the tunnel nest, deep in a bank, where a malachite kingfisher raised its brood.

In Ethiopia Cindy joined her cousin John Buxton (of 'SOS Rhino' fame), to make a one-hour Special about the problems affecting one of the scenically most spectacular wildlife areas on earth – the Simien Mountains. To film the walia ibex and gelada baboons of the Simien Massif, you are frequently perched on crags over five or six thousand foot vertical drops and all this in intense African sunlight beating down in ultra-clear, thin air at between twelve thousand and thirteen thousand feet. At this height there is far less atmosphere to filter the ultra-violet light. We had experienced enough trouble at Shala when filming pelicans at a far lower altitude. For the first few days in the high Simiens Cindy suffered severe sunburn and sunstroke, the ultra-violet light inflicting excruciating burns even through her clothing. She is a courageous girl who deserved a major success for sheer guts.

The story of how she dealt with a tooth abscess while filming in the wild country north of Lake Turkana in Kenya illustrates the tenacity of the lady. There are no dentists in those parts. In fact the nearest one was two days' drive away. Cindy decided that the pain was such that she couldn't wait. Nor, for that matter, could she afford to take four or five days out of her filming schedule at that moment. She eventually found an Asian who had some knowledge of tooth extraction or, anyway, owned a pair of dental forceps. In lieu of an anaesthetic, an African sat on her stomach and held her head, while the 'dentist' struggled with the tooth for twenty minutes before he wrenched it out of the gum. Relief from the pain was instantaneous and the ordeal, Cindy told me, 'well worth it'. However, she got a nasty shock when she at last reached a dentist in Nairobi. He told her that the abscess had been ruptured at the worst time of all and she was lucky not to have become badly infected by the poisons released.

She achieved her major success during the third or fourth year of her wildlife filming career. By then her camera technique had reached a point at which it was able to make maximum use of a unique opportunity. In Zambia there is a huge area of swamp called the Bengweulu. It is about the size of Wales when fully flooded after the rainy season and holds a large population of big animals, including buffaloes, elephants and lions who lie out among the water in isolated clumps of reeds and grass to ambush their prey. The Bengweulu is also home to a large population of marsh-adapted antelope, both black lechwe and sitatunga. But it was none of these that Cindy Buxton came to film.

In a few swampy areas of Africa, notably the southern Sudan, Uganda and the Bengweulu swamp, there exists what must surely be the strangest-looking bird in the world. It is usually called the whale-headed stork and sometimes the shoebilled or boatbilled stork. Its scientific name is *Balaeniceps rex*. It lives in dense reed beds and, since it stands nearly four feet tall, it is surprising that it is not more often seen. The answer is that it is exceedingly shy, rather like our own bittern in this respect. No one had so far observed its nesting behaviour or written a paper about it. Cindy Buxton set out to put the record straight. Except for an occasional visit from a friend, she was isolated in the swamp for over six months. The first problem was to find a nest, the second to film it. Luckily she was able from time to time to borrow an airboat from Ian Manning, a Canadian biologist studying the marsh antelope. For the rest she was left to her own devices. When she did eventually find a shoebill nest, the birds accepted her floating hide remarkably quickly and settled down to hatch two chicks, one of which survived. The *Survival* Special we made about her adventures and achievement was called 'Almost a Dodo', a tribute to the bird's weird appearance. (When the first shoebill skull was discovered, some naturalist suggested it was the fossilized relic of a dodo or dinosaur). The film is the only record of the shoebill's breeding biology. Leslie Brown, the world authority on birds of prey and the first ornithologist to discover where the two million flamingoes of the Rift Valley nested, is at present recording the information gathered in the first scientific paper on *Balaeniceps rex*.

Cindy Buxton comes from what you might call a fairly sheltered, almost feather-bedded English background, yet is perhaps most at home in the bush. All the women in *Survival*'s life, with the possible exception of Joan Root who grew up in Kenya, have a largely urban or anyway not especially open-air background. Jen Bartlett comes from Sydney. Mary Grant, who is now Mrs Plage, worked in a bank in Bath. Her family live in Portsmouth. Liz Bomford who, as I write, has been filming for a year with her husband Tony and three-year-old daughter in the rain forests of Madagascar, is a zoology graduate from Bedfordshire. I have met biologists whose wives had never seen a real wild animal or lived in a tent until they met their husbands and yet are blissfully happy. There is just no telling who will turn out to be a bird in the bush, though you can fairly confidently say who won't. A man in the bush certainly needs at least some home comforts and feminine solace. On the other hand, we have all in our time seen some disastrous exports intended to provide this.

However, though dolly-birds do not as a species thrive in tents, there is no reason why a woman should lose her femininity simply because she is part of a naturalist camera team. *Survival*'s ladies are extremely feminine. This quality reveals itself in many ways. Moira, Rod Borland's South African born wife, insists on some domestic grace-notes, even under canvas. When you return from a long hot day's filming there are wild flowers (when in season) in vases on the camp table. There may even be paper napkins folded in flower shapes. The hairy-chested sleep-under-a-tarpaulin school find this rather ridiculous. Though I would never miss such niceties myself it is easy to see the point. To adapt the old army phrase more politely: 'any fool can live in squalor.' There is absolutely no need to do so. It is refreshing after a day spent in a bouncing vehicle or a furnace of a hide to return to civilized surroundings. It sometimes needs a woman to point this out. The last time my wife and I camped with the Borlands was on a beach in Tongaland on the South Africa–Mozambique border where Rod was filming leatherback turtles. There were flowers on the table that night. A few minutes before we sat down to eat, Moira Borland touched the tentacles of a 'blue bottle', a Portuguese man-o'-war stranded on the beach, was stung and temporarily almost totally paralysed. The flowers and the poisonous 'jelly fish' are not really connected except that between them they in some ways sum up the strange life of a naturalist camerawoman.

I have left Lee Lyon to last because she has a special place. Lee was killed in a freak accident with a young elephant in Rwanda in June 1975.

When the message reached me through the American Embassy that Lee had been killed, my first thought was that in the treacherous weather conditions of the Rwanda–Zaire border she had flown her aircraft into the side of a mountain. But when I went to see the man at the Embassy, the cable he handed me from the US Consulate in Kigali clearly stated that she had been crushed by an elephant. For some reason he gave me a little homily about young girls doing unsuitable jobs. I couldn't answer him or argue with him or tell him that Lee wouldn't have considered any other sort of job suitable because for some reason the impact had just then hit me and I was crying. Throughout the next dreadful week when I spoke each day to Adrien Deschryver on a poorly connected line to Kigali I found myself repeatedly breaking down.

The facts of the tragedy were these. During the frustrating time when *Survival* had been banned from filming in the Zaire parks, Lee had been left without a story. She had got to hear, as we had also heard in London, about a bizarre attempt to save the calves of Rwanda's last herd of elephants. Rwanda is a greatly overpopulated country where every acre of farming land is at a premium. This one remaining elephant herd living in papyrus swamps along the banks of a river was understandably not popular as its members frequently emerged to pillage the local *shambas*, or farms. The villagers took reprisals, often very inefficient reprisals. Many of the surviving adults, therefore, carried old bullet or spear wounds. Some had wire burns or deep scars from broken snares on their legs. The twenty or thirty adult elephants left were not only savage, they were mainly in bad shape. Even had there been an obvious and easy method of capturing and transferring them to Kagera National Park some twenty miles away, few would have been in good enough condition to warrant the exercise. As it is, there is no easy way to translocate a five ton elephant, especially from such a densely populated area. Their calves, however, were something quite different and there were known to be ten to twenty of these of ages varying from a few weeks to two or three years old. The rescue operation had a bad flavour about it. To save the babies it would first be necessary to shoot their mothers, indeed all the adult elephants. Knowing that this was the only hope the calves had, the President of Rwanda sanctioned the undertaking. A team of experts from a game management firm in Kenya was hired as the people most qualified to carry out the task humanely and efficiently. Meantime the authorities in Kagera, a National Park without elephants, prepared a mile-long promontory sticking out into a lake for the baby elephants' reception. A wide lane of bush was cleared across the base of the promontory and a stout electric fence laid across it. This fence was designed to keep lions, the only natural enemies the calves would face, out of their sanctuary. The long-term hope was that the youngsters would grow to maturity on their lion-proof headland and eventually breed to repopulate the park.

The operation from a filming standpoint had one exciting and redeeming feature. In order to minimize stress on the smaller babies, who would have already stood by and seen their mothers slaughtered, helicopters of the Rwandese army would lift the youngsters on slings attached to their winch wires and carry them in a partially tranquillized state to the *bomas*, or pens, in the holding area where they would remain during their two or three weeks' acclimatization period. Whatever shock the drugged babies might feel during their four or five minutes flight would, it was felt, be more than compensated for by the speed at which the transfer was accomplished. The larger calves weighing up to a ton would be ferried in cages on rafts driven by outboard motors down the river that connected the acclimatization camp with the swamp.

Survival in London had heard of this venture through Bernhard Grzimek. At first we had felt that the operation, however necessary, dramatic or effective, was too brutal to show the television viewer. Meantime, without waiting for direct instructions, Lee Lyon had set off in her aircraft to the scene of the action. I gather that she was not entirely welcomed on arrival. Some of the team doing the job felt that there were aspects of the transfer, notably the necessary killing of the adults, that would be seen by a viewing public as inconsistent with what they think of as wildlife conservation. However, Lee's persistence, professionalism and, let's face it, feminine charm won her the day. She had the good sense to cover only what was strictly necessary of the cull, without glossing over the realities, and to concentrate on the positive side of the airlift.

The story, as things turned out, was loaded with emotion from many quarters. Alan Root, for example, who was in London at the time, felt the Rwanda operation was best left uncovered and told me so in his usual forthright way. I did not agree. More to the point, *Survival* did not agree. I had talked Lee's maverick venture over with Aubrey Buxton and he had ruled that provided we presented the facts fairly and without sensationalism, the choppering of baby elephants was too good a story to miss. So Lee was given approval to carry on and film the programme. In view of what was to happen, the situation was given a further personal loading because my daughter Jane, who had been saving up to visit Lee in the field for some time, had joined her at the most exciting part of the venture.

All went well at first. A dozen young elephants were airlifted or rafted from the swamp. The film of the babies 'flying' like Dumbo at the end of the helicopter winch wire was truly marvellous stuff, especially the shots which Lee had got by hanging head downwards out of the chopper to film the airborne elephants dangling below. The babies apparently settled down splendidly in camp. My daughter flew home just before the movement by road to Kagera Park and their release began.

Adrien Deschryver was there to help Lee drive, carry and set up camera gear as he had frequently done since Dieter had left Zaire. The first releases went according to plan. The lorry carrying the crate containing the captives was backed down into a ramp dug out of the ground. The catching team unbolted the rear door of the crate and the young elephant was allowed to wander out in its own time, get its bearings in its new environment and amble away to the shelter and security of the nearby bush. This is exactly what happened with the first batch of releases. One or two of the youngsters made half-hearted threat charges in the direction of the little knot of observers and the camera position but this was exactly what you would expect in the situation. The demonstrations were amusing rather than dangerous. Everyone present had seen baby elephants behave like this many times before. On past experience there were no grounds for expecting any trouble. However, everyone there, including Lee, was only too aware that wild animals are unpredictable and that even a very small elephant is possessed of enormous strength.

It was on a later release that the tragedy happened. Lee had taken every sensible precaution save one. She had drawn up her Volkswagen bus so that it was directly behind her camera position and she had left the door open so that if the extremely unlikely happened, she could dart back inside for protection. Lee, after all, had worked with Dieter among the Manyara elephant herds with the Douglas-Hamiltons, so she was under no illusions about the speed and power of elephants of all ages. The one safety measure she had overlooked may seem particularly extraordinary, because she had been there when Dieter, tethered to his heavy camera and tripod by the lead from his battery belt, had nearly been flattened by the big bull at Vitshumbi. On the face of it this was foolhardy, but to say this is to overlook the nature of cameramen. Convenience and speed when doing an exacting job are their first considerations, that and getting the pictures. In satisfying these basic drives, safety considerations are sometimes overlooked. And so it was in Lee's case.

The elephant concerned was one of the larger calves, weighing perhaps three-quarters of a ton. When the door of its cage was removed it was obviously angry or at least confused. It came out, went back inside again and finally backed out. There was still no indication that it would behave abnormally. After a second or two it broke into the familiar threat charge but this time it kept coming, covering the thirty yards or so towards the Volkswagen and the camera at that deceptively slow-looking pace. There would still have been time for Lee to leave.

Lee Lyon, from California, was killed shortly after this picture was taken in Zaire. She had flown to neighbouring Rwanda to cover the story of the capture and subsequent release in Rwanda's Kagera National Park of that country's last surviving elephant calves. The young elephants were carried from the swamp in which they were caught to the acclimatization camp, slung beneath military helicopters. It was while they were being released that one of the larger calves charged and trampled her. The film, the first she had made entirely on her own as a *Survival* wildlife photographer, was called 'Lee's Story'.

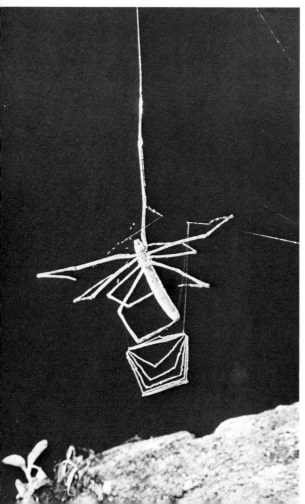

The highly specialized camerawork of Oxford Scientific Films has played a big part in many Survival films. The Oxford team of zoologist photographers pride themselves on being able to film 'The World You Never See', which became the title of a Special in which the spawning trout played a star role. To capture this sequence, a miniature river bed was constructed in the studio and the exact natural conditions necessary for spawning created. The Trinidadian spider, Dynopis, performed her trick in another Special, 'Come Into My Parlour'. Dynopis is weaving a net, seen suspended beneath her. She drops this over her victim and wraps her quarry up before eating it.

It is my belief that she simply did not think the elephant meant business. I doubt whether I would have done so either. She kept filming, thinking no doubt of the shot and seeing only the narrow world revealed by her camera eyepiece. By the time the elephant was within yards of the camera it was too late to unbuckle the battery belt, or release the lead from the camera, and run. The elephant swept her along the side of her vehicle, pushed her a yard or two and knelt on her. Adrien ran with others to try to pull the elephant away. She just had time to look up and say 'Adrien' before she died.

Her death affected me more than any tragedy outside my own family. For weeks I could not trust myself to talk about the circumstances to anyone.

I was determined that the film she had died shooting should be made. There were plenty of good reasons why it should have been forgotten. Sensationalism for one. It is not hard to think of others. It would have been perfectly understandable had *Survival* and Anglia felt sensitive in the extreme. Aubrey sensed the way I felt about Lee's death. I shall always appreciate that he never once interfered while I worked with the editor, Ron Pope, to make the film. I am aware that I must have seemed secretive and unjustifiably possessive about the whole production. That was the way I felt at the time. I wanted the film to be a tribute, neither mawkish nor sensational, to a beautiful and courageous young woman who died doing what she enjoyed doing most in life. The film was called 'Lee's Story'.

Chapter 16

End Titles

Survival has now made a name for itself on television in the USA. Both one-hour network shows and later a syndicated half-hour series introduced by actor John Forsythe, called 'The World of Survival', have become firmly established. Getting production exactly right for a large UK audience had always been our philosophy and aim. But what is right for the UK is almost certainly not right for the States. To expect a half-hour *Survival* to sell in the States exactly as made for transmission on ITV would be almost like sending over British cars with right-hand drive for use on American roads. To make American versions we needed American flair and know-how. We have found it among our colleagues at J. Walter Thompson with whom we have worked since our first US network production, 'The Enchanted Isles'.

First and foremost there is Jack Ball, ex-Princeton man, whose experience lies on the television side of the agency business. Jack knew tracks through the American television jungle that we, unaided, would have had no hope of finding or following. After a few years with *Survival* he even became hooked on wildlife conservation to the extent of taking a safari with some of our leading cameramen in East Africa. One result of this was that he insisted on shooting and editing his own wildlife film called 'Mr Ball Goes to Africa', to which all of us have had to submit on visits to his elegant Greenwich, Connecticut, home.

When Aubrey underwent this ordeal he made two fairly typical observations: 'How long does it last?' and: 'Isn't there rather a lot of music?' It is a standard complaint on this side of the Atlantic that all American versions seem to require wall-to-wall music. There is, in fact, a perfectly good reason for this. US audiences have so many channels to choose from and so many commercial break points in each show at which to change their station that continuous sound is thought essential to hold the viewer's attention. This technique does not apply to 'Mr Ball', however. The audience has no hope of escape. At the end of the showing, Jack sometimes observes that he can't see why it takes a year to make a network show. We are too polite to tell Jack Ball that his is possibly the worst wildlife film ever made. On the other hand, he is far too astute a judge of the medium not to know that.

Without Jack it's difficult to guess exactly where we would have got in the States. He has been the mainspring of our rapid development in the most important of all overseas markets. US sales have enhanced the economy of the whole *Survival* enterprise, enabling us to plan more boldly, to take bigger financial risks on setting up wildlife projects like 'Gorilla', 'Orangutan', 'Tiger' and 'The Year of the Wildebeest'. We might never have undertaken these without the assurance of export sales. While sticking a whole plumage of feathers into Yankee Doodle's cap, let's also put a big one in Anglia's and note that *Survival* has won millions of dollars for the balance of payments and will no doubt continue to do so. The Queen's Award for Industry was won by *Survival* largely through our successful venture in New York with our new allies.

Jack Ball heads Anglia's subsidiary in America in which J. Walter Thompson is the key partner. We owe a lot to the enthusiasm of JWT and particularly to their President, Don Johnson. *Survival* is the only television series in history to have formed its own American company. In doing so, we've been lucky to find an American team that recognizes what we're at and is enthusiastic about conservation as well as about sales.

It would be only too easy for our American partners to try to 'hype' things up (the jargon is catching) to build up the jeopardy element (American TV demands a lot of jeopardy: even if the anaconda doesn't actually eat the host it's nice to think that it *might*). Such distortion could happen to *Survival* in less sensitive hands, either in the US version of the shows themselves or in the essential publicity promoting them before transmission. Happily we are protected on the promotional side by an executive called Delta Willis whose father is a duck-hunter on the Mississippi Delta. Her name does not derive from the Greek alphabet. As a country-raised girl Delta knows the true values of the wildlife product. As to the Americanization of commentaries, we are lucky to have a highly professional writer, Jim deKay, to turn my own and colleague Malcolm Penny's right-hand drive commentaries into left-hand drive narrations and without spilling a drop of the essential truth *en route*.

I think it is fair to say that we sometimes succeed in mystifying each other across the Atlantic. Our American allies often do so by using business terms unfamiliar to us. (For example: what on earth can an executive who is known as Coordinator of Integration actually do?) For our part our apparently insular ways sometimes exasperate Lexington Avenue to the point at which they have been heard to describe us as Nineteenth Century Fox. We take that as rather a compliment. Great time for quality that nineteenth century!

In most cases, a writer knows when a book is finished. With this one, it is impossible to be sure. So many things are happening to *Survival* and its team at this very moment. By the time the book is in the reader's hands, so much will have altered, so much more have taken place. As I have been writing the last few chapters, adventures and misadventures have beset us. Jen and Des Bartlett came close to drowning in the Amazon when their rubber boat was crushed. They were washed half a mile down river and had separately given up hope when each was saved by the kind of luck that is only issued once in a lifetime. Mike Price, working with Dieter Plage, on the tiger Special 'Tiger, Tiger', spent some heart-stopping minutes when a tigress stared at him eyeball to eyeball through the slit of his canvas hide. A new American recruit, David DeVries, who already has a fine record as a naturalist and film-maker in the States, had an unfortunate visit from a bear while shooting a caribou Special with the Porcupine Herd, named after the Porcupine River, in the Yukon Territory of Alaska. The bear dragged his frame tent into a river. David was out at the time but four thousand feet of exposed film was not. The film ended up in the river and was never seen again. It naturally contained some of his best footage. Later on during the same expedition, a member of David DeVries's team fell into an icy river. When they got him out he was suffering from hypothermia. They had struck camp and were walking out to make their rendezvous with a float-plane that was to pick them up, so there was no tent in which to give the frozen and almost certainly dying man shelter. So David and another companion stripped off their clothes and hugged their naked colleague in a sleeping bag to get some warmth back into his body. Though he had relapsed into a coma, their body-warmth saved him.

These are the stories of 'jeopardy' that the public and Press undoubtedly like to hear and, to tell the truth, which one rather enjoys recounting. They emphasize the intrepidity and dedication of the naturalist camera teams, the people in the front line. They also suggest, quite correctly, that *Survival* is a very exciting business to be in.

Thrilling though misadventures may be, they do not make films and everyone concerned would be better off without them. They are counter-productive except, perhaps, in publicity terms. Production is what counts and we are currently producing all over the world.

The New York office keeps an elegant map on the wall that shows where the camera teams are working. It is a piece of front-office window dressing as much as anything else, but it does give a fair picture of the scene.

At this moment that map shows that Des and Jen Bartlett have moved south from Alaska, are currently in Japan and heading for Bali, Port Moresby in New Guinea and back to Australia. After that there are plans for them in southern Africa. In Africa Alan Root, in Kenya, has just finished an epic about everything that happens in and around a termite hill; Bob Campbell and Cindy Buxton have teamed up in Zambia to tell the year-round story of what the mighty Luangwa River does to the Luangwa Valley and its great herds of animals as it floods and then subsides. Liz and Tony Bomford are returning from a fruitful year in Madagascar filming their way home on a catamaran via the Indian Ocean islands. Jeff Foott has just descended from the high Rockies after a spell in Mexico filming the secret wintering ground of thousands of monarch butterflies. Other dots on the map represent projects nearer base, in the Swiss Alps, Perthshire, Oxford and Norfolk. Dieter Plage and his wife Mary are returning to a concentrated programme in Nepal, India and Ceylon that includes Everest.

I can only repeat the remark made to Aubrey Buxton and myself after we made our very first *Survival* of all, 'The London Scene' in 1961. 'Yes,' said the doubting well-wisher, 'I can see that there may be two more programmes but what are you going to do after that?'

That was roughly three hundred *Survivals* ago. Three hundred *Survivals* from now, it is conceivable that a similar question may be asked. Whoever happens to be running the unit at that date might as well have his answer ready. May I suggest that he says: 'Why, three hundred more, of course.'

Appendix

International Awards Won by SURVIVAL

Golden Nymph at the Monte Carlo Film Festival for 'The New Ark', 1963.

Silver Medal of the London Zoological Society to Aubrey Buxton for his contribution to the appreciation of natural history, 1967.

Golden Nymph at the Monte Carlo Film Festival for the best colour production, 'The Enchanted Isles', 1968.

Finalist's Plaque of the National Academy of Television Arts and Sciences for 'The Enchanted Isles', 1968.

Royal Television Society's Silver Medal to Aubrey Buxton for outstanding artistic achievement in television, 1968.

Golden Hugo Award at the Chicago International Festival for the top documentary, 'Secrets of the African Baobab Tree', 1972.

Honourable Mention at the San Francisco Film Festival for 'Secrets of the African Baobab Tree', 1972.

Christopher Award for 'Secrets of the African Baobab Tree', 1973.

Emmy Award to Des and Jen Bartlett for cinematography in 'The Incredible Flight of the Snowgeese', 1973.

Emmy Award to Les Perry for editing 'The Incredible Flight of the Snowgeese', 1973.

Certificate of Merit from the British Association for the Advancement of Science for 'The Flight of the Snowgeese', 1973.

Ohio State Award for 'The Incredible Flight of the Snowgeese', 1973.

Eddie Award made by the American Cinema Editors to Les Parry for editing 'The Incredible Flight of the Snowgeese', 1974.

Golden Scissors Award to Les Parry for editing 'The Incredible Flight of the Snowgeese', 1974.

SAS Prince's Special Prize at the Monte Carlo International Television Festival for 'The Empty Desert', 1974.

The Royal Geographical Society's Mrs Patrick Ness Award for zoological investigations, awarded to Iain Douglas-Hamilton, 1974.

The Royal Geographical Society's Cherry Kearton Medal for travellers engaged in the study/practice of natural history through the medium of photography, cinematography and television, awarded to Des and Jen Bartlett, 1974.

The Queen's Award to Industry, 1974.

Golden Gate Award at the San Francisco Film Festival for the best network documentary Special, 'The World You Never See', 1974.

Special Jury Award at the San Francisco Film Festival for the best network documentary, 'Trial by Wilderness', 1974.

Diploma in the Popular Science section of the 29th International Scientific Film Congress in Miskolc, Hungary, for 'Inside Story', 1974.

Golden Gate Award at the San Francisco Film Festival for the best network documentary Special, 'The Great Migration: Year of the Wildebeest', 1975.

Special Jury Award at the San Francisco Film Festival for the best network documentary, 'Gorilla', 1975.

Diploma at Ekofilm, Czechoslovakia, for 'Gorilla', 1975.

Christopher Award for 'The Great Migration: Year of the Wildebeeste', 1976.

Ohio State Award for 'Magnificent Monsters of the Deep', 1976.

Special Jury Award at the San Francisco Film Festival for the best network documentary, 'Come Into My Parlour', 1976.

Silver Plaque Award at the Chicago International Festival for 'Search for the Shinohara', 1976.

Christopher Award for 'Come Into My Parlour', 1977.

Ohio State Award for 'Come Into My Parlour', 1977.

Certificate of Merit from the British Association for the Advancement of Science for 'Come Into My Parlour', 1977.

Christopher Award for 'Orangutan: Orphans of the Wild', 1977.

Ohio State Award for 'Orangutan: Orphans of the Wild', 1977.

Royal Television Society's Gold Medal to Aubrey Buxton for outstanding work behind the camera, 1977.

Index

Note : Page numbers in italics indicate references in captions
Entries in single quotes, followed by the letter *S* indicate films
in the *Survival* series

aardvark, 186
abalones (molluscs), *168*
Abbaye, Lake, 107
Abiata, Lake, 101–2, *103*, 105
Acacia tortilis woods (Manyara,) *164*,
  166
Addis Ababa, 100, 102, 106, 113
'Africa's Little Game' (*S*), 54–5
'Airlift', (*S*), 106
albatross, 60–1, 65
Albermarle Island, 64
Albert, Lake, 21, 61
Aldabra Island, 59
'Almost a Dodo' (*S*), *72*, 188
Amboseli National Park (Kenya), *72*
Amin, Idi, 17, 37, 39, 45
Among the Elephants (Douglas-Hamilton), 161, 163
Angemeyer, Carl, 64
Anglia Television, 12, 15–16, 25–6,
  29, 56, 80, 195
antelope, 21, 27, 30, 97–8, 188; gemsbok (oryx), 97–8; pronghorn, 94
arachnids, 82
'Arctic Summer' (*S*), 145 fn
Argulus (crustacean), 81–2
Armand Dennis Productions, 28, 35,
  89–90
Asaita (Danakil country), 107, 109–10,
  114
Associated Rediffusion, 11–14, 26, 56
Australia, 31–3
avocet, 15, 58
Awash National Park, 100, 106;
  River, 106–7

baboons, 30, 187
Baker, Lady, 61
Baker, Samuel, 61

Baker, Stanley, 37
Balaeniceps rex (stork), 188
Ball, Jack, 122, 124, 146, 175, 194–5
ballooning, 153–7
Bartlett, Des, 9, 28, 35–8, 43, 56, 78,
  84, 89–97, 122–4, 126–30, 132–3,
  135–6, 138–40, 145–8, 160, 185,
  196–7
Bartlett, Jen, 10, 28, 35–7, 90–5, 122,
  126–30, 132, 135–6, 140–1, 143,
  145, 147–8, 160, 184–6, 189, 196–7
Bartlett, Julie, 35–7, 90–2, 94
Bartlett, Les, 128–30, 132, 137, 142,
  144, 145
BBC, 11, 13, 27, 28, 55, 77–9, 149,
  152–3; Natural History Unit, 16, 77
Beagle, the, 64, 68, 74
bears, 122, *169*, 196; polar, 127, 131,
  143–5
Beauchene (Falkland Isles), 60
beavers, 91, 122–5
beetles, dung, 54; tok-tokky, 99
Bell, Martin, 156–8
Benguela current, 99
Bengweulu swamp, 188
Bernstein, Sydney, 13
bison, 62
Bitter Lakes Refuge, 94
bittern, 17, 188
Blakeney, 11, 28–9, 56–8, 186
Bohorok (Sumatra), *121*, 178–81, 183
Bokara tribe, 47
Bomford, Liz, 10, 189, 197
Bomford, Tony, 189, 197
boobies, 64–5, 71–2
Borland, Moira, 98, 189
Borland, Rodney, 95, 97–9, 102, 160,
  189
Borneo, 178

Borner, Monica, *121*, 178–81, 183
Bosque de L'Apache, 94
Boswell, Jeffrey, 77–8
British Antarctic Survey, 59
Brown, Leslie, 100–1, 103–4, 188
Bryce Canyon, 93
Budongo Forest, 37
buffaloes, 34, 62, *72*, 167, 188
Bukavu, 169, 173, 176–7
bushbuck, 164, 185
butterflies, 11
Buxton, Anthony, 17
Buxton, Aubrey, 9–17, 20, 25, 27–8,
    33–5, 38–9, 43–5, 50, 56–7, 63–4,
    68–9, 74–5, 78, 95, 100, 106–8 113,
    122, 126, 146–7, 177, 186, 191,
    193–4, 197
Buxton, John, 10, 17–21, 24–5, 62, 187
Buxton, Lucinda (Cindy), 10, *72*,
    186–8, 197
Buxton, Maria, 35

Campbell, Bob, 9–10, 43, *72*, 154, 156,
    197
Campbell, Glen, 146–9
caracel (lynx), 186
cattle egret, *72*
'Central Flyway' (*S*), 145 fn
Chambura River, 18
chameleons, 54
Charles, H.R.H. Prince, 76
Chiricahua Canyon, 93
Chitawan jungle, 116; National Park,
    169, 182–3
Churchill (Canada), 127–31, 134, 137,
    140, 142
Churchill, Randolph, 125
Churchill, Winston, 125
'Cloud over Paradise' (*S*), 83
Collins, Sir William, 161
Commonwealth Forestry Institute, 78
'Continuous Performance' (*S*), 57
controlled shooting, 66–7, 124
Cooke, John, 81
Coppard, Denys, 74
cormorants, 65, 105
Cortez, Sea of, 93
Countryman programme, 12, 56
Cowen, Bill, 37–8
coypu, 12, 56
cranes, sandhill, 129–30, 133, 141,
    145, 147–8
Crater Highlands, 162
'Creatures from Another World' (*S*),
    82
crocodiles, 158–9

Daily Express, 83
Daily Mirror, 78
Daily Telegraph, 83
Dakota, North, 130, 138
Danakil, Depression of, 112; Desert,
    100, 106–7, *120*; Sultan of, 107–13;
    tribe (Afars), 106–10, 110 fn, 111–
    114, *120*
Dankworth, John, 14, 25, 29–30, 74–5
Darnton, Iris, 61–2
Darnton, Rupert, 61–2
dartons, 105
Darwin, Charles, 63–5, 68–9, 73,
    75–6, *168*
Darwin Research Institute, 64, 68
'Death Trap Lake' (*S*), 54
deer, 27, 30
deKay, Jim, 195
de la Bat, Barnabe, 97
Dennis, Armand, 28, 35–6, 43, 89
Dennis, Michaela, 28
Deschryver, Adrien, *121*, 168–73, 177,
    192–3
De Soto Refuge (Iowa), 132, 137
DeVries, David, 196
dikdik, 185
diseases, tropical, 177–8, 181–3; Hos-
    pital for, 177, 183
Disney, Walt, 67
Djibouti, 107
Dodinga people, 39–40
Douglas-Hamilton, Iain, *73*, 151–2,
    161–7, 192
Douglas-Hamilton, Oria, *73*, 151,
    161–4, 166–7, 192
Dreschfield, Ralph, 17
ducks, 11, 13, 57, 105
Dudwa National Park, *169*
dune crickets, 99
'Dusts of Kilimanjaro, (S), *72*

eagles, fish, *25*, 103, 185; bald, *25*;
    tawny, 88, 103
Eales, Betty, 57
Eales, Ted, 56–9, 186
East African Wildlife Society, 53
East Anglia, 10, 15, 28–9
Eastman, Ron, 77–8
Eastman, Rosemary, 77–8
Eburru Volcanics, 152
echidnas, 32
Ecuador, 63–65
Edward, Lake, 18, 174
Edwards, Fiola, 182
Edwards, George, 58–60
Edwards, Jim, 182
egrets, 105

'Eighth Wonder of the World' (S), 43–4
eland, 43
Elementeita, Lake, 152
elephants, 40–1, 54, *73*, 161, 163–7, 174–5, 188–93
'Elephants Have Right of Way' (S), 34
Elizabeth II, H.M. Queen, 76
elk, 91
'Empty Desert' (S), 99, 100
'Enchanted Isles' (S), 74–6, 122, 124, *168*, 194
Entebbe, 17, 18, 37
Ethiopia, 100, 106, 108, *120*; revolution in, 113
Etosha National Park, 97–8
'Explorers' Nile' (S), 37
Eyeasi, Lake, 162

Falkland Islands, 59–61
flamingoes, 51–3, 187–8
'Family That Lives with Elephants' (S), *71*, 151, 161, 163
'First Catch your Unicorn' (S), 98
Flanagan, Peter, 97–8
'Flight of the Snowgoose' (S), 126–49
'Floating World of Naivasha', (S), 187
Fonda, Henry, 125
Foott, Jeff, 9, 91, *168*–9, 197
'Forbidden Desert of the Danakil', (S) 113
Ford, John, 94
Forsythe, John, 194
Fosbrooke, Henry, 44
foxes, 13, 14
Frankfurt Zoological Society, 168, 178
Frey, Regina, *121*, 178–81, 183
frigate birds, 64

Galapagos, the, 16, 55, 63–71, 74–5
Galapagos, The (Nelson), 72, *168*
Gallico, Paul, 149
gannets, 64
Gannon, Frank, 125
gazelle, 43
geckos, 99
geese, 57, 60; blue, *24*, 130; Canadian, 130; kelp, 61; snow *24*, 94, 126 ff
Gelai, Mount, 162
George, Lake, 18
giraffes, 43, 54, 164
gliding, and vultures, 85–7
godwits, 58
Gol Mountains, 87–8
Goma (Zaire), 175–7
Goodall, Jane, 167
Gooders, John, 80

'Gorilla' (S), *121*, 171, 177, 195
gorillas, *121*, 168–72
Graham, Alaister, 155
Granada Television, 16, 28
Grand Canyon, 94
griffins, 88
Grzimek, Professor B., 38–9, 53, 85–8, 95, 167–9, 174, 178, 191
Grzimek, Michael, 38, 43
gulls, 93, 129, 137

Harris, Dr Mike, 64
Harris, Richard, 149
Harris, Rolf, 31–3, 54–5
Hay, Mike, 59, 84–7
Hell's Gate Gorge, 151–2, 161
Hemingway, Ernest, *25*
herons, 14, 58, 105
hippopotami, 18, 20, 34, 54, 157–9, 174, 185–6
Hood Island, 64–5, 69
Hopcraft, John, 187
hornbill, 67
Horsey, 11, 17
Hosking, Eric, 59
'How the West Was Lost' (S), 62
Hudson Bay, 126, 129–30, 140
'Humpbacks, the Gentle Giants' (S), *120*
Hungarian Festival of Films, 79, 80
Hunt, Peter, 11
Huxley, Sir Julian, 53
hyenas, 53, 186
Hylan, Bill, 123

ibex, 187
ibis, 103
Idi Amin, Lake, 21
iguanas, 65, 69
'Inside Story' (S), 80
Isabella Island, 64
Issas tribe, 110, 110 fn
Issylmeer (Holland), 58

jackdaws, 11
Jackson (U.S.A.), 91
'Jackson Hole' (S), 91
jaegers, 129, 137
Jakarta, 181–2
Jamestown, 134, 138
Jie tribe, 45, 48
Johnson, Don, 195
Joseph, Stanley, 26–7, 29–31, 34, 44, 54, 70, 74–5

Kabarega National Park, 15, 16, 18, 20, 25

Kagera National Park, 190–2
Kahuzi-Biega National Park, *121*, 168–70, 172
Kamembe, 172
Kampala, 18, 35, 37
kangaroos, 31–3
kangoni 39
'Karamoja' (S), 42 ff, 122
Karamoja Bell, 40; cattle scheme, 46–7; region, *24*, 39, 45–6
Karamojong people, *24*, 39, 45–7
Kariba, 30
Karum, Lake, 112
Katmandhu, 181–2
Kazinga Channel, 18
Kenya, 42, 54, 154, 185, 187, 197; Mount, 42
kestrel, 11
Kidepo National Park, 39, 40
Kidney Island, 60
Kigali, 172–3
Kilaguni Lodge, 54–5, 159
Kilimanjaro, Mount, *25*, 42, *72*, 154
kingfishers, 77, 105, 187
Kinshasa, 177
Kinyala, 18, 19
Kivu, Lake, 174–5, 177
Koobi Fora, 152
kudu, 164

Labwor, 49
Lack, David, 79
Lagaja, Lake, 162
lake fly, 104
Lamprey, Hugh, 88
'Land of the Loon' (S), 145 fn
Langata (Nairobi), 28
Lango, 49
Lawrie, Andrew, 182
Leakey, Richard, 152
'Lee's Story' (S), 193
Lengai, Mount, 162
Lerai Forest, 44
Lincoln, Abraham, 125
Lindup, David, 29, 74
Linnean Society of London, 76
lions, 33, 43, 54, 167, 188
Lilliput, 11
Living Desert, The (Disney), 67
lizards, 54, 65; *Aporosaurus*, 99–100
London, shooting in, 12–14; Zoological Gardens, 28
'London Scene' (S), 14, 27, 197
Look programme, 28–9
Luangwa River, 197
lungfish, *72*
Lynch, Johnny, 138

Lyon, Lee, 10, *73*, 91, *120*, 128–30, 132, 160–1, 163, 165, 168–71, 173–5, 177, 189–91

Maasai nomads, 43–4, *72*, 151, 163
McConnell River, 126-7, 129–31, 137, 140
MacDermot, Brian, 107–8
McInnes, Charles, 126-8, 132
MacMillan, John, 12
McNeil River, *169*
MacPhail, Ian, 78
Madagascar, 189, 197
Madi District, 15, 21
Magadi, Lake, 50–3; Soda Company, 50–1
'Making of a Natural History Film, The' (S), 79
Malan, Dr, 182
mallard, 14, 57
Man Alive programme, 13
Manning, Ian, 188
Manyara, *73*, 161–4, 166
Margach, Chiels, 18, 19–20, 25, 37–8
marriage customs, tribal, 47
marsh harriers, 17
Masindi, 18
Meyers, Farlan, 146–7
migration, animal/bird, 47 fn, 149–50, 164
Mississippi Delta, 126, 134, 195
Mitchell Cotts, 107–9, 111–12
Moar, Ian, 81
Mobuto, President, 168
mocking birds, 65
moles, golden, 99
'Monument in the Mangroves' (S), 90
Monument Valley, 94
Moroto, Mount, 49
Morris, Desmond, 16, 28
Morton, Bill, 13–15, 27
'Mow the Kangaroo Down' (S), 31
Murchison Falls National Park, 15–16, 18, 20, 25
Murgett, Frank, 12
Murray, Stephen, 75
music, use of, 14, 25, 30–4, 119–20
Mzima Springs, 156–7, 186
Mzima Springs' (S), 150

Nairobi, 28, 35, 38, 42–3, 50–2, 112, 151, 154, 159, 173, 185, 188
Naivasha, Lake, 50, 67, 91, 150–1, 153, 185
Nakuru, Lake, 52, 187
Namibia, 95, 97–9, 102
Namib Desert, 97–100

National Trust Nature Reserve, 56
Natron, Lake, 50, 52, 162
Ndala River, 162–3, 167
Nelson, Dr Bryan, 64–5, 71–2
Nelson, June, 64
'New Ark' (S), 70
New Island, 61
Ngorongoro Crater, 38, 43–4, 54 note
Nightingale Island, 60–1
Nile, West, 15, 21
Niven, David, 154
Norwich, 12, 28, 80
'Nothing Going on' (S), 54–5
Nyerere, Dr (later President) Julius, 53, 156
Nyirangongo, Mount, 174–5

Obote, Milton, 17, 45
Observer, the, 11
O'Connell, Pat, 21–4
Okavango Swamp, 25, 114
Olduvai Gorge, 150, 152
'One that Came Back, The' (S), 15, 27
'On the Trail of the Snowgoose' (S), 145 fn
Opotipot (Uganda), 39
Orange River, 90
'Orangutan, Orphans of the Forest' (S), 121, 161, 195
orangutans, 178, 180–1, 183
oribi, 39
Origin of Species, The (Darwin), 63–4, 68
Ovambo tribe, 98
Owen, John, 43
owls, 11, 57
oxen, 48–9
Oxford Scientific Films, 79–81
oyster catchers, 57

Paling, John, 81
Parker, Ian, 155
Parks, Peter, 80–1
parrots, 19
Parry, Les, 135, 145, 147
Pas, The (Canada), 127–8, 144
'Passing of Leviathan' (S), 120
Payne, Roger, 84
Pearson, John, 43, 50–1, 53, 54 note, 86–7
'Pelican Flyway' (S), 106
Pelican Island, 90, 103
pelicans, 64, 87, 101–6, 174, 187
penguins, 61
Penny, Malcolm, 195
Pennycuik, Colin, 85–7
Perry, Roger, 64

pheasants, 57
Philip, H.R.H. Prince, 63, 68–73, 76, 100, 152, 168, 177
Pian tribe, 45, 47
Picture Post, 11
pigeons, 13, 14, 85
Plage, Dieter, 9, 25, 39, 84, 95–8, 100, 102–6, 109–13, 115–16, 120–1, 154, 156, 160–1, 163, 165–9, 169, 170–1, 173–83, 192, 196–7
Plage, Mary (née Grant), 189, 197
plankton, 81
platypus, duck-billed, 32
plover, 57, 104
Pope, Ron, 80, 193
Poppleton, Frank, 35, 37, 156, 182
Poppleton, Inge, 182
Porcupine River, 196
Portuguese man-o'-war, 189
Prairie Waterfowl Research Center, 134, 138
Price, Mike, 169, 178–9, 182, 196
'Private Life of the Kingfisher', 78
ptarmigan, 129
puffin, 13

Quaker Oats Company, 122–3, 125
Queen Elizabeth National Park, 35, 37–8

Randall, Ken, 21–4
Raza Island, 93
redshank, 11, 57
reed buck, 39
Reucassel, Dick, 86
rhino-catchers, 18, 20–1, 23–4
rhinoceroses, 16, 20–1, 43, 182–3; white, 15, 21–5
Rhodes, Mike, 79
Ricciardi, Mirella, 161
'Richest Sea in the World' (S), 128
Rift Valley, 50, 52–3, 85, 100–1, 103, 112, 162, 166–7, 185, 188
'Rivers of No Return' (S), 169
Robertson-Glasgow, James, the late, 75
Robinson, Dick, 123
Root, Alan, 35, 38–46, 47 fn, 50–5, 63–8, 71, 76, 91, 95, 107, 150 ff, 161–3, 168, 185–6, 191, 197
Root, Joan, 10, 25, 35, 39–42, 44–6, 52–3, 63–5, 69, 76, 95, 155–9, 161–3, 184–6, 189
Rosewell, 94
Royal Society for the Protection of Birds, 27, 59

Rudolf, Lake (Lake Turkana), 152, 187
ruffs, 58
Rukwa, Lake, 101
Russell, Osborne, 91
Rwanda, 172–4, 177, 189–91

'Safari by Balloon' (S), 154, 157
'Saga of the Sea Otter' (S), 168
St Kilda, 59
salmon, sockeye, 169
Salthouse, 11
Samburu (Kenya), 88
Sand Lake Refuge 134, 142, 147–8
Santa Cruz Island, 64
Savidge, John, 20–1
scaup, 130
Scientific American, 87
scorpions, 67, 186
Scott, Peter, 14, 15, 28, 53, 149
seahorses, 89–90
sea lions, 65, 69
'Sea of Cortez' (S), 128
sea otter, 168
seals, 57, 61; Antarctic, 65
sea urchins, 168
'Secrets of the African Baobab Tree'
  (S), 67, 150
Serengeti National Park, 44; Plains,
  43, 150–1, 153, 161–3, 167; Re-
  search Institute, 88
'Serengeti Shall Not Die', (S), 38
Seychelles, the, 59
Shala Lake, 100–2, 105–8, 187
shearwaters, 61
sheep, Karakul, 97
shoebills, 72, 188
'Shotgun Wedding' (S), 57
siamangs (gibbons), 179
Sielmann, Heinz, 63
Signy Island, 59
'Silent Wings' (S), 86
Simien Mountains, 187
Skeleton Coast, 97, 99
Skinner, Eric, 78–80
Sklair, Sam, 147, 149
skuas, 57
Smith, Tony, 152–3
snakes, egg-eating, 54
Sonjo tribe, 163
'S.O.S. Rhino' (S), 15–26, 28, 37, 54,
  62, 67, 187
South Island, 152–3
spiders, 81–2; trap-door, 99
spoonbills, 58
Spurn Head, 59
Squaw Creek Refuge, 132–3

squirrels, 54
Sri-Lanka (Ceylon), 83
Stewart, Ken, 21–2, 24
sticklebacks, 79, 81
storks, 72, 87, 102, 126, 174; whale-
  headed, 188
Suk tribe, 45, 47
Sumatra, 121, 178, 182

TAM ratings, 30
Tanzania (Tanganyika), 38, 52–3,
  101, 154–6, 162; National Parks,
  43, 47 fn, 166
Taylor, Forbes, 154, 156
Tendaho, 106, 109
termites, 48, 54
terns, 57–8, 93, 129–30
Test, River, 77
Teton Mountains, 91, 122
Thesiger, Wilfred, 106–7, 109, 113
This Week programme, 11–13, 15
Thompson, David, 81
Thompson, Gerald, 78–81
Thompson Company, J. Walter, 122–
  125, 146, 194–5
Thoren, Ken, 147–8
Throw Out Two Hands (Smith), 153
tigers, 116, 169, 179, 196
'Tiger, Tiger' (S), 116, 169, 195–6
tiliapa fish, 25, 50
tits, blue, 79
'Tomorrow May be Too Late' (S), 30
Tongaland, 189
Tonight programme, 11
Tors, Ivan, 78
tortoises, 64–5, 69
Trimmer, Bombo, 18, 19
Tristan da Cunha, 59, 61
Tsavo National Park, 54, 67, 164
Tucson (Arizona), 91, 93, 122, 127,
  129, 138, 160; Desert Museum, 92
Turkana, Lake (Lake Rudolf), 152,
  187
turtles, 189
tussac birds, 61

Uganda, 15 ff, 39 ff; National Parks,
  15–18, 35, 37–9, 182
Urban, Emil, 100–1, 103, 105–6
US Wildlife Refuges, 90, 138

van Lawick, Hugo, 167
Victoria, Lake, 17
Victoria Nile, 37
vipers, side-winding, 99
Virunga National Park, 173–5, 177;
  volcanoes, 174–5

Vitshumbi, 174, 192
vultures, 52–3, 85–8, 102–3

waders, 10, 15, 50
Walker, Lewis Wayne, 93
wallabies, 31
wasps, 54; alder wood, 78–9
Wedd, Louie, 21–4
Welles, Orson, 120
whales, 120, *120*
Wichita Mountain Refuge, 90
Wiggin, Maurice, 14
wildebeest, 37, 43, 47 fn, 150
'Wilderness at Bay' (*S*), 90
Williams, John, 52–3
Willis, Delta, 195
windhoek, 95
'Wings Over the Rift' (*S*), 87
wombats, 32

Wood Buffalo Park, 62
woodpecker finch, 16, 64–7, *168*
World of Survival (U.S.A.), 194
'World of the Beaver' (*S*), 124–5
World Wild Life Fund, 68, 78, 178
Wyoming Rockies, 90

'Year of the Wildebeest' (*S*), 47 fn,
  162, 195
Yellowstone Park, 90–1
Yukon Territory, 196

Zaire (Congo), 21, *121*, 167–8, 172–7,
  190
Zambia, 188, 197
zebra, 33, 39, 43
Zoo Time programme, 28
Zubert, Christian, 161